PENGU...

The Penguin History...

and Birmingham (Ph.D. in Economics). Since 1996 he has been
Professor of the History and Philosophy of Economics at the Univer-
sity of Birmingham, where he has taught since 1980. Previously he
taught Economics at University College London (1975–7) and the
University of Keele (1977–9). From 1998 to 2000 he held a British
Academy Research Readership. He has also taught courses in the
history of economics at the universities of Bristol, Buckingham and
Oporto. He is Associate Editor of the *Journal of the History of
Economic Thought* and Editor of the *Journal of Economic Method-
ology*. As well as contributing articles on economics to numerous
journals, he is the author and editor of many books, including *A
History of Modern Economic Analysis* (1985), *Economists and the
Economy* (1988; second edition, 1994), *Keynes: Contemporary
Responses to the General Theory* (1999), *Exemplary Economists*
(co-editor with Roger Middleton, 2000) and *Toward a History of
Applied Economics* (co-editor with Jeff Biddle, 2000).

The Penguin History of Economics

Roger E. Backhouse

PENGUIN BOOKS

PENGUIN BOOKS

Published by the Penguin Group
Penguin Books Ltd, 80 Strand, London WC2R 0RL, England
Penguin Putnam Inc., 375 Hudson Street, New York, New York 10014, USA
Penguin Books Australia Ltd, 250 Camberwell Road, Camberwell, Victoria 3124, Australia
Penguin Books Canada Ltd, 10 Alcorn Avenue, Toronto, Ontario, Canada M4V 3B2
Penguin Books India (P) Ltd, 11 Community Centre, Panchsheel Park, New Delhi – 110 017, India
Penguin Books (NZ) Ltd, Cnr Rosedale and Airborne Roads, Albany, Auckland, New Zealand
Penguin Books (South Africa) (Pty) Ltd, 24 Sturdee Avenue, Rosebank 2196, South Africa

Penguin Books Ltd, Registered Offices: 80 Strand, London WC2R 0RL, England

www.penguin.com

First published 2002
5

Set in 9.5/12.5 pt PostScript Adobe Sabon
Typeset by Rowland Phototypesetting Ltd, Bury St Edmunds, Suffolk
Printed in England by Clays Ltd, St Ives plc

Contents

Contents

Acknowledgements

Most of this book was written during my tenure of a British Academy Research Readership from 1998 to 2000. I am grateful to the British Academy for its support, and to several colleagues who read various drafts of the manuscript and whose detailed comments have helped me remove many errors and improve the argument. These are Mark Blaug, Anthony Brewer, Bob Coats, Mary Morgan, Denis O'Brien, Mark Perlman, Geert Reuten and Robert Swanson. I also wish to thank those subscribers to the History of Economics Society's email list who answered my requests for bits of information (usually dates) that I could not find myself (Bob Dimand proved a mine of information). I am also very grateful to Fatima Brandão and Antonio Amoldovar for inviting me to teach a course at the University of Oporto, which helped me to sort out my ideas on how to organize the material in the second half of the book. Stefan McGrath, at Penguin Books, encouraged me to embark on this project, and was patient when I overshot the initial deadline by a long time. He also provided helpful suggestions, as did Bob Davenport, whose editing of the final draft was exemplary and saved me from many mistakes. None of these people, of course, bears responsibility for any errors that may remain. Last, but definitely not least, I would like to thank my family: Alison, Robert and Ann.

Prologue

The History of Economics

This book is about the history of attempts to understand economic phenomena. It is about what has variously been described as the history of economic thought, the history of economic ideas, the history of economic analysis, and the history of economic doctrines. It is not, except incidentally, concerned with the economic phenomena themselves, but with how people have tried to make sense of them. Like the history of philosophy or the history of science, this is a branch of intellectual history. To illustrate the point, the subject of the book is not the Industrial Revolution, the rise of big business or the Great Depression – it is how people such as Adam Smith, Karl Marx, John Maynard Keynes and many lesser-known figures have perceived and analysed the economic world.

Writing the history of economic ideas involves weaving together many different stories. It is clearly necessary to tell the story of the people who were doing the thinking – the economists themselves. It is also necessary to cover economic history. Natural scientists can assume, for example, that the structure of the atom and the molecular structure of DNA are the same now as in the time of Aristotle. Economists cannot make comparable assumptions. The world confronting economists has changed radically, even over the past century. (Maybe there is a sense in which 'human nature' has always been the same, but the precise meaning and significance of this are not clear.) Political history matters too, for political and economic events are inextricably linked, and economists have, as often as not, been involved in politics, either directly or indirectly. They have sought to influence policy, and political concerns have influenced them. Finally, it is necessary to consider changes in related disciplines and in the underlying intellectual climate. Economists' preconceptions and ways of thinking are inevitably formed by the culture in which they are writing. The history of economics has therefore to touch on the histories of religion, theology, philosophy, mathematics and science, as well as economics and politics.

What makes the problem difficult is that the relationships between these various histories are not simple. There is no justification for claiming, for example, that connections run solely from economic or political history to economic ideas. Economic ideas feed into politics and influence what happens in the economy (not necessarily in the way that their inventors intended); the three types of history are interdependent. The same is true of the relationship between the history of economics and intellectual history more generally. Economists have sought to apply to their own discipline lessons learned from science – whether the science of Aristotle, Newton or Darwin. They are influenced by philosophical movements such as those of the Enlightenment, positivism or postmodernism, as well as by influences of which we are completely unconscious. However, links also run the other way. Darwin's theory of natural selection, for example, was strongly influenced by the economic ideas of Malthus. In short, economic ideas are an integral component of culture.

One factor that contributes to the interdependence of economics and other disciplines and intellectual life in general is that, at least until recently, economics was not an activity carried out by a group of specialists called 'economists'. Modern disciplinary boundaries simply did not exist; also, the role of universities in society has changed almost beyond recognition. The people responsible for developing economic ideas included theologians, lawyers, philosophers, businessmen and government officials. Some of these held academic positions, but many did not. For example, Adam Smith was a moral philosopher, and his economic ideas formed part of a much broader system of social science, rooted in moral philosophy. Furthermore, the people who wrote the conventional canon of economic literature occupied various positions in the societies in which they lived, which means that comparisons across time have to be made with great care. When the thirteenth-century writer Thomas of Chobham wrote about trade and finance, he was offering guidance for priests taking confession. Perhaps the present-day counterpart to his work should be sought not in modern academic economics, but in papal encyclicals. Gerard Malynes and Thomas Mun, both of whom wrote in seventeenth-century England and are considered to have contributed to our understanding of foreign trade and exchange rates, were respectively a government official and a merchant. Perhaps they should be considered the forerunners of people like Jacques Polak at the International Monetary Fund, or the financier James Goldsmith.

When writing history of economics that covers over any period longer than about the last century, we have no choice but to select from a great variety of literature, written by different people for different purposes under different circumstances. Indeed, one of the most interesting things about the history is to see what has happened to ideas as they have been taken up by different writers and used for different purposes. This means that we have to be careful not to treat past writers as though they were modern academic economists.

What is Economics?

The discussion so far has rested on the assumption that we know what economics and economic phenomena are. But economics is notoriously difficult to define. Perhaps the most widely used definition of the subject is the one offered by Lionel Robbins: 'Economics is the science which studies human behaviour as a relationship between ends and scarce means which have alternative uses.'[1] The phenomena we associate with economics (prices, money, production, markets, bargaining) can be viewed either as consequences of scarcity or as ways in which people try to overcome the problem of scarcity. Robbins's definition goes a long way towards capturing the features common to all economic problems, but it represents a very specific, limited view of the nature of such problems. Why, for example, should the operations of multi-national corporations in developing countries, or the design of policy to reduce mass unemployment, be seen as involving choices about how to use scarce resources? It is perhaps ironic that Robbins's definition dates from 1932, during the depths of the Great Depression, when the world's major economic problem was that vast resources of capital and labour were lying idle.

A more natural definition is that of the great Victorian economist Alfred Marshall, who defined economics as the study of mankind in the ordinary business of life.[2] We know what he means by this, and it is hard to disagree, though his definition is very imprecise. It could be made more precise by saying that economics deals with the production, distribution and consumption of wealth or, even more precisely, is about how production is organized in order to satisfy human wants. Other definitions include ones that define economics as the logic of choice or as the study of markets.

Perhaps as important as what these definitions say is what they do *not* say. The subject matter of economics is not defined as the buying and selling of goods, markets, the organization of firms, the stock exchange or even money. These are all economic phenomena, but there are societies in which they do not occur. It is possible, for example, to have societies in which money does not exist (or performs only a ceremonial function), in which production is not undertaken by firms, or in which transactions are undertaken without markets. Such societies face economic problems – how to produce goods, how to distribute them, and so on – even though the phenomena we normally associate with economic life are missing. Phenomena such as firms, the stock exchange, money and so on are better seen as institutions that have arisen to solve more fundamental economic problems, common to all societies. It is better, therefore, to define economics in relation to these more fundamental problems, rather than in relation to institutions that exist in some societies but not in others.

Anyone writing a systematic 'principles of economics' has to decide on a specific definition of the subject and work within it. The historian, however, does not have to do this. It is possible, instead, to start with those ideas that make up contemporary economics – ideas that are found in economics teaching and are being developed by people recognized as economists. These, however, do not provide a precise definition, for the boundaries of the discipline are indistinct. Academics, journalists, civil servants, politicians and other writers (even novelists) all develop and work with economic ideas. The boundaries of what constitutes economics are further blurred by the fact that economic issues are analysed not only by 'economists' but also by historians, geographers, ecologists, management scientists, and engineers. (Such writing may not be what professional economists would consider 'good' or 'serious' economics, and it may be ridden with fallacious arguments, but that is a different matter – it is still economics.) Approaching the subject in this very pragmatic way might seem less desirable than defining economics in terms of its subject matter. In practice, however, it is a workable approach and probably corresponds with what most historians actually do, even if they profess to work within a tight analytical definition of the subject.

Having decided on what constitutes contemporary economics, it is possible to work backwards, tracing the roots of the ideas that are found there, as far as it is decided to go. Some of these roots will clearly lead outside the subject (for example, to Newtonian mechanics or the Reformation), and the historian of economics will not pursue these further. Others will lead to ideas that the historian decides still count as economics, even though their presentation and content may be very different from those of modern economics, and these will be included in the history. The result of such a choice is that, the further we go back into history, the more debatable it becomes whether or not certain ideas are 'economic'. When people argue, as they have, that a particular individual or group is the 'founder' of economics, they are claiming that earlier writers should not be considered to be economists.

This raises two major questions about writing the history of economics. Where should it begin? And is our perspective on the past distorted through being obtained through the lens provided by present-day economics?

Some historians have argued that proper economics does not begin until we enter the modern world (say the fifteenth or sixteenth century), or even till the eighteenth century, when Adam Smith systematized so much of the work of his predecessors. Economics, the argument runs, is about analysing human behaviour and the way people interact through markets and respond to changes in their economic environment. Early writers, it is claimed, had quite different concerns, such as moral and theological issues about the justice of market exchange or lending at interest, and their work should not be classified as economics.

There is, however, a big problem with this argument: it is simply not possible to draw a clear dividing line between what constitutes economic analysis and what does not, or between what constitutes 'proper' or 'real' economics and what does not. For example, the moral and theological arguments of medieval theologians about the justice of commercial activities presuppose an understanding of how the economy operates. The economic content of such writing may be half-hidden or obscure, but it is there. The view underlying this book is that economic ideas were present even in antiquity, and that those ancient ideas are relevant in trying to locate the origins of modern economics. Furthermore, even in the present century, economics deals with normative questions (questions about what ought to be done), some of which parallel those tackled by the ancients. Economists are forever arguing that this policy or that will improve the welfare of society. It may be unfashionable to think of this as involving ethics, or morality; nonetheless, ethical presuppositions underlie modern economics just as much as they underlay Aristotle's thinking about the market. The Old Testament contains many economic ideas, as does the poetry of Homer. In a general history of economics, it may not be necessary to dwell long on these texts, but they are part of the story.

My argument can be summed up by saying that economics does not have a beginning or a 'founder'; people have always thought about questions that we now consider part of economics. In this book I start with ancient Greece and the world of the Old Testament, for it is necessary to start somewhere, but these do not represent the beginning of economic thought.

Viewing the Past through the Lens of the Present

The approach outlined above, focusing on what has been termed 'the filiation of economic ideas', is now unfashionable. In a postmodern world, the fashion is to stress the historical relativity of ideas and to decry any attempt to view past ideas from the perspective of the present. However, anyone who writes a history of economic thought *necessarily* views the past, to some extent, from the perspective of the present. Simply to focus on 'economic' ideas is to select past ideas according to a modern category. However much we try to do so, we can never completely escape from our preconceptions attached to the questions we are trying to answer. It is better to state these preconceptions as explicitly as possible rather than to pretend that they do not exist. The objective of this book is to explain how economics got where it is today, at the beginning of the twenty-first century.

A common approach is to write a history that covers the accepted canon of 'important' writings on economics. However, to do this is simply to rely on judgements that others have made in the past. It does not avoid the problem of one's choice of material being influenced by one's interests. What usually happens is that historians start with a conventional canon – a list of the works, figures or movements that are considered to represent the economics of the past. They then modify this, increasing the emphasis in some places, reducing it in others in response to the questions that interest them and the evidence they find. As economics has changed, so too have views about what constitutes the appropriate canon.

To approach the past from the perspective of the present can, however, result in stories that make very unconvincing histories. When the story told is one of progress from crude beginnings to the 'truth' reached by the historian's friends, contemporaries or other heroes, the result is what has come to be called 'Whig history', after the nineteenth-century Whigs who told the story of Britain in this way, and readers are right to be sceptical. Nevertheless, the Whigs' attitude is shared by many economists, some of whom write histories of economics. They find it hard to accept that their own generation's theories and techniques (to which they may themselves have contributed) may not be superior to those of earlier generations. Critics of such work are right when they argue that this approach misses the important historical questions and frequently results in a caricature of what actually happened.

However, to examine the past in order to understand the present need *not* mean telling the story as one of progress. The reasons why ideas evolved as they did will include historical accidents, vested interests, prejudices, misunderstandings, mistakes and all sorts of things that do not fit into accounts of progress. The story may involve certain lines of inquiry dying out, or moving away from what is currently considered economics. We may discover, when we look back, that earlier generations were asking different questions – perhaps even questions we find it hard to understand – with the result that the notion of progress becomes problematic.

The Story Told Here

The story told in this book clearly reflects certain conventional views about what constitutes economics – certain topics are included because it is 'obvious' that they should be there. The publisher (not to mention many readers) would have been unhappy if it said nothing about Adam Smith, David Ricardo, Karl Marx or John Maynard Keynes. It is recognizably a history of economics, as the term is commonly understood. However, it departs from the conventional canon both in the relative importance attached to different figures and in many of the topics that are included. It also tries to place people in an appropriate historical context – one that they might have recognized.

The book is not organized around the 'great figures' of the past, as was once common. Chapters typically start with a discussion of the historical context, and proceed from there to the economic ideas that emerged. The emphasis on economic, political and intellectual history varies throughout the book, and is generally less prominent as the story unfolds. The most important reason for this is that when we are discussing periods when economics was less clearly distinguished from other disciplines it is more important to discuss ideas outside economics. As economics developed, during the nineteenth century, into an academic subject, the problems economists tackled were increasingly ones that arose within the discipline. Also, throughout the book, there is an emphasis on the communities and circumstances out of which economic ideas emerged, rather than simply on individuals: on what could loosely be called the sociology of the economics profession. The position of economists (or, more accurately, the position of people reflecting on economic matters) in society has changed, and this has influenced the way in which ideas have developed. Chapters dealing with early material therefore contain much general history. However, as the story develops, economic ideas become much more prominent and general history plays a smaller part. By the twentieth century, when economics had become a predominantly academic discipline, economic ideas were changing for reasons that were substantially internal to the discipline.

The book does cover the conventional canon, but this is challenged in many ways. The Islamic world enters the medieval story. Political philosophy and the Hobbesian challenge are an important element in the chapter on seventeenth-century England. Smith is viewed as a moral philosopher and is set in the context of the Scottish Enlightenment. Malthus is portrayed not just as a pure economist, or demographer, but as someone who contributed to contemporary political debates. Theoretical contributions of early-nineteenth-century French and German writers are placed alongside those of their English counterparts. Chamberlin is discussed in the context of US industrial economics, not that of the British cost controversy. The list could be continued. The most significant change, however, is that the twentieth century is a major part of the story (almost half the book). In covering it, I have attempted to give as broad a picture of the subject as possible. Given that my main aim is to explain how the discipline reached its present state, developments within its theoretical 'core' are clearly prominent. However, they are not the whole story.

In telling this story, I have inevitably drawn on accounts written by specialists in the various periods the book covers. The 'innovations' mentioned in the previous paragraph are all taken from such works. The number of places where I have been able to depart from the conventional story reflects, at least in part, the range of recent work on the history of economic thought – and this is particularly true of the twentieth century. My main debts are acknowledged in the suggestions for further reading at the end of the book.

1

The Ancient World

Homer and Hesiod

Plato suggested that Homer educated Greece, his epic poems providing
the values by which life should be lived. In the literary papyri found in
Egypt, Homeric scrolls outnumber those by all other authors put
together. Even today, stories of Hector, Achilles, Troy and the journeys
of Odysseus form part of Western culture. It is not clear whether the
Iliad and the *Odyssey* should be regarded as the work of a single
individual or as compilations of the work of many poets, but in either
case they represent the writing down, somewhere around 750–725 BC,
of a long oral tradition. The Homeric epics, together with the poems
of Hesiod (*c.* 700 BC), are as far back as the written record takes us in
Europe.

The society described in the *Iliad* and the *Odyssey* probably reflects,
in part, the Mycenaean (Bronze Age) world of Troy around 1400–1100
BC, and in part Homer's own time. It was ordered and hierarchical,
based not on market relationships, but on the distribution of wealth
through gifts, theft, prizes for winning competitions, plunder received
in war, and tribute paid by defeated cities to their conquerors. Troy
might have fallen earlier, it has been suggested, if the Greek army had
not been so intent on pillaging. Trade was viewed by Homer as a
secondary, and inferior, way of acquiring wealth. Heroes were aristocratic warriors, rewarded strictly according to their rank. Gifts were
governed by a strict code of reciprocity, in which it was important that,
when gifts were exchanged, those involved should hold the same rank
after the exchange as before. Hosts were obliged to provide hospitality

and gifts for their guests, who in turn had an obligation to provide gifts, perhaps to the hosts' families, at a later date in return.

The basis for this economy was the household, understood as the landowner, his family and all the slaves working on an estate. Owners and slaves would work alongside each other. Prosperity was seen by Homer as the result of being in a well-ordered, rich household. On the other hand, there was suspicion of excessive wealth – households should be rich, but not too rich. There were, of course, traders and craftsmen (we read of Greek soldiers exchanging their plunder for provisions, and craftsmen were brought in to do certain tasks on landed estates), but they were less important than landed estates. Even if he gained his freedom, a slave who lost his place on a landed estate might lose his security. The acquisition of wealth through trade was regarded as distinctly inferior to obtaining it through agriculture or military exploits.

Of the two poems attributed to Hesiod, the one that is seen as having the most substantial economic content is *Works and Days*. He starts with two creation stories. One is the well-known story of Pandora's box. The other, undoubtedly influenced by Mesopotamian creation stories, tells of a descent from the golden age of the immortals, 'remote from ills, without harsh toil',[1] to a race of iron, for whom toil and misery are everyday realities. Hesiod offers his readers much advice about coping with life under these conditions. *Works and Days* is a poem within the tradition of oriental wisdom literature, moving seamlessly between advice that would nowadays be seen as ritualistic or astrological and practical advice on agriculture and on when to set sail in order to avoid being lost at sea. Though they fall within the same tradition, however, when compared with the Babylonian and Hebrew creation stories, Hesiod's stories (like those of Homer) are comparatively secular. It is Zeus who provides prosperity, and Hesiod regards morality and pleasing Zeus as the main challenges that men have to deal with, but the stories are the product of the author's own curiosity, not the work of priests.

Hesiod can be read as having realized that the basic economic problem is one of scarce resources. The reason men have to work is that 'the gods keep men's food concealed: otherwise you would easily work even in a day enough to provide you for the whole year without working'.[2]

Choices have to be made between work (which leads to wealth) and leisure. Hesiod even suggests that competition can stimulate production, for it will cause craftsmen to emulate each other. However, though these ideas are clearly present in *Works and Days*, they are not expressed in anything like such abstract terms. Hesiod describes himself as a farmer, and says that his father was forced to emigrate owing to poverty. The virtues he sees as leading to prosperity are thus – not surprisingly – hard work, honesty and peace. His ideal is agricultural self-sufficiency, without war to destroy the farmer's produce. This is far from the aristocratic disparagement of work and support for martial virtues that can be found in Homer, but the two poets share the idea that security is bound up with land.

Hesiod's poetry provides a good illustration of the earliest writings on economic questions. Economic insights are there, but nothing is developed very far and it is difficult to know how much significance to attach to them.

Estate Management – Xenophon's *Oikonomikos*

The period from the seventh to the fourth centuries BC saw great literary, scientific and philosophical achievements. Thales (*c*. 624–*c*. 546 BC) proposed the idea that water was the primal substance underlying all forms of life, and the notion that the earth was a disk floating on water. Anaximander (*c*. 610–*c*. 546 BC) drew the first map of the known world and composed what is believed to be the first treatise written in prose. We know little of their reasoning, for very little of what they wrote has survived, but the important point is that they were trying to reason about the nature of the world, liberating themselves from mythology. Towards the end of the sixth century Pythagoras (*c*. 570–*c*. 490 BC) used theory and contemplation as means of purifying the soul. Though he was engaged in what we would now see as a form of number mysticism, in which numbers and ratios have mystical properties, he and his followers made enduring contributions to philosophy and mathematics. The fifth century saw the emergence of playwrights, Aeschylus (*c*. 525–456 BC), Sophocles (*c*. 495–406 BC) and Euripides (*c.* 480–406 BC), and historians such as Herodotus (*c.* 485–*c.* 425 BC) and Thucydides (*c.* 460–*c.* 400 BC).

These developments form the background to the world of Xenophon (*c.* 430–354 BC) and Plato (*c.* 429–347 BC). For this period there is virtually no economic data. Our knowledge of it therefore comes solely from political history. But we do know that the economy of this period was, like that of Homer's day, still based on agriculture, with landed estates as the main source of wealth. There had, however, been enormous political and economic changes in the intervening centuries. Among the most important of these were the reforms introduced in Athens by Solon, appointed *archon*, or civilian head of state, in 594 BC. These curtailed the power of the aristocracy, and laid the basis for democratic rule based on the election, by the property-owning classes, of a council of 400 members. Land was redistributed, laws were codified, and a silver currency was established. The Athenian merchant fleet was enlarged, and there was an expansion of trade. Specialized agriculture developed as Athens exported goods – notably olive oil – in return for grain. The old ideal of self-sufficiency began to break down.

Though intended to bring stability, Solon's reforms resulted in class divisions and political upheaval. Athens and the other Greek cities also became involved in a series of wars with the Persians. In 480 BC Athens itself fell to the Persians, but the Persian fleet was defeated at Salamis. The following year the Persian army was defeated by the Spartans at Plataea and hostilities came to an end. The legacy of the Greek naval victory was that Athens became the leader of a maritime alliance of Greek states, exacting tribute from them. In effect, Athens was the centre of an empire, her great rival being Sparta. The strengths of Athens were trade and sea power; Sparta's position was based on agriculture and its army. War eventually broke out between the two states in 431 BC – the start of the Peloponnesian War that ended with the defeat of Athens, in 404 BC, and the dissolution of the naval league.

For the fifty years from the end of the Persian Wars till the start of the Peloponnesian War, Athens was essentially at peace. The result was a period of great prosperity known as the Periclean Age, after Pericles, who led the more democratic party from 461 to 430 BC. Piracy was removed from the eastern Mediterranean, trade flourished, and commercial agriculture and manufacturing developed, along with many of the activities now associated with a commercial society: banking, credit, money-changing, commodity speculation and monopoly trading. One historian has written of Athens being 'a commercial centre with a complex of economic activities that was to remain unsurpassed until post-Renaissance Europe'.[3] The resulting prosperity was the basis for great building projects, such as the Parthenon.

Athenian democracy was direct, involving all the citizens – i.e. adult males of Athenian parentage. Even juries could involve hundreds of citizens, and the fondness of Athenians for litigation – in which plaintiffs and defendants had to speak for themselves – meant that it was important for people to be able to defend their own interests, and argue their case. There was thus a demand for training in rhetoric, which was provided by the Sophists. The Sophists were itinerant, travelling from one city to another, and, though the main requirement was for skills in public speaking, many of them believed that their pupils needed to know the latest discoveries in all fields. The Sophists were thus the first professional intellectuals in Greece – professors before there were universities.[4] The first and greatest of the Sophists was Protagoras (c. 490–420 BC), who taught successfully for forty years before being banished for his scepticism about the gods.

Socrates (469–399 BC) emerged against this background of 'professional intellectuals'. Because they travelled, they could stand back from the laws and customs of individual cities. They engaged in abstract thought, and, though many paid respect to the gods, they looked for non-religious explanations of the phenomena they saw around them. What stands out about Socrates is his method: relentlessly asking questions. It was this that attracted to him pupils as able as Plato and Xenophon. He was, however, the butt of Aristophanes' satire in *The Clouds*, in which his questioning of the gods' responsibility for rain and thunder is ridiculed. As he wrote nothing himself, our knowledge of Socrates stems only from Aristophanes and, above all, from the dialogues of Plato and Xenophon. We can be confident about much in their accounts; however, it is often hard to know precisely which ideas should be attributed to Socrates himself and which come from Xenophon or Plato using him as a mouthpiece.

Xenophon came from the Athenian upper classes and, like all Socrates' pupils, was well off. For some reason (maybe linked to his association with Socrates, who was tried and executed in 399 BC) he left Athens, and in 401 BC he joined a military expedition to Persia, in an attempt to help Cyrus the Younger take the throne from his brother. The attempt failed, and Xenophon, if we are to believe his account of the event, was responsible for leading the troops back to Greece. From 399 to 394 BC he fought for Sparta, after which he lived, under Spartan protection, on a country estate, till he returned to Athens in 365 BC. Most of his writing was done in this more settled period of his life.

Oikonomikos, the title of Xenophon's work, is the origin of the words 'economist' and 'economics'. It is, however, better translated as *The Estate Manager* or *Estate Management*. Taken literally it means *Household Management*, '*oikos*' being the Greek word for 'household', but by extension the word was used to refer to an estate, and Xenophon's *Oikonomikos* is in fact a treatise on managing an agricultural estate. Familiar Socratic themes such as an emphasis on self-discipline and training people to wield authority are found in the book, but its main theme is efficient organization. Given the Greeks' emphasis on the human element in production (perhaps a feature of a slave society), efficient management translated into effective leadership.

The prime requirement of an effective leader was to be knowledgeable in the relevant field, whether this was warfare or agriculture. Men would follow the man they saw as the superior leader, Xenophon claimed, and willing obedience was worth far more than forced obedience. Though he illustrated this with examples taken from war, Xenophon saw the same principles as applying in any activity. The other requirement for efficiency was order. Xenophon used the example of a Phoenician trireme (a ship propelled by three banks of oars) in which everything was so well stowed that the man in charge knew where everything was, even when he was not present. This was how an efficient estate should be run – with stores efficiently organized and accounted for. It was commonly believed that good organization could double productivity.

Seen from this perspective, Xenophon's emphasis on efficiency seems simply an exercise in management, applied to an agricultural estate rather than to a modern firm. His conception of the 'administrative art',[5] however, was much broader than this, extending to the allocation of resources in the state as a whole. He makes this clear when he discusses the way in which Cyrus the Great organized his empire, with one official in charge of protecting the population from attack and another in charge of improving the land. If either failed to do his job efficiently, the other would notice, for neither could perform his task properly if the other was not doing so. Without defence the fruits of agriculture would be lost; and without enough agricultural output the country could not be defended. Though officials were given the right incentives, it was still necessary that the ruler took an interest in all the affairs of the state – agriculture as well as defence. Administrative authority, not the market mechanism, was the method by which resources would be efficiently allocated and productivity maximized.

Because it is something to which subsequent economists and historians have paid great attention, it is necessary also to mention Xenophon's account of the division of labour. He observes that in a small town the same workman may have to make chairs, doors, ploughs and tables, but he cannot be skilled in all these activities. In large cities, however, demand is so large that men can specialize in each of these tasks, becoming more efficient. Turning back to the estate, Xenophon argues that division of labour can be practised in the kitchen, anything prepared in such a kitchen being superior to food prepared in a smaller kitchen where one person has to perform all tasks.

Xenophon's model is of men interacting with nature – not with each other through markets. Productive efficiency involves managing the use of natural resources so as to get the most from them. His is a static world in which it is taken for granted that nature is known and understood. Trade and markets are peripheral. Given the development of trade and commerce in Athens by this time, it is perhaps surprising that agricultural estates are as central to Xenophon's view of economic activity as they were for Homer's. This can be explained by his position as a soldier and, for thirty years, a landowner under Spartan protection. For some of his contemporaries, such explanations are harder to defend.

Plato's Ideal State

The background to Plato's *Republic*, which attempts to provide a blueprint for the ideal state, is the political turmoil that engulfed Athens and the other Greek city states in the fifth and fourth centuries BC. Experience had taught Plato that neither democracy nor tyranny could provide a stable society. Leaders in a democracy would not do what was just, but would use their office to gain support. Tyrants, on the other hand, would use their power to further their own interests, not those of the state as a whole. But without any leadership there would be chaos. Plato's solution to this dilemma was to create a class of philosopher-kings – the 'guardians' – who would rule the state in the interests of the whole society. These would be self-appointed, for they would be the only ones capable of understanding how society should be organized. In the ideal state their whole upbringing and way of life would be designed to train them for their role and to ensure that they fulfilled it properly. To ensure that the guardians would not become corrupt, pursuing their own interests, they would be forbidden to own property or even to handle gold and silver. They would receive what they needed to live as a wage from the rest of the community. Unlike tyrants, they would have to put the interests of the state first.

Plato's vision was concerned with the efficient organization of society – with a just society organized on rational principles. Like other Greek writers, he saw efficiency as involving the human element in production. Men should specialize in those activities for which they were naturally suited, and should be trained accordingly. Indeed, the origins of cities (states) lay in specialization and the dependence of people on one another. He took the physical endowment of resources and technology for granted. His was a static world, in which everyone had a fixed place, maintained by efficient administration undertaken by disinterested rulers. Though he saw a role for trade, the role for markets in his ideal state was very limited. Consumer goods might be bought and sold, but property was to be allocated appropriately (on mathematical principles) between citizens. There would be no profits or payment of interest.

This view of the state presumed that cities would remain small. In a later work, Plato argued that the optimum number of households in a city was 5040. The reason for this number was that it was divisible by the first ten integers, and so allowed division into an optimal number of administrative units. The idea that cities should remain small was consistent with the experience of Greek cities, constrained by the availability of agricultural land and resources. When populations rose, a city would organize an expedition to found a colony. This colony would become a new city in which the Greek way of life would be maintained. Such colonies, which often became independent of the cities from which they stemmed, were to be found throughout the Mediterranean, notably in southern Italy, Sicily and North Africa.

Plato was an aristocrat, involved in Athenian public affairs, who fought several military campaigns. In his early life he had travelled widely, visiting the Pythagorean communities in Italy, from which he probably acquired his interest in mathematics. While in Sicily, he became involved with the ruler of Syracuse, unsuccessfully trying to train Dionysius II for leadership after the death of his father, Dionysius I, in 367 BC. In around 375 BC he founded his Academy (in the grove sacred to the hero Academus just outside Athens) in order to train statesmen to become philosophers. Unlike the school founded a few years earlier by Isocrates, which emphasized the teaching of rhetoric, Plato believed that it was more important to teach principles of good government. Several of his students became rulers (tyrants), and Plato saw the task of his Academy as offering advice to such people. In at least one case, a tyrant is believed to have moderated his rule in response to Plato's teaching.

Aristotle on Justice and Exchange

Aristotle (384–322 BC) was a son of a physician and a student of Plato. He joined the Academy at the age of seventeen, and remained there till Plato's death twenty years later.

The influence of Aristotle on subsequent generations was such that, for many, he was simply 'the philosopher'. His writing encompassed philosophy, politics, ethics, natural science, medicine and virtually all other fields of inquiry, and it dominated thinking in these areas for nearly 2,000 years. His contributions to what are now thought of as economic issues are found in two places: Book V of the *Nichomachean Ethics* and Book I of the *Politics*. In the former he analysed the concept of justice, and in the latter he was concerned with the nature of the household and the state.

In the Athenian legal system, men who were in dispute with each other had to go first to an arbitrator, who would try to reach a fair or equitable settlement. Only if the arbitrator's decision was unacceptable to one of the parties would the dispute go to court, in which case the court would have to decide on a settlement in between the limits set by the two parties' claims, or in between that set by the arbitrator and that claimed by the aggrieved party. In Book V of the *Nichomachean Ethics* Aristotle was considering the principles of justice that ought to apply in such disputes. This perspective is important, because it immediately establishes that he was thinking of principles that should apply in judicial decisions, and that he was dealing with cases of isolated exchange (in which individual buyers and sellers negotiate with each other about specific goods). He was not dealing with exchange in organized, competitive markets. Indeed, it is likely that, though trade was well developed in Athens by the fourth century BC, competitive markets were few and far between. There is much evidence that prices of standard commodities were regulated (even the price of singers was regulated – if demand for the services of particular singers was too high, they would be allocated by a ballot), and the quality of manufactured goods was probably sufficiently variable that the price of each item would have had to be negotiated individually, as in isolated exchange.

When dealing with exchange and the distribution of goods, Aristotle distinguished between three types of justice. The first is distributive justice. This requires that goods (or honours, or whatever is being distributed) are distributed to people in proportion to their merit. This was a common problem in Aristotle's day, for much was distributed by the state – booty from war, silver from the mines at Laurium, and many other goods. Aristotle's concept of distributive justice was a very elastic notion, for merit can be defined in different ways in different settings. After a battle, merit might be measured by the contribution of soldiers to the victory. Within a partnership, justice would require that goods be distributed in proportion to the capital that each person had invested. Furthermore, different criteria may be used to assess merit: in a democracy it might be assumed that all citizens should receive an equal share, whereas in an oligarchy the oligarchs would be thought to merit larger shares than other citizens. The second type of justice is rectificatory justice – putting right previous injustices by compensating those who had lost out. Rectificatory justice restores equality. Finally comes reciprocal (or commutative) justice, or justice in exchange.

If two people exchange goods, how do we assess whether the transaction is just? One way, commonly understood in ancient Greece, is to argue that if exchange is voluntary it must be just. Xenophon cited the example of two boys – one tall and with a short tunic, the other short and with a long tunic – who exchanged tunics. The conventional view was that this was a just exchange, for both boys gained from it. Aristotle recognized, however, that in such exchanges justice does not determine a unique price, but merely a range of possible prices in between the lowest price the seller is prepared to accept and the highest price the buyer is prepared to pay. There is therefore still scope for a rule to determine the just price within this range. His answer was the harmonic mean of the two extreme prices. The harmonic mean has the property that if the just price is, say, 40 per cent above the lowest price the seller will accept, it is also 40 per cent below the highest price the buyer is prepared to pay. Justice involves finding a mean between extremes, neither of which is just.

The principle that justice involves finding a suitable mean also applies to the two other forms of justice. Distributive justice involves proportionality, or geometric proportion, and is associated with the geometric mean. (The geometric mean of two quantities is found by multiplying them together and taking the square root of the result.) Rectificatory justice involves arithmetic proportion (compensation should equal what has been lost). We thus find that Aristotle has related the three types of justice to the three types of mean that were known to him: the geometric, arithmetic and harmonic means. This was far from accidental. Aristotle, like Plato, was strongly influenced by the Pythagoreans, who worked out the mathematical relationship between musical notes. It was believed that similar harmonies and ratios could explain other phenomena, and it is therefore not surprising that there were close parallels between Aristotle's theory of justice and the mathematics of ratios and harmonies.

The influence of Pythagorean mathematics on Aristotle's account of exchange extends even further. By Aristotle's time it was widely accepted that all things were built up from common units (atomism). Geometry was based on points, arithmetic on the number '1', and so on to the physical world. It was believed that this meant that different phenomena were commensurable in the sense that they could similarly be expressed as ratios of whole numbers. This was why it had been a great blow to the Pythagoreans to discover that there were irrational numbers like π or $\sqrt{2}$ that could not be expressed as ratios. Exchange of one good for another was important because it made the goods commensurable – shoes could be measured in terms of wheat. But if the shoemaker did not want wheat, or the farmer did not want shoes, exchange would not take place, making it impossible to compare the two goods. How was this problem to be resolved? Aristotle's answer was money. The shoemaker and the farmer might not want each other's produce, but they would both sell it for money, which meant that shoes and wheat could be compared through taking the ratio of their money prices. It is demand that makes goods commensurable, and money acts as a representative of demand.

Aristotle and the Acquisition of Wealth

However, although money was fundamental to Aristotle's thinking, he believed that there were clear limits to the legitimate role of commercial activity. His argument was based on a distinction between two types of wealth-getting. The first was a part of estate management. A man should know things such as which type of livestock would be most profitable, or whether to engage in planting wheat or bee-keeping. These were natural ways in which to acquire wealth. In contrast, the second type – getting wealth through exchange – was unnatural, for this involved making a gain at someone else's expense. Unnatural ways to acquire wealth included commerce and usury (lending money at interest). Somewhere in between came activities such as mining.

The Socratic philosophers, including Xenophon, Plato and Aristotle, held that citizens should aim at a good life. This was the life of the *polis*, or independent city state in which citizens played an active part in civic life. To do this they needed material resources, provided by their estate. Natural ways of acquiring wealth were ones that increased the stock of goods needed to live the good life. Though estate management was fundamental, trading to obtain goods that could not be produced at home and exchanging one's surplus produce for something of which one had greater need were perfectly natural. But an important part of such a life was that wants were limited, and that once a man had enough wealth to live in the right manner he would have no need for further accumulation of wealth. High levels of consumption were not part of the good life. There was therefore a limit to the natural acquisition of wealth.

What disturbed Aristotle about commerce was that it offered the prospect of an unlimited accumulation of wealth. This was something of which Athenians were well aware, for, although the self-sufficient city state was the ideal, there had been several crises when the city had been forced to raise money from traders. Typically, merchants were not citizens, so raising money in this way meant going outside the *polis*. The puzzle was that, even though they did not do anything useful, traders and speculators managed to create so much wealth that they could help out cities in times of crisis. How was this possible? Aristotle's answer was that goods can be either used or exchanged. Of these, the former is a proper, natural procedure, as is exchange between people who need goods different from what they currently possess. On the other hand, exchange simply for the purposes of making money is unnatural, for goods are not being used for their proper purpose. The unnaturalness of such activities is revealed in that creating wealth by exchange suggests that wealth could be accumulated without limit – something Aristotle believed to be impossible. Men might be rich in coin, he argued, yet starve through lack of food.

The view that there are limits to the proper acquisition of wealth and the use of exchange simply in order to make money fits in with

Aristotle's theory of justice. The essence of natural acquisition of property is that it enables men to live a good life in the *polis*. It has a clear objective, and is not being pursued for its own sake. Similarly, when he turned to the question of justice in the *Nichomachean Ethics*, Aristotle was dealing with the injustice that arises 'not from any particular kind of wickedness, such as self-indulgence, cowardice, anger, bad temper or meanness, but simply from activities for which the motive is the pleasure that arises from gain'.[6] In making this distinction, one can see Aristotle separating out one sphere of life – one that it is tempting to describe as 'economic' – money-making. What is significant, however, is that Aristotle did not see this sphere as covering even the major part of those activities that we now think of as economic, for production and the most important types of trade were excluded. Even more significant, he did not see markets and money-making activities as providing a mechanism that could regulate society. Order was produced not through individuals pursuing their own ends, but through efficient administration.

Like Plato, Aristotle was a teacher. In 342 BC he was appointed tutor to Alexander the Great, and in 335 BC he returned to Athens to found his own school, the Lyceum. It was Alexander who finally destroyed the independence of the Greek city states, so weakened by the Peloponnesian War, as he expanded his Macedonian Empire to include not only the rest of Greece, but also Egypt and much of the Persian Empire, right across to India. Though Alexander's empire was relatively short-lived, disintegrating after his death in 323 BC, its major effect was to spread Greek culture throughout the ancient world. The age of independent city states was over, and the Empire's administration was run along lines taken over from the Persian and Egyptian empires that preceded it. Greek became the official language, and was widely spoken in the towns (though not in the countryside), and Greek mathematics, science, medicine and philosophy flourished in cities such as Alexandria in Egypt. The writings of the Greek philosophers, though rooted in the Greek city state, reached a far wider audience.

Rome

At the time of Alexander's death, the Roman republic controlled no more than a small area on the west coast of the Italian peninsula. During the following three centuries this grew into an empire that covered most of Europe and North Africa. On the death of Augustus (AD 14) the Roman Empire stretched from Spain to Syria, and from the Rhineland to Egypt. It reached its greatest extent in the reign of Trajan (98–117), and, though it lost territories, notably to the Frankish tribes in the north, it retained much the same boundaries till the end of the fourth century. Roads, cities and other major public works were built on an unprecedented scale. Rome was without any doubt the greatest civilization the Western world had seen.

Rome produced armies that conquered the world, and architecture that produced a sense of awe in those who later looked upon its ruins. Latin became the language of the educated classes in Europe. Yet the centre of the Empire was always in the East. Rome relied on Egypt for its supplies of grain. The Empire's largest cities and much of its population were in the eastern provinces in Asia Minor. In contrast, the Western Empire remained largely rural. The cultural centre of the Empire was also in the Eastern Empire – in Hellenized cities such as Antioch and Alexandria, in which Greeks continued to make advances in science and philosophy. Roman writers readily acknowledged their debts to the Greeks, with the result that the Romans themselves are widely believed to have contributed little to economics. They are said to have been doers rather than thinkers – engineers rather than scientists. However, while there may not have been contributions comparable with those of Plato or Aristotle, this view is far from justified. Roman writers made a different type of contribution, the explanation for which is to be found in the structure of Roman society.

The Roman constitution linked political power to the ownership of land and to military service. War and conquest were a major source of wealth, and soldiers were rewarded with grants of land, associated with political power. Romans were expected to be willing to endure the hardships and risks of war in order to preserve their wealth. It followed that the rich, who had more wealth to preserve, should face the greatest risks. The poor man gained little from war and should therefore neither pay taxes nor be required to fight. Trade offered a route to wealth, but this wealth had to be converted into land if it were to bring political power. Land, therefore, was the pre-eminent form of wealth.

The philosophies that gained most adherents in Rome, especially among the upper classes, both originated in Greece: Cynicism, founded by Diogenes of Sinope (*c.* 410–*c.* 320 BC), and its offshoot, Stoicism, founded by Zeno of Citium (*c.* 335–263 BC). The last great exponent of Stoicism was Marcus Aurelius, Roman emperor from AD 161 to 180. Cynicism, like the later teaching of Epicurus (*c.* 341–270 BC) emphasized the here and now. Freedom from want was to be achieved through reducing one's needs to the barest minimum, living in what ordinary men would consider poverty. The Stoics believed that happiness resulted not from material possessions, but from virtue. Moral virtue was the only good, which meant that a man who had done the best he could had nothing to regret. For both the Cynics and Stoics, virtue involved following nature. They were thus responsible for the idea of natural law, by which human laws and institutions could be judged.

The concept of natural laws, applying to the whole of humanity, provided the foundation for the field where the Romans made perhaps their greatest contribution to social thought – jurisprudence. Roman law has exerted a major influence over subsequent legal systems. More important, many significant economic ideas were articulated in Roman commercial law. The Romans had great respect for property, and the law contained many provisions to safeguard ownership. The idea of the corporation, having an existence independent of the individuals involved in it, goes back to Roman law. The law on contracts permitted trade, and guaranteed property and allowed it to be transferred. However, though trade was allowed, wealth acquired from trade remained more controversial than wealth from landed estates. There was always a sense that wealth from trade, which appeared almost to arise out of nowhere, was tainted in a way that wealth derived from the land was not. Stoic ideas were the origin of the concept of reasonableness as it appeared in much commercial law.

Of particular importance was the idea, going back to Aristotle, that if all parties had agreed to a contract voluntarily, that contract must be just. For a contract to be valid, all that was necessary was that the parties had consented to it, not that a particular ritual or formula had been followed. This focused attention on the circumstances under which an action was voluntary – on the point at which coercion rendered an action involuntary. If someone could show that he had entered into a contract under threat, he might be able to get it annulled on the grounds that he had not entered into it voluntarily. In general, however, a threat was held to invalidate a contract only if it were sufficient to scare a *vir constans*: a man of firm character. It would normally, if not always, have had to involve a threat of physical violence. The need for consent was the reason why wilful fraud rendered a contract invalid. For example, someone did not truly consent to a contract if he was misled about the quality of good being offered. Normal bargaining over a contract, however, was allowed.

Conclusions

The world of ancient Greece and even Rome can seem very remote. However, the ideas developed there are more important than their remoteness might suggest. Greek philosophy has exerted a profound influence on Western thought, and the economic thought discussed in this book forms part of that broader tradition. Our way of reasoning goes back to Plato and Aristotle. Plato argued for the existence of universals – ideal, pure forms that could be understood only through abstract reasoning. Aristotle, in contrast, saw concrete facts as fundamental, and general principles had to be derived from these through a process of induction. These two different attitudes still beset modern economics. Roman law has been similarly influential. In addition, the Classics formed an important part of many economists' education, at least until the twentieth century, with the result that many of the writers discussed in the following chapters will have been directly influenced by them.

The ancient world was dominated by self-sufficiency and isolated exchange. As the terms of such exchanges were clearly something over which men had control, it was natural that great attention should be paid to whether they were just. However, although there was no market economy in the modern sense, commercial activity was sufficiently developed and sufficiently prominent to provide a significant challenge. On the whole, the thinkers whose views are known to us (we have less evidence of how merchants themselves viewed things) were suspicious of commerce. These two themes – justice and the morality of commerce – dominated discussions of economic issues right up to the seventeenth century, by which time the existence of a market economy and a commercial mentality had come to be accepted.

2
The Middle Ages

The Decline of Rome

The ancient world is conventionally thought to have ended with the fall of Rome and the Roman Empire. This was a long-drawn-out process, with its end commonly dated to the fall of the Western Empire in 476, though the Empire continued in the East, based on Constantinople (Byzantium), for almost another 1,000 years. The modern world is thought to have begun in the fifteenth century. This was the century of the Renaissance, when Europe rediscovered classical humanism and Portuguese explorers discovered the New World and sea routes to the Far East. An important symbolic date was that of the fall of Constantinople to the Turks, in 1453. In between we have the so-called Middle Ages.

Dated in this way, the Middle Ages span nearly a millennium of European history during which profound economic, social and political changes occurred. The way in which men made sense of these changes cannot be understood separately from religion. The key event here was the adoption of Christianity as the religion of the Roman Empire. The emperor Constantine (c. 272/3–337) was converted to Christianity in 312, and under Theodosius (c. 346–95) Christianity became the official religion, with non-Christians and heretics being persecuted. Religion and politics remained entangled for centuries, for outsiders to the ruling elite typically favoured non-orthodox versions of Christianity. For example, Arian Christianity (heretical in relation to the official religion of the Empire) was widespread in the countryside. After Rome fell and Islam had come into being, the conflict between Christianity and Islam overshadowed the many disputes within Christianity.

Economic problems played an important role in the fall of the Roman Empire, even though attacks by waves of barbarian invaders provide the popular explanation of what happened. A critical period for the Empire was the third century. Population fell by a third, partly due to plague brought in by eastern invaders. The supply of gold fell, possibly because there were no longer new imperial conquests, a major source of gold in the past. Alternatively, the reason may simply be that commerce was failing. With the fall in the supply of gold, trade to the East collapsed. Furthermore, given that the Empire was held together only by the army and that there were many people in the cities who needed to be pacified with distributions of food, taxation rose. At times the authorities had to requisition food directly to feed the army and the poor. Some of the money needed was raised by debasing the coinage. In the time of Augustus coins were pure silver, but by 250 the silver content had fallen to 40 per cent, and by 270 to 4 per cent. Despite attempts at financial reform by a series of emperors, culminating in Diocletian's famous edict of 301 in which he sought to fix prices and wages, inflation continued.

An important economic and social change during the last years of the Empire that became even more marked during the Middle Ages was the decline of the towns. Cities in the Western Empire were essentially colonial towns, whereas those in the Eastern Empire were larger and generated much wealth. As trade declined, so did the position of towns in the Western Empire. There was a general retreat from them, symbolized by the fact that for Christian aescetics such as St Jerome (c. 347–420) abandoning worldly possessions meant retreating into the desert.

To understand the economic thought of the Middle Ages, it is necessary to understand not simply the Greek and Roman ideas discussed in the previous chapter but also two other strands of thought: Judaism and early Christianity. This involves going back to the time of the Old Testament.

Judaism

The economic thinking of the early Christian Church owed much to Judaism. In the Old Testament tradition it was thought that restricting one's wants was an important way to cope with the problem of scarcity. As in ancient Greece, there was also great suspicion of trade, and hostility to lending money at interest. There were, however, some distinctive features in the biblical teaching on economics. Man was seen as a steward, with a responsibility to make the best possible use of what God had entrusted to him. Work was seen as good – a part of the divine plan for mankind. Adam was told to multiply and fill the earth, and even in the Garden of Eden he was to work the soil and to look after it.[1] Abraham was amply rewarded for his faith. These texts can be read as favouring economic growth – those who follow the Lord accumulate wealth.

The Old Testament also contains many laws that regulated economic activity. Charging interest on loans to fellow Israelites was forbidden. After working for six years, slaves were to be set free and given enough capital to make a new start. Even more radical, all debts were to be cancelled every seventh year (the sabbatical), and in every fiftieth year (the jubilee) ownership of all land was to revert to its original owner. There is no evidence that the jubilee was ever enforced, and certainly by the time of the monarchy (*c.* 1000–900 BC) there was considerable inequality. This was partly due to the king's imposition of taxes, requisitioning of goods, and forced labour. (The state of the poor was a major theme in the writings of the prophets.) The provisions of the law nonetheless helped keep alive the view that men were only stewards, not outright owners, of their lands.

Though wealth was the reward given to the righteous man, the pursuit of individual wealth was criticized as leading people away from God. For Moses, worship of the Golden Calf was incompatible with the worship of God. Similarly, when Isaiah wrote of Israel being crowded with foreigners and traders, and (presumably as a result) being filled with gold and silver, he observed that the land was also filled with idols and that people bowed down in front of the work of their own hands.[2] Throughout the Old Testament, seeking to increase one's own wealth is associated with dishonest business practices and the exploitation of the poor. This attitude was clearly expressed by the prophet Amos (eighth century BC):

Listen to this, you who grind the destitute and plunder the humble, you who say, 'When will the new moon be past so that we may sell our corn? When will the sabbath be past so that we may open our wheat again, giving short measure in the bushel and taking overweight in the silver, tilting the scales fraudulently, and selling the dust of the wheat; that we may buy the poor for silver and the destitute for a pair of shoes?'[3]

In the same way, moneylenders were seen, along with traders and retailers, as behaving unjustly – exacting interest in advance and depriving people of essentials such as the cloak under which they need to sleep.[4]

There was thus a clear distinction between the *pursuit* of wealth, which was castigated, and the wealth that arose through following God's commands. As obeying God's commands involved working and acting as a responsible steward, this was far from a condemnation of all economic activity. The objection was to bad practices, not to the acquisition of wealth itself. Pursuing wealth was wrong because it encouraged such practices. Thus, so long as they looked after their own people and behaved justly, the Israelites were encouraged in their business activity. The book of Ecclesiastes even encourages people to engage in foreign trade and gives advice on taking (and hedging) risks: 'Send your grain across the seas, and in time you will get a return. Divide your merchandise among seven ventures, eight maybe, since you do not know what disasters may occur on earth.'[5] The Old Testament is not about withdrawing from the world. Money corrupts only when it becomes people's sole motive.

Early Christianity

In the New Testament the emphasis is different. Jesus was steeped in the Old Testament, and much of his teaching followed the laws of Judaism very closely. In the parable of the talents, he spoke of stewardship and risk-taking, and he taught that the righteous would be rewarded. But he was a working man, many of whose followers came from the poorest parts of Jewish society and had no hope of bringing about major economic, social or political change. Thus he required his followers to give up their possessions, warned that the rich might find it impossible to obtain salvation, and taught that rewards for righteousness would be found in heaven rather than on earth.

For the earliest Christians, notably St Paul, who was responsible for transforming Christianity from a Jewish heresy into a religion open to all races, Christ's second coming, and with it the end of the present world, was imminent. This meant that the idea of economic progress found in the Old Testament was pushed aside. Even the importance of good stewardship of resources was played down. Paul wrote that those who have wealth should not count on keeping it, or even on having time to use it to the full. His advice was that people should carry on as they were, the imminence of the end of the world meaning that there was no point in starting anything new. This was an environment in which economic thought was clearly not going to develop. However, when it became apparent that the end of the world would not happen within the lifetime of the original Apostles (Peter is believed to have died in Nero's persecutions in AD 65), the Church began to think again about economic development. There are some hints of this in the later books of the New Testament, notably the Revelation of St John.

The early Fathers of the Church were therefore confronted with a tension between the views of the Old and New Testaments. On the whole they opted for retreating from the world, possibly influenced by their Cynic and Stoic contemporaries. Poverty and detachment from worldly possessions were encouraged, and we have the examples of hermits and saints who gave up everything, retreating to a life of poverty. The Old Testament injunction to work was explained away by arguing that the problem had been that idleness would lead to corruption. Work was desirable because it prevented people from being idle, but if one could resist temptation this was even better.

The outstanding figure of this period was St Augustine, Bishop of Hippo, in North Africa (354–430). His *City of God* was written to rebut the charge that the fall of Rome to Alaric and the Goths in 410 was retribution for the Empire's having adopted Christianity. The book is significant because it looks forward to the possibility of creating a new society, rather than simply looking back to preserve, or re-create, the past. Unlike Plato, Augustine did not seek to establish a blueprint for a new society, for it is impossible to create a perfect society on earth. Instead he saw progress as trying to get closer and closer to a perfect society.

Wealth, Augustine argued, was a gift from God; but, though it was good, it was not the highest good. It should be regarded as a means, not an end. Though he considered it best not to own property at all, he recognized that not everyone could do this. Private property was, for Augustine, entirely legitimate, but it was important for people to abstain from the love of property (which would cause it to be misused). In the same way Augustine distinguished between the trader and his trade: there was nothing wrong with trade in itself, for it might benefit people through making goods available to those who otherwise would not have them, but it was open to misuse. Sin was in the trader, not in trade. There was, however, an unresolved conflict between this teaching about the legitimacy of private property and the natural-law doctrine of communal property. Private property was the creation of the state, which therefore had the right to take it away.

Augustine took many ideas from Greek thought, but his horizons were incomparably broader. Whereas Xenophon and even Aristotle were concerned with the *polis* or city state, Augustine dealt with a people defined not by birth or locality, but by agreement on a common interest. Depending on the nature of this shared interest, the community might progress or regress. He broadened out the Old Testament notion of development to make it relevant to Christendom, not simply Israel, and provided a perspective on history that proved influential in the emerging societies of western Europe.

Islam

The Western Empire ceased to exist in 476. Though this event was of great symbolic importance, little changed. The barbarian kingdoms that emerged in western Europe sought not to overthrow the Roman Empire, but to become part of it. They still looked up to the Roman emperor, even though that emperor was now in Constantinople, not Rome. The significant event marking the end of the ancient world was not the fall of Rome, but the rise of Islam and the Muslim conquest of Arabia, the Persian Empire, North Africa and much of Spain. The Muslim advance across Europe was stopped only in 732, by Charles Martel at Poitiers. It was at this time that European society was cut off from the Mediterranean and had to reorganize itself. It was now, for example, not with the fall of the Western Empire, that Syrian traders disappeared from western Europe. In contrast, in the Muslim lands trade flourished and a great civilization was established, absorbing Persian culture in addition to the Hellenistic culture brought by Alexander. Centres of learning were established in cities such as Baghdad, Alexandria and Cordoba, and there the legacy of Greece was preserved at a time when it was lost in the rest of Europe. Plato and Aristotle first entered the Latin West through translations from Syriac and Arabic.

The Islamic economic literature of this period falls into two categories: the literature of the 'golden age' of Islamic dominance (750 to 1250) and that of the crisis years which followed (1250 to 1500), by the end of which the Moors had been driven out of Spain and the European nations were embarking on voyages of discovery. The background to this literature was the Koran. Like the Old and New Testaments, this contained no systematic exploration of economics, but it did discuss isolated, practical economic issues. It said that income and property should be taxed in order to support the poor. The taking of interest on loans was prohibited. Inheritance was regulated, so that estates had to be broken up instead of being passed on to a single beneficiary. Beyond this there was little. While these rules presented a challenge, given the highly developed urban civilization that Islam had taken over, Islamic society was very traditional, and the role for economics was rather limited.

In the Islamic golden age, two main types of literature can be found. One is the so-called 'mirror for princes' literature. The mirror books were open letters, usually written by scholars and viziers, which presented rulers with an image of efficient and just government and advised on how commerce and public administration might best be organized. One of the most economically developed examples was by al-Dimashqi (in the ninth century), who explained how the merchant could contribute to the good of the community by linking parties who have surpluses or shortages of particular products. He argued, however, that for the merchant to benefit society he must refrain from speculation and the desire to accumulate wealth. He might take a normal profit, but no more. Another type of writing concerned the organization of either the city or the household. It was written by lawyers and civil servants – sometimes by the sheriffs responsible for ensuring that markets functioned in an orderly manner. They analysed the conflict between free markets (supported in the Koran) and the desire for administrative control of markets and prices – something for which there was great pressure when shortages threatened to make goods too expensive for the urban poor to survive. Such writing frequently discusses economic problems such as pricing, factors influencing consumption, and the supply of goods.

The potential conflict between the Greek heritage and Islamic thought is illustrated by Averroes (Ibn Rushd, 1126–98), writing near the end of the golden age, the last in a line of outstanding Muslim philosophers. His father and grandfather had held the position of chief judge in Cordoba, and in 1169 he was appointed to the same position in Seville. Part of his life was spent in Marrakesh, including a spell late in life as chief physician to the Emir. His commentaries on Aristotle were probably written in Cordoba in the 1170s, and are particularly important because it was through these, translated from Arabic into Latin, that Aristotle came to be known in the Christian West.

Though he had sympathies with Plato's ideal of a strong ruler, Averroes followed Aristotle in seeking to establish ethical principles through reasoned argument. This brought him into conflict with religious traditionalists, who were not happy with the way in which he sought to reconcile ethics based on reason with the revealed ethics of the Koran. At one point the Emir banished him from Marrakesh, and his many books on Greek philosophy were burned.

Perhaps the point where Averroes departed furthest from Aristotle was in his treatment of money. Aristotle had recognized three functions of money: means of exchange, measure of value, and a store of value for future transactions. To these, Averroes added that of being a reserve of purchasing power: unlike other goods that could also serve as a store of value, money could be spent at any time without having first to be sold. He also took a different view from Aristotle on the question of whether money is a commodity like any other. Writing in the twelfth century, Averroes took monetary transactions for granted in a way that Aristotle did not: the economy could not function without it. Money was thus unique. Furthermore, the value of money had to be unchangeable, for two reasons. One was that money is used to measure all things. Like Allah, also the measure of all things, it must be unchangeable. The other was that, if money is used as a store of value, changes in its value are unfair. The money a ruler makes by reducing the amount of precious metal contained in coins is pure profit that he has done nothing to earn, similar to interest on a loan, and is as such unjustifiable. Averroes thus broke with Aristotle's view that the value of money is a convention that the ruler might alter at will.

In the thirteenth century the situation changed. Following the Mongol advance into Europe, much of Persia and Asia Minor fell to the Seljuk Turks. The Catholic princes of Aragon, Castile, Navarre and Asturias managed to reclaim much of Spain from the Moors. This was the background to the writings of Ibn Khaldun (1332–1406), who came from a Moorish-Andalusian family but who migrated to North Africa after the fall of Seville to the Catholics. He pursued a varied career as a civil servant, jurist and historian – at one point he accompanied the Sultan of Egypt to negotiate a peace treaty with the Mongol conqueror, Tamerlane. He was well educated in the science and philosophy of his day. But though he was a member of the ruling class, with close connections to emirs and sultans, his Spanish upbringing gave him the attitude of an outsider to North African civilization.

Ibn Khaldun's major work is a history of civilization in which he wove together economic, political and social changes. It was a work in social science, or the science of culture, in which his aim was not to derive moral precepts, but to explain the organization of society. He was familiar with Greek philosophy, but became sceptical about very abstract theorizing, on the grounds that it could lead to speculation and a failure to learn lessons from past experience. Inquiries had to be exhaustive if their results were not to be misleading.

Civilization, according to Ibn Khaldun, went through a series of cycles. His theory has been summarized by one historian as follows:

A new dynasty comes into being and as it acquires strength, it extends the area within which order prevails and urban settlement and civilization can flourish. Crafts increase in number and there is greater division of labor, in part because aggregate income rises, swelled by increase in population and in output per worker, and provides an expanding market, a very important segment of which is that supported by governmental expenditure. Growth is not halted by a dearth of effort or by a shortage of demand; for tastes change and demand rises as income grows, with the result that demand keeps pace with supply. Luxurious consumption and easy living serve, however, to soften both dynasty and population and to dissipate hardier qualities and virtues. Growth is halted by the inevitable weakening and collapse of the ruling dynasty, usually after three or four generations, a process that is accompanied by deterioration of economic conditions, decline of the economy in complexity, and the return of more primitive conditions.[6]

Though this might be seen as a political theory, explaining the rise and decline of dynasties, and though sociological factors (such as the contrast between the values acquired in Bedouin 'desert' life and 'sedentary' city life) are in the forefront of the story, economic factors are nonetheless equally important. Though not discussed separately, concepts such as the effect of division of labour on productivity, the influence of tastes on demand, the choice between consumption and capital accumulation, and the impact of profits (and hence taxation) on production are all analysed as part of the story.

Ibn Khaldun's account of the process of economic development is a remarkable achievement. When taken together with the other Muslim literature of this period, it shows how great an understanding of economic phenomena existed among certain circles of Islamic society in the fourteenth century. Trade and science both flourished in the Islamic world, and men such as Ibn Khaldun, involved in the legal and administrative systems, were able to use their own experience and the traditions handed down to them to amass a large stock of economic knowledge. Ibn Khaldun's work had little lasting influence in the Islamic world, however. It was in western Europe, not North Africa, that the next major developments in economic thought were to arise.

From Charles Martel to the Black Death

The golden age of Islam was the dark age of Christian Europe. In the south, Muslims controlled most of Spain and were at the gates of Constantinople, while in the ninth century Vikings dominated the north. Flows of gold into much of Europe ceased, and there was a lapse into rural self-sufficiency. Yet Christian Europe survived, primarily through the development of two institutions. One was the monastic cell, in which Christianity was kept alive. By 700, Benedictine monasteries in the rest of Europe had fallen to invaders, but Christian learning, including knowledge of Latin and Greek classics, was kept alive in monasteries in Ireland and Northumberland. By the time these were sacked by the Vikings, Christianity had spread back to France and Germany.

The second vital institution was the system, sometimes referred to as 'feudalism', by which grants of land were linked to military service. ('Feudalism' is a term invented many years later, and meant different things in different parts of Europe, so has to be used with care.) The invaders threatening Europe were horsemen. To defeat them it was necessary to follow the Persian and Byzantine example and use heavily armoured men on great horses, specially bred for their strength. The problem of how to support such horsemen, which had imposed a serious economic drain on the Persian and Byzantine empires, was solved by Charles Martel (ruler of the Franks in 719–41), who used lands confiscated from the Church to endow a new class of warriors. These received rights over land in return for an obligation to put a knight (or a certain number of knights) into the field when called upon to do so by the king. Around this grew up an entire social and economic system based on relationships between land-holding and military service. At the same time Charles Martel brought monks from England and Ireland to reorganize the Frankish church. Monasteries were established, along more puritan lines than the old Benedictine foundations. An alliance at all levels of society was formed between State and Church, the most notable sign of which was the concordat between the ruler and the Pope, and the coronation of Charlemagne (742–814) as Emperor in Rome.

The combination of military power and highly disciplined religious orders provided the basis for a period of European expansion. Norman knights conquered England (1066) and southern Italy (1057–85) and were, together with the monks of Cluny (in Burgundy), instrumental in organizing the 'reconquest' of Spain from the Moors (1085–1340). Between 1096 and 1291 the crusades (inspired by the Church, but undertaken by Frankish knights and their followers) established Christian states in Palestine. The twelfth and thirteenth centuries saw the colonization of the plains of northern Europe. This involved both knights (the Teutonic Knights – the order of St Mary's Hospital in Jerusalem) and religious orders. The Cistercians were particularly active: monasteries set up colonies, usually further east, bringing wasteland under cultivation. In the same way, towns set up new towns further east. Other towns were established by kings. Long-distance trade was revived by the crusades, Venice and other Italian trading cities providing much of the finance and transport, and gold began to be coined again in Europe. Expansion of trade with the Far East was made possible by the Mongol conquests in Asia, which established a unified, tolerant and peaceful empire stretching from eastern Europe to China.

In the fourteenth century, however, this expansion halted. Jerusalem and the other conquests in Palestine were lost by the West, advance in the East was halted, and the Moors managed to halt the reconquest of Spain for two centuries. The eastern Mediterranean was ruled not by knights organized on the Frankish model but by Italian trading cities. Archers (including those of the English at Crécy) began to defeat armoured knights. Trade began to fall, bringing about the collapse of many of the great banking houses of Europe. Then in 1347–51 the Black

Death spread throughout Europe. Population fell by a third, and in some areas by a half. Labour became scarce, and conflicts between labourers and landlords became endemic, with peasant rebellions, legislation to control labour, and attempts by the Church to recover lands it had lost. Feudal society, once the means of expansion, became conservative and inflexible.

The Twelfth-Century Renaissance and Economics in the Universities

But before this, in the midst of the process of expansion, there took place what has been called the twelfth-century renaissance. Perhaps linked to rising prosperity, conflicts between emerging powers (notably Church and State), the loosening of the feudal system, and the emergence of an urban middle class, there arose a demand for learning. Peripatetic teachers, not unlike the Sophists of ancient Greece, emerged. In the first half of the twelfth century, Peter Abelard (1079–1142) argued for the use of reason and against censorship. Conquests of parts of Europe previously controlled by the Moors made Arabic learning available, and via this route Europeans rediscovered the Greek classics. The commentaries of Averroes were enthusiastically taken up, and through them Western scholars were introduced to Aristotle. This ferment led to the establishment of a new institution, the university: Bologna, Paris and Oxford were the first, and by 1400 there were a further fifty-three.

It was from these universities that the period's economic writing emerged. The scholars involved formed a mobile, international community centred on one university: Paris. The economics they produced – usually referred to as 'scholastic' economics – was concerned primarily with ethics. Ethical questions, however, inevitably required people to think about the way in which economic activities actually worked.

The earliest scholastic writings on economics are found in manuals for confessors – books on how priests should advise people who came to them for confession. Economics figured prominently because many priests were unfamiliar with the business practices on which people sought spiritual guidance. An example of such a manual is the *Summa*

Confessorum, by Thomas of Chobham (*c.* 1163–1235), written around 1215 – the year in which it became compulsory for all adults to go to confession at least annually. Economics comes into the book when Thomas reviews the moral hazards of various professions, including that of the merchant. His list of capital sins includes both usury and avarice. However, he provides a strong defence of commerce, missing from many earlier writings:

Commerce is to buy something cheaper for the purpose of selling it dearer. And this is all right for laymen to do, even if they do not add any improvement of the goods which they bought earlier and later sell. For otherwise there would have been great need in many regions, since merchants carry that which is plentiful in one place to another place where the same thing is scarce. Therefore merchants may well charge the value of their labour and transport and expenses in addition to the capital laid out in purchasing the goods. And also if they have added some improvement to the merchandise they may charge the value of this.[7]

He goes on to place merchants alongside craftsmen (a favoured occupation, since Joseph was a carpenter). Thomas warned, however, that it was sinful to deceive the buyer or to charge more than the just price.

Thomas brought several arguments to bear on the question of usury. (1) When money is lent, ownership of the money passes from lender to borrower, so usury involves the lender profiting from property which belongs to someone else. (2) The usurer sells time, which belongs to God. (3) Lending for a share of profits is sinful unless the lender also shares expenses and losses in the same proportion. Thomas did not allow interest to be paid as compensation for opportunities lost by the lender during the period of the loan, but it was acceptable to seek compensation for losses incurred through a borrower's failure to repay a loan on time.

A significant advance in such thinking was made by William of Auxerre (*c.* 1140–1231) – the theologian who, in 1230, is thought to have played a part in persuading Pope Gregory IX not to ban Aristotle's work. William based ethics on natural law, in the sense of 'that which natural reason dictates to be done either without any deliberation or without much deliberation'.[8] A modern scholar has written:

The importance to social philosophy of a concept like this is hard to overestimate. It provides a set of more or less self-evident *rational* postulates on which further arguments are based. The conclusions reached via such arguments (provided they are logically correct) are rationally valid, but they are also normative since they are based on law.[9]

William paid much attention to private property, concluding that it was a necessary evil – subject to the qualification that, in times of need, those with property were obliged to share it with those who had none. In a similar vein, he argued that the use of coercion, including the bargaining power that might result from a borrower needing a loan, rendered a contract invalid. It could not be argued that payment of interest was morally acceptable because the borrower had entered into the contract voluntarily.

The major figures in scholastic economics, however, are usually considered to be Albert the Great (Albertus Magnus, *c.* 1200–1280) and Thomas Aquinas (*c.* 1225–74), both Dominican friars. By the time of their work, economic thought was found not just in confessional manuals but also in commentaries on Peter Lombard's *Sentences* and on Aristotle, both of which were very common literary forms.

Aristotle (*Nicomachean Ethics*, V.5) argued that justice was served if the ratio of shoes to food equalled that of shoemaker to farmer, or if the ratio of houses to shoes was that of builder to shoemaker. This passage has provoked enormous controversy, because the meaning of 'shoemaker to farmer' and 'builder to shoemaker' is far from clear. Albert, in his commentaries on this passage, suggested that it should be read as meaning that the value of one good in terms of another should be in proportion both to the relative need for the two goods and to the labour involved:

As the farmer is to the shoemaker in labour and expenses, thus the product of the shoemaker is to the farmer's product . . . [It is] with regard to communal toil and trouble, they are sufficiently measured.

Exchange is to be made . . . according to a proportion between the value of one thing and the value of the other thing, this proportion being taken with regard to need, which is the cause of exchange.[10]

In the first of these sentences, Albert is saying that the values of shoes and food should be proportional to the labour and expenses of the shoemaker and the farmer. In the second he brings in need as what should determine relative values. When taken together, these passages can be read as explaining why labour should be rewarded: if the bed-maker does not receive enough to cover his expenses, no more beds will be produced. Values should thus be related both to the need for goods and to the costs of producing them. Albert starts with an ethical question, and on the basis of an obscure passage from Aristotle he reaches a conclusion about what prices must obtain if society is to be supplied with the goods it requires.

Thomas Aquinas was a pupil of Albert the Great, and in much of his work he sought to simplify and clarify his teacher's writings. Like Albert, he brought together ideas from Aristotle and the Church Fathers, such as Augustine. This is well illustrated by his teaching on property. This contains all the major arguments used by the scholastics, many of which originated in Aristotle. These include the need for private property if people are to be in a position to exercise liberality, the argument that people will take more care over their own property than over the property of others, and the argument that private property leads to order. But it is in the argument from peace that Aquinas's skill in bringing together patristic and Aristotelian ideas is perhaps best illustrated. The argument is Aristotelian, but Aquinas Christianizes it by arguing that private property is necessary for peace only because of the corrupt state of man following the Fall. However, though Aquinas recognizes that property must of necessity be private, the fruits of that property are common and must be shared, either through giving one's surplus goods to those in need or through buying and selling.

To understand their attitudes towards property and wealth, it is important to remember that many of the scholastic writers were mendicant friars who were committed to a life of poverty. They did not consider wealth to raise the quality of life, let alone to be an end in itself. On the other hand, they recognized that most poor people had not chosen to live in poverty. They also recognized that if everyone were poor there would be no one who could support them. This explains why Aquinas, for example, warned against an excess both of poverty and of wealth. Wealth was beneficial only if used in a way that was consistent with the demands of justice and charity.

One demand of justice was that, where goods were used for exchange, buying and selling must take place at the just price – that there must be commutative justice, or justice in exchange. Here the scholastics took over from Roman law the idea that something is worth as much as it can be sold for without fraud. They were, however, unwilling to draw from this the conclusion that it was just to sell a good for the highest price that could be obtained for it. It was agreed that wilful misrepresentation of a good or its quality was unjust. However, this argument from Roman law presumed that both parties consented to the terms on which the goods were being exchanged, which raised the question of how much information about a good the seller had to provide. Aquinas allowed that a seller could hide some information. If there were an obvious defect, it was enough to charge a suitable price, and the seller did not have to tell everyone about the defect (which might result in the good selling for less than the just price). It was accepted that haggling took place – that buyers and sellers would always try to outwit each other. There was also no requirement for a seller to tell a buyer about factors that might lower the price in future. For example, the owner of a ship full of grain did not have to tell buyers about other ships that would shortly be arriving. The just price was the price that was appropriate in the present, not the one that would prevail in future.

The main idea underlying scholastic discussion of the just price was that the market offered protection against economic compulsion. If the value of a good to its seller were more than its normal value, it could be sold for this higher value, otherwise the seller would experience a loss. However, it was unjust for a seller to take advantage of circumstances affecting the buyer. (Indeed, there was a long tradition in natural law that said that in cases of severe need, such as famine, taking what one needed did not constitute theft – that property became communal.) Competition between sellers, as occurs in public markets, was recognized as protecting buyers.

What the scholastic writers were doing in their discussions of issues such as property and the just price was providing arguments based on natural law to support and interpret (or qualify) the teaching of the

Church on economic matters. Their focus was continually on injustice arising from people being under compulsion, and the need for the victims of compulsion to be compensated. In discussing these problems, they developed and clarified many economic concepts. Nowhere is this more obvious than in their teaching on usury. The injunction in the Sermon on the Mount to 'Lend without expecting any return' was widely cited,[11] as was St Ambrose's claim that 'If someone receives usury, he commits robbery',[12] but they also tried to find rational arguments to support their case.

The fundamental idea underlying all discussions of usury was that money is sterile. Making money from money is unnatural. Thus, if a borrower makes a profit using money he or she has borrowed, this is because of his or her efforts, not because the money itself is productive. This idea of the sterility of money was reinforced by the legal concept of a loan. In law, most loans took the form of a *mutuum*, in which ownership of the thing lent passes to the borrower, who subsequently repays in kind. The original goods are not returned to the lender. This can apply only to fungible goods, such as gold, silver, wine, oil or grain, that are interchangeable with each other and can be measured or counted. Because ownership passed to the borrower, it followed that any profit made using the goods belonged to the borrower, and that the lender was not entitled to a share.

The main qualification to the prohibition of any payment by the borrower was that the lender could seek compensation if he or she suffered a loss because the borrower failed to repay on time. Thomas of Chobham, for instance, gave the example of a lender who needed the money to trade at the fair, to pay his rent, or to provide his daughter with a dowry. Compensation for an actual loss was widely accepted. Controversy began when the idea was extended to cover an expected loss caused by default (*damnum emergens*), or to cover the loss incurred by the lender within the period of the loan (*lucrum cessans*). Aquinas, for example, rejected the argument for *lucrum cessans* on the grounds that, as ownership passed to the borrower, the lender who took money was effectively selling something that was not his to sell. One problem with these qualifications was that, if they were allowed, they could be used systematically to get round the prohibition on usury. A penalty clause could be included in a loan contract on the understanding that the borrower would default and that the penalty would be paid.

Nicole Oresme and the Theory of Money

The scholastic economic tradition was an evolving one, and, though Thomas Aquinas provided what was in many ways its definitive statement, it continued to evolve in the centuries that followed. The framework laid down by the Church Fathers and, from the twelfth century, by Aristotle was all-pervasive, but it still left room for change and the exploration of new lines of inquiry. Nowhere is this more evident than in fourteenth- and fifteenth-century writings on money. Aristotelian ideas provided the analytical framework, but new ideas were developed in response to new problems.

The fourteenth century was a time of economic, political and social upheaval. For example, feudal institutions such as the links between military service and rights over land were declining, and commerce was expanding. New forms of credit and banking were being developed. In the middle of the century the Black Death produced a chronic shortage of labour, substantially changing the relations between the different classes of society. Kings found themselves short of income and made increasing resort to measures such as debasement (reducing the gold and silver content of the coinage) to increase their revenues. Questions of money and its role in the economy therefore became much more prominent.

The way in which the Aristotelian tradition could be developed to deal with these new problems is well illustrated by Nicole Oresme's *Treatise on the Origin, Nature, Law and Alterations of Money*. This was written in Latin in the mid fourteenth century by a Frenchman, born around 1320, who studied in Paris, served as adviser to Charles V of France, and died as Bishop of Lisieux in 1382. It was unusual in being written as a short tract on the evils of altering the currency, but it drew heavily on Aristotle and probably reflects ideas that, by this time, were widely accepted by scholastic writers. In the *Treatise*, Oresme puts forward the Aristotelian arguments about the origin of money (in exchange) and condemns 'unnatural' uses of money. There are, however, emphases not found a century earlier. Debasement is condemned as undermining trust in the currency (Oresme regards it as worse than usury, which in turn is worse than making money through exchange). Clipping of coins (in order to melt down and sell the metal clipped off) is also harmful, because the clipped coins circulate as if they are of full weight. In both cases, Oresme's argument is that the action leads to confusion about the value of the currency, and that this is harmful. He cites Aristotle's contention that the thing that should be most stable in character is money.

Another issue to which Oresme pays attention is the ratio of gold to silver in the currency. This, he argues, should reflect the natural scarcity of the two metals – because gold is scarcer, it should be valued more highly than silver. Implicit in this is the idea that scarce commodities are more valuable than those that are more abundant. When the relative scarcity of metals changes, the ratio of gold to silver in the coinage will have to change too. However, such changes, Oresme believes, are rare, and most attempts by rulers to change the currency are arbitrary and designed solely to raise revenue. He likens attempts to raise the value of a scarce metal to a monopolist's charging a high price for his product, and condemns it accordingly.

Oresme's main argument, however, is that money is intended for the community, to be used at a price set by the ruler. In the same way that people may own property but the community has a right to the fruits of that property, the ruler has the right to coin money, and to set its price, but is required to exercise this right in the interests of the community. Thus, although it is wrong for a ruler to alter the value of money for his own ends, it is legitimate for him to do so on behalf of the community:

Since money belongs to the community . . . it would seem that the community may control it as it wills . . . And if the community has great need of a large sum of money for a war or for the ransom of its prince from captivity, or for some other emergency, then it might raise it by altering the money, and this would not be contrary to nature or usurious, since it would not be the act of the prince alone, but of the community to whom the money belongs.[13]

The significance of this passage is explained by an event that happened in 1356. The King of France, Jean le Bon, was captured by the English at Poitiers, and the Dauphin was faced with a demand for 4 million crowns as his ransom. This sum was so large that to pay it threatened the stability of the French currency. The Dauphin (who became Charles V) turned to Oresme for economic advice.

There is, in Oresme's work, a tension between different ways of thinking about economic activity. The first idea is that it is the prerogative of the ruler to determine the value of money. This implies that people should accept clipped coins at full value and not value them according to their intrinsic value (as natural riches). Against this, Oresme recognizes that men do what they find profitable: they ignore the price set by the ruler and sell money 'as if it were natural riches'. This practice leads to precious metal being transported abroad, when it is lost to its proper purpose – to finance trade in the country where it was minted. Oresme thus glimpses the power of the market, for he sees that undervalued money will be exported, causing economic difficulties at home. He also sees that it is important for a ruler to retain the public's trust in a currency, for by this time money had ceased to depend solely on the value of the silver it contained. In other words, money had become more than a piece of precious metal marked with a stamp to save people the trouble of weighing and testing it. However, when Oresme challenges the way in which rulers alter the value of money, his objection is the moral/political one that the interests of the community must be placed above those of the ruler himself. It is thus moral or political constraints, not economic forces, that constrain what the ruler should do. Although the context is much more modern, the underlying argument is thoroughly Aristotelian.

Conclusions

The idea that the Middle Ages produced no significant economic thought is far from the truth. The underlying framework remained an ethical one, informed by theology and law. However, the scholastic writers tried to find rational arguments for their moral judgements – to develop ideas based on natural law. To do this, they had to develop and analyse economic concepts. They were led into exploring what determined the value of a commodity and the role of competition in regulating prices. They also explored the nature of money, and paid attention to the development of new commercial institutions. They used the concepts of expected profit or loss and of opportunity cost, though not everyone accepted that these could justify the payment of interest. Thus, although the scholastics' focus was on morality, they could and did analyse the way in which the economy worked.

3

The Emergence of the Modern World View – the Sixteenth Century

The Renaissance and the Emergence of Modern Science

Medieval society did not suddenly disappear. In parts of Europe, feudal institutions continued into the eighteenth and nineteenth centuries. Serfdom, for example, was not abolished in Russia until 1861. Medieval views of the world, in which religion, science and mysticism exist alongside one another, have lasted even longer. In many respects, however, the fifteenth century marks the beginning of the modern world. This is symbolized by the fall of Constantinople to the Turks in 1453, which marked the end of the Roman Empire in the East. In the second half of the century the Portuguese explored the African coastline, and reached India in 1498. The West Indies were reached in 1492, and within a few years the continents of North and South America had been discovered. The world could no longer be seen as centred on the Mediterranean.

Dramatic as the new discoveries were, however, they were only a part of an even more extensive transformation of European society that took place between the fifteenth and seventeenth centuries. Central to this process was the artistic, literary and cultural flowering, centred on Italy, known as the Renaissance. This would never have been possible without the rediscovery of the Greek and Latin classics. In the fourteenth century Petrarch (1304–74) had looked back on the preceding thousand years as a 'dark age' in comparison with the highly developed cultures of Greece and Rome and had started the process of rediscovering ancient literature. The scholastics of the Middle Ages had, of course, rediscovered much ancient writing, but, whereas they had been interested primarily in philosophy, and above all in Aristotle, Petrarch sought to learn from the entire corpus of classical writing – poetry, history and biography as well as philosophy and science. Classical scholarship (*literae humaniores*) provided an alternative source of moral inspiration to that provided by the Church.

Even in artistic works commissioned by the Church – which were extensive (work on St Peter's Basilica in Rome was started in 1506) – there was an increased interest in humanity. Less and less did major works of art have a religious theme, and, when such themes were treated, the impact of the rediscovery of the classics and the new humanism was clear. To illustrate this, it is enough to cite the names of Leonardo da Vinci (1452–1519), Michelangelo (1475–1564) and Raphael (1483–1520). The same was true of music. Art and music were no longer being used solely in support of religion.

As people rediscovered classical literature, they discovered new perspectives on science, many deriving from Plato rather than Aristotle. It was a view of the world where science, astrology and pagan gods all had a place. A significant part of this was the Neoplatonic association of the sun with divinity, from which it was a short step towards seeing the world as going round the sun rather than vice versa.

The man who took this step, Copernicus (1473–1543), was driven by a Pythagorean search for a simple, mathematical formula that would explain the motion of the planets. What he objected to in the geocentric cosmology he inherited from Aristotle and Ptolemy was its inelegance as much as its inaccuracy – though deriving a more accurate system was of crucial importance because of the urgent, practical problem of reforming the calendar. (Because the calendar year was not exactly the same length as the solar year, the seasons were moving away from their traditional places in the calendar.) Copernicus turned to classical writers other than Aristotle and Ptolemy, and found there the idea of a sun-centred universe whose implications he worked out. Though the predictions of such a system were still far from satisfactory, Copernicus was nonetheless able to produce results that were superior to those derived from the old system. However, although displacing the earth from its position at the centre of the universe involved a radical break with tradition, the rest of his cosmology was medieval. Heavenly bodies still travelled in circles, at constant speed, moved by crystalline spheres. Postulating a moving earth was anomalous in that Copernicus could not answer obvious objections, such as why, if the earth was moving, objects on its surface did not fall off.

Further movement away from the medieval world view towards that of modern science occurred during the following two centuries. Kepler (1571–1630), working with the more accurate astronomical observations provided by Tycho Brahe (1546–1601), discovered that elliptical orbits, with the sun at one of the foci, fitted the data far better. He too was inspired by the Neoplatonic search for harmony and pattern in the universe. However, he still did not answer the main objections to the idea of a moving earth, nor provide any theoretical explanation of why the earth should move. It was left to Galileo (1564–1642) to develop new methods of inquiry (such as turning a telescope on the stars) and to postulate a uniformity between the motion of bodies on the earth and in the heavens. Descartes (1596–1650), again developing ideas from classical writers, took the step of seeing heavenly bodies as particles moving freely in an infinite space. Taking his lead from Galileo, he provided the first statement of the law of inertia. The system was then completed by Isaac Newton (1642–1727), who added the law of gravity. Newton was able to use his laws of motion to explain not only the movement of the planets but also that of bodies on the earth's surface. For the first time, there was a coherent and complete alternative to medieval cosmology. The universe was seen no longer as being kept in motion by God but as governed by mechanical laws. God might play a role in setting it in motion (a divine clock-maker), but thereafter his role was at an end.

Such a brief account of the rise of modern science is necessarily oversimplified, but it is enough to make several important points. The Scientific Revolution involved a profound transformation in how the world was viewed, with implications not only for the way in which natural phenomena were thought of but also for thinking about religion and society. A change of this magnitude was a long-drawn-out process. At its beginning, anticipations of the Scientific Revolution can be found in the *via moderna* (modern way) stemming from the work of William of Ockham (*c.* 1285–*c.* 1349), with its separation of the spheres of human reason and divine revelation. Towards the end of the transformation, even Newton retained a belief in astrology that cannot be separated from his astronomy.

The Reformation

The sixteenth century was also the time of the Reformation, when the Protestant Churches separated from the Roman Catholic Church. This event, or series of events, had profound political and social consequences. Although this has been disputed, it may even have been an important factor underlying the economic growth in England and the Netherlands, two Protestant countries, during the seventeenth and eighteenth centuries. However, it did not involve any significant break with traditional economic thinking, for it was essentially a conservative movement – a reaffirmation of Judaeo-Christian morality and theology against the humanistic-pagan influences of the Renaissance. The event that provoked Luther's publication of his ninety-five theses in 1517 was the arrival of a friar selling indulgences to pay for the building of St Peter's Basilica.

One of the factors that made Luther's stand against the Church hierarchy more far-reaching than the many similar protests that had been made in earlier centuries was the invention of printing. The Gutenberg Bible was printed in 1455, and by the end of the fifteenth century the number of books printed probably exceeded the number written by scribes in the previous thousand years. Printing meant that Protestant ideas could spread rapidly within Europe. Luther's protest thus became much more than a single monk's quarrel with the Church. The other factor underlying the success of the Reformation was the emerging nationalism within Europe. In the German states, Luther found protectors against both the papacy and the Habsburg Empire. Religious differences could be used as weapons in political battles.

The major figures in the Reformation – Martin Luther (1483–1546), Jean Calvin (1509–64) and Ulrich Zwingli (1484–1531) – were conservative on economic questions. Luther strictly upheld the prohibition of usury and the doctrine of the just price, even rejecting some of the exceptions that had come to be accepted. As money was sterile, for example, it was wrong to demand a premium for late payment. He endorsed the idea of a hierarchically ordered society, in keeping with medieval thinking. In general, however, Luther had little interest in economic questions and certainly no curiosity about economic matters. Similarly, although Calvin relaxed the teaching on usury, he too held strongly to the idea of the just price. Businessmen were expected to make only moderate profits, and were not to seek all they could get. Even on usury, however, his thinking was in practice close to scholastic doctrine. While he accepted that the payment of interest was legitimate, he hedged it with qualifications: people should not be professional moneylenders, they should not take advantage of the poor, and they should obey legal restrictions on interest rates. Such doctrines were all firmly in the scholastic tradition.

The Reformation had a very direct impact on political thought. In the medieval world view, good laws were judged by their conformity with God's law. Sovereignty derived from God. Thus it was on the authority of the Pope, Christ's vicar on earth, that Charlemagne was crowned Holy Roman Emperor in 800. Though there were continual disputes between secular and ecclesiastical authorities, neither side sought to dispense completely with the other. Conflict between the two jurisdictions was a defining feature of medieval politics, not something that could be eliminated. On the other hand, given the need to resolve such conflicts, a large literature grew up on the claims that secular and ecclesiastical authorities might rightly make. Radicals entertained the notion that sovereignty might come from the people, though at the same time seeking to reconcile this with the idea that God was sovereign over all.

This situation was transformed with the Reformation. There was no longer any single ecclesiastical authority to which everyone owed allegiance. If a ruler became Protestant, there was a problem for those of his subjects who remained loyal to the Catholic Church. Individual Protestants living under a Catholic ruler were in a similar situation. It was possible to conceive how subjects might find themselves in a situation in which religious scruple called for disobedience to their

55

ruler. In short, there was now a problem of political obligation. A new basis for political structures was required. One way to obtain this was to appeal to the idea of natural law. Though stemming from Stoic and Roman thought, and developed by the scholastics, the idea of natural law was taken up by Protestant lawyers and philosophers. This had implications for economic thought, though it was not until the seventeenth century (with the work of Grotius, Pufendorf, Hobbes and Locke – see pp. 74–5, 80–82 and 108) that these were explored. In the sixteenth century, novel economic thinking arose from a different quarter.

The Rise of the European Nation State

Alongside these cultural and religious changes was a fundamental change in the way in which society was organized. Medieval society was one where a variety of powers competed with each other for supremacy. This was most clearly represented in the long struggle between the emperors (first the Roman emperor, later the Holy Roman Emperor) and the papacy. Alongside these, numerous local princes also claimed allegiance. There had, of course, been monarchies for centuries, but they rarely ruled over lands that had any strong national identity, and their power was frequently limited by the power of nobles living within their realms: kings had no monopoly over military force. However, from the fifteenth century, this began to change. There emerged several powerful nation states, each of which comprised a defined geographical area in which the inhabitants shared a common national identity and were ruled by a king who held a monopoly of military power and hence political power. The power of the nobility became subject to that of the monarch. This process was most advanced in England, which had a defined national boundary and was secure from foreign invasion, but France and Spain – much larger and then more powerful – were not far behind.

These emerging nation states had extremely meagre resources available to them. They had to raise armies and maintain navies, but their administrative apparatus and tax powers were very limited. Maintaining a permanent national army was beyond the economic capacity of any government, and rulers had to resort to such expedients as employing foreign mercenaries. Kings, even of the most prosperous parts of Europe, were chronically short of money. Thus not only did people increasingly think in national terms, they also started to consider ways in which the economic power of nations could be increased. There were changes in the economic environment too. The geographic discoveries made by the Portuguese and Spanish changed trade patterns. The opening of long-distance maritime trade routes had an enormous effect and arguably marked a turning point in western-European economic history. Spanish conquests in America brought large quantities of gold and silver to Europe. Prices, which had fallen steadily through the fourteenth and fifteenth centuries, began to rise in the sixteenth. The changing role of the Church in society meant that the state had to take on new responsibilities. The Poor Law, introduced by Elizabeth I of England in 1597–1601, to provide support for the destitute, was something that had not been needed a century earlier.

These changes were associated with two significant shifts in the economic balance of Europe. The first was the decline of independent city states. The cities that grew most rapidly during the sixteenth century were capital cities. For example, the population of London rose from less than 50,000 in 1500 to around 575,000 in 1700. Other cities did not grow to the same extent. Venice, for example, declined in importance relative to London, Paris and Amsterdam. The second shift was the increased prosperity of the countries bordering on the North Sea and the decline of the Mediterranean. It has been argued that by the end of the seventeenth century conditions were such that it is inconceivable that the Industrial Revolution could have occurred anywhere other than in England or the Low Countries. It would be difficult to come to this conclusion looking at the situation two centuries earlier.

Mercantilism

The rise of the European nation state is often associated with 'mercantilism'. This term has been used to describe the economic thought of the entire period from the end of the Middle Ages to the Age of

Enlightenment – from the fifteenth century to the eighteenth – but the word 'mercantilism' (along with its synonym 'the mercantile system') was not used until the second half of the eighteenth century. Its inventor was the Marquis de Mirabeau (see p. 100), in 1763, but the person who popularized it was Adam Smith, who used it in his *Wealth of Nations* in 1776 (see p. 121). Smith used it as a label for a set of policies he was criticizing. It was then taken up by economists and historians, who used it to refer to different things. As often happens when terms develop in this way, Smith grossly oversimplified his predecessors' thinking, and many of these oversimplifications were carried over into the ensuing literature. However, although some historians have argued that it would be better to avoid using the term, it can be used to describe certain broad sets of ideas and policies.

Mercantilist policies include the use of state power to build up industry, to obtain and to increase the surplus of exports over imports, and to accumulate stocks of precious metals. These stocks of precious metals, which could readily be turned into money, were believed to be important for national power. They might bring economic advantages (for example, a larger supply of money might stimulate production and employment), and they were needed to pay armies.

Mercantilist economics, unlike ancient or medieval economics, was centred on the nation state, which was viewed as being in a competitive struggle with other nations. However, the so-called 'mercantilist' era spanned three or possibly four centuries during which major economic and social changes took place. It covered countries ranging from the prosperous, growing economies of England and the Netherlands to much more backward regions such as those in eastern Europe. There were also great differences in social and political institutions within Europe. To see why these matter, consider some of the goals that have been proposed to explain mercantilist policies. These include (1) unification of the state through a system of national protective tariffs and internal free trade; (2) provision of sufficient revenue for the state through developing the economy; (3) high employment, through encouraging trade and increases in the money supply; and (4) accumulation of treasure and wealth through trade policy. The problem is that different aims applied in different countries and at different times. Unification through customs policies was unnecessary in England, and was not achieved in Germany till the late nineteenth century. Provision of state revenue through economic development characterizes the policy of Colbert under Louis XIV in France (see pp. 89–90), but does not fit the policies pursued in other countries. Not surprisingly, therefore, it can be argued that policies have to be explained in terms of responses to particular problems rather than as the result of governments seeking to achieve some larger aim.

There is also the problem that the term 'mercantilism' is used to denote both the economic policies pursued and the economic ideas that were used to analyse those policies. It refers both to the actions and ideas of statesmen such as Colbert and to the people who developed ideas about how the economy worked – the so-called 'mercantilist' writers. Like mercantilist policy-makers, mercantilist writers were generally responding to immediate practical problems. Their thinking was strongly influenced by the context in which these problems arose, and by the perspectives from which they tackled them. Contributors to the mercantilist literature include academics working in the scholastic tradition (natural-law philosophers), lawyers, government officials or 'consultant administrators', merchants, speculators and adventurers. It is therefore not surprising that there was no uniform mercantilist doctrine. It is for this reason that the term 'mercantilism' will be used very sparingly in this and following chapters. Though many of the writers discussed could be labelled 'mercantilist', in most cases it is preferable to focus on other aspects of their work and to refrain from categorizing them in this way. Sometimes, however, it is hard to avoid using the term.

Machiavelli

The best-known political thinker of the sixteenth century and of the Renaissance was Niccolò Machiavelli (1469–1527) author of *The Prince* (written in 1513). Although Machiavelli's approach has much in common with the approaches of seventeenth-century writers, his book was a response neither to the problems of emerging nation states nor to the Reformation's undermining of medieval conceptions of sovereignty. Machiavelli – writing before the Reformation – was responding to the situation facing certain Italian city states.

His book broke with the past in many ways. The interests of the state were clearly separated from religion, and the science of politics was seen as separate from morality. Machiavelli offered an analysis of how rulers could most efficiently achieve their objectives – typically to increase state power. Though subsequent commentators have often focused on his precepts concerning the ruthless use of power by rulers, it is arguably the way in which he approached the problem that was more important. His methods involved both observation – drawing conclusions from the results of policies pursued by rulers in the past – and deduction from general assumptions about human nature. He based his advice on the assumption that people would behave unscrupulously, in a self-interested way – not because he believed that men had no moral principles, but because this was the safest and most reliable assumption to make. Men might behave morally or altruistically, but it was foolish for rulers to rely on this.

The School of Salamanca and American Treasure

Scholastic thought continued through the sixteenth and seventeenth centuries, though its content changed in response to new circumstances. One place where it remained strong was Spain, where the pre-eminent school was at Salamanca. Here, theologians and jurists continued to write in the traditional scholastic style – full of questions, objections, distinctions, solutions and conclusions, quoting extensively from Aristotle and Aquinas. Their economic analysis began with Aristotle, but, despite this, they were responsive to the new problems posed by the growth of commerce and the influx of vast quantities of treasure from the New World into what was a backward part of Europe. The main problems facing the School of Salamanca were usury, prices and money, where it was necessary to bring Thomistic doctrines into line with contemporary business practices, and to explain the dramatic changes that American treasure was having.

An important figure in the line of Salamancan writers was Martín de

Azpilcueta Navarro, or Navarrus (d. 1586), a Dominican who had taught law at Toulouse and Cahors before moving to Spain. Navarrus's account of the value of money is contained in 'Comentario resolutorio de usuras', an appendix to a theological manual published in 1556. He began from Aristotle's observation that the purpose of money is to facilitate trade. However, where earlier writers had condemned other uses of money as unnatural, Navarrus argued that changing it for profit was an important secondary use of money. In the same way that it was just for merchants to make moderate profits from buying and selling goods, money-changing was lawful if done to obtain a moderate living. He also took a more relaxed view of usury, allowing a greater range of compensation for loss.

However, how could someone make a profit at the same time as always dealing in money at its just price? Navarrus's answer was that the value of money was not constant, determined simply by its tale (the stamp on it) or the quantity of precious metal it contained. The value also depended on money's scarcity and the need for it, as well as on factors such as uncertainty about whether it would be raised or lowered in value, or even repudiated. Though it was wrong for money-changers to create artificial shortages in order to make a large profit, it was legitimate to take advantage of normal variations in the value of money, buying monies where or when they were cheap, and selling where or when they were dear.

These moral assertions rested on a supply-and-demand theory that was applied to money as well as to other commodities: that

all merchandise becomes dearer when it is in great demand and short supply, and that money, in so far as it may be sold, bartered, or exchanged by some other form of contract, is merchandise and therefore becomes dearer when it is in great demand and short supply.[1]

This, Navarrus contended, was why prices rose 'after the discovery of the Indies, which flooded the country with gold and silver'.[2] Though it might look as though all other goods had become more expensive, this was because money had fallen in value. He went on to explain changes in the relative price of gold and silver in a similar way.

One of the problems faced by Spain was that, though it received vast quantities of treasure from America, little of it remained in the country. Money flowed out to the rest of Europe: it was most abundant in cities such as Genoa, Rome, Antwerp and Venice. One response to this was to impose laws forbidding its export. Thomas de Mercado (d. 1585), another member of the School of Salamanca, used exactly the same arguments as Navarrus to claim that such laws would fail to keep money in. If money was being exported it was because it was more highly valued abroad than at home – in Antwerp rather than Seville, say – and so the only way to stop it leaving the country was to increase its domestic value relative to other commodities. Like Navarrus, Mercado argued that these natural variations in the value of money in different places justified making profit through engaging in foreign-exchange transactions.

The idea that scarcity makes goods dear and plenty makes them cheap has a history going back to ancient times, so it is not surprising that the Salamancans were not alone in seeing a link between American treasure and rising prices. Another to do so was Jean Bodin (1530–96), a lawyer and official in the French government. Bodin noted that prices of all goods and also the price of land had risen. He claimed that the principal reason for this was not scarcity or monopoly (two reasons often given for high prices), but the abundance of gold and silver. Bodin cited historical examples, from biblical and ancient times, to support this claim. One way in which his *Response to the Paradoxes of Malestroit Concerning the Rising Prices of All Things and the Means to Remedy the Situation* (1568) stands out from the Salamancan works is in its detailed factual discussion of monetary conditions in different parts of Europe, which enabled him to discuss with some authority how trade caused money to flow from one country to another.

England under the Tudors

The end of the Middle Ages in England is usually dated to the accession to the throne of Henry Tudor, in 1485. Though the Tudor monarchy confronted many of the problems facing other European rulers of the period, such as inflation and a chronic shortage of revenue, defining national boundaries was not one of them. The most interesting economic work from the Tudor period is *A Discourse of the Common Weal of This Realm of England*, probably written by Sir Thomas Smith (1513–77), a Cambridge don, lawyer and government official, in 1549 and revised in 1581.[3] It takes the form of a conversation between a doctor (the leading figure), a knight, a merchant, a craftsman and a husbandman (farmer), in which many of the social and economic problems of the day are discussed – the major ones being inflation and the enclosure of common land so that it can be used for grazing sheep.

Inflation was, as in the rest of Europe, a serious problem in sixteenth-century England. In earlier centuries prices had fluctuated, but there had been no long-term tendency for prices to rise, whereas by the end of the sixteenth century wheat prices were between four and five times higher than they were at its beginning. The author of the *Discourse* clearly sees the difference between real and money incomes, for he points out that rising prices harm only those people on fixed incomes: landlords whose rents are fixed by pre-existing contracts, and workers who work for fixed wages. Those who buy and sell gain from rising prices. He also points out that it does not make sense to complain about foreign goods being more expensive if the goods that are exported to buy them have also risen in price.

People were very familiar with the idea that scarcity, or 'dearth', could cause high prices, but the problem now was that prices were rising even when goods were plentiful. The explanation offered by Smith was debasement of the currency – hardly surprising, given that the first version of the *Discourse* was written in the middle of the so-called 'Great Debasement' of 1542–51, during which the silver content of the shilling was reduced to a sixth of its previous amount. Such changes in the value of the currency were roundly condemned. In 1581, perhaps because Smith had by now read Bodin, a new explanation of inflation was introduced: an increase in the quantity of money caused by imports of gold and silver from the Indies and other countries.

Enclosure of common land was associated with the expansion of sheep farming, to satisfy the growing demand for wool caused by rising exports of English cloth. Wealthy landlords were seen to be fencing off common land to graze sheep, causing a dearth of food and depriving poor people of their livelihoods. Not surprisingly, enclosure was bitterly controversial and was the major issue discussed in the *Discourse*. Smith's explanation was that enclosure was the result of the price of wool being high relative to the price of grain. He argued that men would not engage in difficult or dangerous work unless they received an appropriate reward.

Take these rewards from them . . . [and] what man will plow or dig the ground or exercise any manual art wherein there is any pain? . . . [I]f all these rewards were taken from them all these faculties must decay, so if part of the reward be diminished the use of those faculties shall diminish . . . and so they shall be the less occupied, the less they be rewarded and esteemed.[4]

Smith argued that it was necessary for 'the profit of the plow to be as good, rate for rate, as the profit of the grazier and sheepmaster', otherwise 'pasture shall ever encroach on tillage for all the laws that ever can be made to the contrary'.[5] The way to stop the expansion of sheep farming, therefore, was not to legislate against it, but to make it less profitable. The way to do this was to remove the tariffs that made it so profitable to export wool.

Smith saw the importance of the balance of trade, and frowned upon importing unnecessary luxuries, or goods manufactured from English raw materials. He encouraged the introduction of new industries that would create work and bring treasure into the country. These are all policies that can be labelled 'mercantilist'. However, he showed a keen awareness of the price mechanism, assuming that men were motivated by self-interest. In this, his work marks a major break with scholastic economics.

Economics in the Sixteenth Century

The rise of the European nation state had an enormous impact on economic thinking. Economic strength was vital to national power, and much thought was given to designing policies that would achieve this.

There was a change in the focus of economic thinking. It was also important to tackle the new problems thrown up by the Spanish conquests in America and the expansion of commerce and finance. In the longer term, the Renaissance and the Scientific Revolution were to have a major impact on economic thinking, but in the sixteenth century their influence was much less. The movement away from earlier ways of thinking was gradual – there was no sudden revolution in economic thought.

The School of Salamanca ended up with an attitude towards commercial activities that was very different from that of Aristotle or Aquinas, but its methods lay squarely within the scholastic tradition. Men of affairs, such as Jean Bodin and Sir Thomas Smith – both lawyers cum government officials – moved even further from the medieval view. To a still greater extent, moral questions were pushed aside in favour of analysing what was actually going on in the world and what could be done. Instead of disputing the morality of profit, such writers were beginning to take profit-seeking behaviour for granted and attempted to work out its implications, in much the same way that Machiavelli had worked out the implications for statecraft of people taking those actions that were in their own interests.

4

Science, Politics and Trade in Seventeenth-Century England

Background

Seventeenth-century England produced an explosion of pamphlets dealing with economic questions. In most of them, merchants and businessmen sought to defend their own interests and to argue for policies that were to their own advantage. Trade was organized through trading companies (such as the Merchant Adventurers and the East India Company) which regulated trade to parts of the world in which they were given monopoly privileges. Each of these companies had its own interests, as did outsiders who were opposed to the companies' privileges. The result was a proliferation of new economic ideas. However, the fact that most writers were motivated by self-interest did not preclude careful and subtle analysis, with the result that great progress was made. The rise of this literature can be related to the economic problems facing the country and to a political system that gave people the incentive to provide rational arguments for the policies they wanted to see adopted. Underlying it was an increasingly secular outlook, reflected in new attitudes to both science and politics which had profound effects on the way in which people thought about economic questions.

Science and the Scientists of the Royal Society

Two figures dominated seventeenth-century thinking on science. The first was Francis Bacon (1561–1626), whose *Novum Organum* (1620) provided a manifesto for experimental, empirical, science. He called for a reconstruction of knowledge on the basis of two principles: natural history (the detailed, systematic collection of facts about nature) and induction (deriving laws of nature from these facts). Scientists were to be servants and interpreters of nature. Bacon was critical of Aristotle and other ancient authorities for creating elaborate arguments based on premises that were not based on careful observation and that were frequently contrary to nature. He was far from being the first to make these complaints, but his views were widely discussed.

The second dominant figure was René Descartes (see p. 53). Like Bacon, Descartes challenged scholastic philosophy and sought to establish firm foundations on which knowledge could rest. He is most famous for his phrase '*Cogito ergo sum*' ('I think, therefore I am') – the only thing that cannot be doubted is that I am doubting. However, in the scientific context, the most significant aspect of his thought is the importance he attached to reason. Whereas Bacon sought to base knowledge on experimental science, Descartes sought, in the manner of mathematics, to base it on a set of simple, self-evident truths. Using deductive logic, more complex truths could then be derived from these. The result would be a body of knowledge that was certain and free of internal contradictions.

Bacon and Descartes both challenged traditional authority and offered methods that they believed would provide secure foundations for knowledge. The methods they offered were radically different, in that Bacon emphasized induction and Descartes deduction. However, there were similarities. Descartes argued that the simplest, most comprehensible view of the world was to see it not as a single organism but as made up of various parts. It was to be understood in terms of the way those parts moved and interacted – as a mechanical system. The scientist should rely not on subjective judgements about the world but on qualities that could be measured. Despite their differences, which were substantial, Descartes's belief in measurement paralleled Bacon's belief in experimental science. They were united in rejecting authority as the basis for knowledge.

Bacon's programme was taken up by the Royal Society, which received its charter in 1662 and included most of the leading scientists of the period, such as Robert Boyle (1627–91 – the leading figure), Isaac Newton, Robert Hooke (1635–1703), John Locke and Samuel Pepys (1633–1703). Its motto, '*Nullius in verba*' ('On no man's word'), echoed Bacon's rejection of arguments from authority, and the Society laid down procedures about how experiments were to be conducted and reported if their results were to be accepted. There were serious difficulties with the inductive part of the programme (even the concept of induction was ambiguous). The Society's critics (such as Thomas Hobbes (1588–1679)) raised justifiable questions about its experimental procedures; some of the fact-gathering was pointless, and some of the experiments performed by the 'virtuosi' merited the scorn poured on them by writers such as Jonathan Swift (1667–1745). However, despite these problems, the Royal Society was undoubtedly extremely successful. The achievements of Boyle and Newton alone are enough to establish that.

From the start, economic questions formed part of the Society's programme. Bacon had called for natural histories of different trades – of 'nature altered or wrought'. The major figure here was William Petty (1623–87). Petty studied medicine in Holland and France, served for a short time as an assistant to Hobbes (who himself may at one time have been an assistant to Bacon), and then returned, in 1646, to Oxford. There he met Boyle and became involved in the circle from which the Royal Society developed. However, having become established as Professor of Anatomy at Oxford, and Professor of Music at Gresham College in London, he took leave of absence in order to go to Ireland as physician to Cromwell's army. Cromwell was faced with the task of dividing Irish lands to reward his soldiers and financiers. In 1655–8 Petty undertook the task of surveying, and produced some of the best maps of any country at the time. Through buying land from soldiers who wanted to sell the land they had been given, he established himself as a major landowner, though he had to spend much time defending his titles.

Petty's thoroughly Baconian approach to economics is stated clearly in the Preface to his *Political Arithmetick*, written in the 1670s though not published until 1690, after his death: 'Instead of using only comparative and superlative words, and intellectual arguments, I have taken the course . . . to express my self in terms of number, weight or measure; to use only arguments of sense, and to consider only such causes, as have visible foundations in nature.'[1] His objective in writing the book was to show that, contrary to much popular belief, England was richer than ever before. He tried to achieve this by providing arguments based on numbers and arithmetic calculations.

Central to Petty's claim about England's wealth was an argument about the value of labour. Wealth comprised people as well as land (of which France clearly had more than England) and capital. Starting from the observation that people each spent £7 per annum and assuming a population of 6 million, he calculated that national income must be £42 million. Deducting £8 million for rents and a further £8 million for profits on 'personal estate' (housing, ships, cattle, coins and stocks of goods), this left £26 million which had to be produced by labour. This gave the following national accounts:

Expenditure		**Income**	
Personal spending	£42 million	Wages	£26 million
		Profits	£8 million
		Rents	£8 million
Total	£42 million	Total	£42 million

Petty went on to compute the value of the population itself. He made the assumption that the rate of return for labour was the same as that for land. He further assumed that its value was 20 times the annual revenue that could be derived from it (implying a rate of interest of 5 per cent per annum), and deduced that, if labour contributed £26 million a year, its value must be 20 times that – namely £520 million. Dividing by the population, this gave him a value for the population of £80 per head. This could then be used to calculate such things as the value of the population lost in the Great Plague.

In his other works, Petty produced more detailed national accounts.

In *Verbum Sapienti* (1665) he derived his figures for average annual spending from assumptions about the distribution of spending (that one-sixth of the population spent 2d. per day, another sixth spent 4d. per day, and so on), the number of days worked in a year (287), and the proportion of the population that worked (50 per cent). He also derived his figure for rents by assuming that England had 24 million acres of land yielding rents of 6s. 8d. per acre. Even more detailed accounts were prepared in *The Political Anatomy of Ireland* (1672), in which he analysed the distribution of landholdings, house sizes and occupations.

Simple as these national accounts were, they involved major conceptual advances. Expressing these in modern terminology, these included the following ideas. (1) National expenditure (or output) and national income are equivalent. (2) National income is the sum of payments received by all factors of production (land, labour and capital). (3) The values of all assets are linked by a common discount rate to the incomes received (i.e. the ratio of rent to the value of land is the same as the ratio of profits to the value of capital). This was clearly a major achievement. However, the accuracy of the numbers involved in these calculations was, to say the least, highly dubious. Petty estimated population from bills of mortality (parish records of deaths from different causes) without discussing the assumptions he had to make in order to do his calculations or the reliability of the underlying data. Even worse, many of his figures were pure guesswork. He admitted as much in the preface to *Political Arithmetick*, where he wrote that many of his observations were 'either true, or not apparently false . . . and if they are false, not so false as to destroy the argument they are brought for; but at worst are suppositions to shew the way to that knowledge I aim at'.[2] In short, by modern standards he was cavalier about his figures. The reason for this may have been that he was not interested in completely precise figures. His aim was just to establish magnitudes sufficiently precisely to make the points he wished to make.

Petty's economics was mercantilist in the sense that he believed that a nation benefited from accumulating treasure, and that taxes on imports might help to achieve this. However, he did not simply confuse treasure and wealth. He recognized that foodstuffs were riches too, and he had a theory about why money was particularly important. What was different about silver, gold and jewels was that they were not perishable and thus were wealth 'at all times and all places'. Furthermore, money was needed to drive trade. This is why it might benefit a country for plate to be melted down and coined. The amount of money that was needed depended on how quickly it circulated. Here again Petty turned to a numerical example. If 6 million people spend £7 per annum each, their total spending amounts to some £800,000 per week. If 'every man did pay his expence weekly', money would circulate within the week and £1 million would be enough. On top of this, however, rents of land (amounting to £4 million) are paid half-yearly, requiring a further £4 million, and the rent of housing (another £4 million a year) is paid quarterly, which requires a further £1 million. In total, therefore, £6 million is required by the nation. Petty also argued that increases in the quantity of money led to falls in the rate of interest. Over the previous forty years, he claimed, the interest rate had fallen from 10 per cent to 6 per cent per annum, this being 'the effect of the increase of mony'.[3]

It is easy to look at Petty's data and conclude that he failed to match the achievements of his contemporaries in the Royal Society, such as Boyle and Hooke. His arguments were mercilessly satirized by Jonathan Swift in *A Modest Proposal, for Preventing the Children of Poor People in Ireland from being a Burden to their Parents or Country; and for Making them Beneficial to the Publick* (1729). It is possible to argue that Petty failed to live up to his Baconian methodology – that his deductions were not about causes that had 'visible foundations in nature', that they were no less speculative than those of his predecessors, and that his use of arithmetic was no more than a rhetorical device. This, however, is to miss the point that his methodology did lead him to ask new questions. Merely to ask about the size of labour's contribution to national wealth, the amount of money needed to drive trade, or the effects of different taxes was to view economic phenomena in a new way. In asking these questions Petty was indeed being faithful to the methods of Bacon and the Royal Society. His involvement in surveying Ireland provided him with some data and stimulated much of his work. However, given the extreme paucity of information available to him and the complexity of the problems he was trying to tackle, it was inevitable that his statistics were unreliable.

Though historians of economics associate the term 'Political Arithmetick' with Petty, he was not alone in applying such methods. John Graunt (1620–74), a close friend of Petty, was elected a fellow of the Royal Society in 1662 on the basis of his book *Natural and Political Observations . . . made upon the Bills of Mortality* (1662). He studied data on births and deaths to estimate the population of London and to construct the first survival table (showing how many people lived to various ages). Towards the end of the century, his work and Petty's were followed up by Gregory King (1648–1712). Having more data available, King produced improved estimates of population and much more detailed national accounts than Petty had been able to construct. He calculated national savings, dividing the population into those classes that saved and those with expenses in excess of their incomes. He also produced comparative accounts of income, population and income per head for England, France and Holland, for 1688 and 1695. These and several of his other calculations were motivated by his interest in understanding the potential of these countries to continue in their then state of war. For the case of England he estimated the sources of war finance, calculating the amounts met from increased production, reduced consumption and disinvestment. He calculated, in 1695, that war could not be sustained beyond 1698. (Peace was negotiated in the summer of 1697.) Finally, mention should be made of Charles Davenant (1656–1714), who studied the distribution of taxes across different regions and was responsible for publishing King's work after the latter's death.

The twentieth-century creators of national-income accounts saw Graunt, Petty, Davenant and King as pioneers. However, interest in their work fluctuated greatly. Adam Smith, like many eighteenth- and nineteenth-century economists, was sceptical about the value of 'Political Arithmetick', with the result that it had little influence on the discipline. It was only when the resources of the modern twentieth-century state were applied to the task that it became possible to construct systematic, reasonably reliable national accounts.

Political Ferment

England was in a state of political turmoil for much of the seventeenth century. The early Stuart kings, James I (r. 1603–25) and Charles I (r. 1625–49), were obliged to turn to Parliament when they needed more funds than they could raise from the royal estates and from established forms of taxation such as customs duties. For a time (the 'eleven years' tyranny', 1629–40) Charles tried to rule without Parliament altogether. The country then experienced a period of civil war (1642–9), which was eventually followed by the Protectorate under Oliver Cromwell. The Stuarts were restored in 1660 and, though it was now clear that they could not revert to the absolutism of their forebears, constitutional conflict persisted. This came to a head when Charles II (r. 1660–85) was succeeded by James II (r. 1685–8), a Catholic. James was forced to flee England in 1688 after William of Orange (r. 1689–1702) landed at Torbay. William took the crown as a strictly constitutional monarch. All this political turmoil raised fundamental questions about the basis on which society was organized.

Lying behind such questioning was a deeper change in men's attitudes towards what were, at the time, known as the passions: greed, envy, lust and so on. By the seventeenth century it had become accepted that such destructive passions could not be contained by religious or moral teaching, and that it was necessary to look for an alternative explanation of how society might be held together. One possibility was that one passion might be used to keep others under control. Bacon had argued that, just as a hunter uses one animal to catch another, or rulers use one faction to control another, so one 'affection' could be used to master another. (This approach can clearly be traced back to Machiavelli.) Hobbes believed that the destructive passions (the desire for riches, glory and domination) could be checked by countervailing passions (the fear of death, the desire to live comfortably, and the hope of achieving this through work). These countervailing passions came to be known as 'interests'.

However, at the same time as people started thinking that society was held together by interest, there was a profound shift in the way in which the term was understood. In the late sixteenth century 'interest' was synonymous with 'reasons of state', and was seen as lying in between passion and rationality. In England, during the Civil War, the concept of interest began to be applied not simply to the national interest but to individuals and groups within the nation. At this time, the term covered all human aspirations (glory, security and honour as well as material comfort) and implied an element of reflection and calculation about how these were to be achieved. By the end of the seventeenth century, however, interest had begun to take on a more narrowly economic interpretation. The same changes happened in France. Thus in 1661 Cardinal Richelieu's secretary could write, 'the name of interest has remained attached exclusively, I do not know how, to the interest of wealth'.[4] Thus by the eighteenth century we find writers regularly assuming that people are motivated by, as it was put by David Hume (see pp. 114–16), 'avidity of acquiring goods and possessions' or, more simply, the 'love of gain'.[5]

One of the most widely debated contributions to this process was that of Thomas Hobbes in *Leviathan* (1651). This was influential not because people agreed with it but because, although his conclusions were intensely disliked, Hobbes's arguments seemed so compelling that they could not be ignored. *Leviathan* offended all sides. It offended royalists by arguing against the divine right of kings. At the same time the book alienated the opponents of monarchy in arguing that sovereignty must of necessity be absolute.

Hobbes's argument was that civil society is possible only if there is a government to make and enforce laws. Without government, society would revert to a state of nature in which every man had to look after himself. Hobbes went so far as to describe such a state of nature as a state of war. Every man would be free to do as he liked, there being no government to stop him. Furthermore, every man would be aggressive towards his neighbours, in order to defend himself. Human behaviour would be unpredictable, and the result would be universal fear and insecurity. Property would be insecure, contracts would be unenforceable, and economic life would be impossible. Hobbes worked on *Leviathan* during a decade (1641–51) spent in France after fleeing England to avoid the Civil War. While England's descent into civil war after

Parliament had challenged the King's sovereignty may have influenced his views, it seems likely that Hobbes was influenced as much by what happened in Germany. During the Thirty Years War (1618–48) Germany descended into economic as well as political chaos as competing rulers fought each other while seeking to establish their own claims to sovereignty.

The way out of such a situation, Hobbes argued, was for men to choose a sovereign (either one man or a body of men) who would become both lawgiver and law-enforcer. If they did this, civil society would become possible. In itself, this is a standard social-contract theory of sovereignty. What distinguishes Hobbes's theory from other social-contract theories is his argument that sovereignty must be absolute – that it cannot be divided or limited. To impose limitations on sovereignty, Hobbes argued, would create conflict, ultimately resolvable only by war. The sovereign therefore must have the right to administer justice, to appoint and reward his servants (for it is physically impossible for one man to rule alone), and to censor political and religious opinions. The last of these was inevitable given that religious divisions were one of the major sources of conflict both in the Thirty Years War and in seventeenth-century England.

Hobbes's argument about sovereignty is important in the history of economic thought because in *Leviathan* he was tackling the fundamental question of what it is that holds society together. Though he saw this as a political question, many of those who responded to him began to see it as an economic one. Almost as important is Hobbes's method. His conclusion that civil society requires an absolute sovereign is based not on theological arguments but on rational deductions from assumptions about human nature – that, in the absence of restraints, people will be aggressive towards their neighbours in pursuing their own security. This is a resolutely secular outlook on society. It resembles Machiavelli's approach to politics, but it goes a step further. Whereas Machiavelli argued that it was prudent for rulers to base their actions on the assumption that men might behave in this way, Hobbes works out his whole theory of sovereignty on the assumption that they will do so.

Economic Problems – Dutch Commercial Power and the Crisis of the 1620s

In the fifteenth and sixteenth centuries the economic heart of Europe was northern Italy. The city state of Venice dominated trade in the Mediterranean, and was a thriving manufacturing centre. Trade across the Atlantic was dominated by Seville. In the seventeenth century, however, economic power shifted decisively from the Mediterranean to north-west Europe. During the seventeenth century the population of northern and western Europe (Britain, Ireland, the Low Countries and Scandinavia) rose by a third, while that of the Mediterranean countries (Italy, Spain and Portugal) fell by 4 per cent. After 1600 Venice entered a period of decline. The Dutch acquired the spice trade, the Counter-Reformation created difficulties for book publishing, and the Thirty Years War in Germany took away important markets. Currency debasement in Turkey raised the cost of cotton and silk, two vital raw materials for the textile industry. In Spain, the inflow of American silver declined and the government of Castile faced a series of financial crises. The previous century's prosperity had not been accompanied by any sustainable industrial growth. In contrast, though they experienced severe economic crises, notably in the early 1620s, the economies of northern and western Europe did experience a period of growth, the most successful economy being that of the Netherlands. The *fluitschip*, first launched in 1595, with its long flat hull and simplified rigging, which was much cheaper to build and run than comparable ships from other countries, was perhaps the main symbol of this success.

Like the Netherlands, England was very dependent on overseas trade, and the Dutch were seen as clear rivals to the English. Naval wars, in which trade was the main bone of contention, were fought in 1652–4, 1665–7, 1672–4 and 1680–84. People sought to understand why the Dutch were so prosperous. In particular, were the low interest rates on loans in Amsterdam the cause or the result of Dutch prosperity? If they were the cause, then this could be used to support measures to lower interest rates (such as usury laws); but if they were the result, then such measures might be harmful.

From 1620 to 1624 England experienced an acute commercial crisis, the immediate cause of which was a decline in sales of cloth to Europe. The number of cloths exported from London by English merchants fell from 102,300 in 1618 to 85,700 in 1620. Two years later sales had fallen to 75,600, and it was not until 1628 that they returned to their 1618 level. Unemployment was widespread. Though the underlying long-term cause of the crisis was the growth of foreign competition, the short-term cause was a sudden loss of markets – first in Germany and the Baltic, and later in the Netherlands.

The crisis provoked a large number of pamphlets arguing about its causes and proposing remedies, with different groups seeking to defend their own interests and to blame people other than themselves. Some located the cause of the crisis within the cloth industry itself – the growth of foreign competition and a fall in the quality of English cloth. Others blamed merchants, criticizing the monopoly privileges of the Society of Merchant Adventurers, which accounted for over half of England's cloth exports. The most significant discussions, however, were to do with money. There was a widespread view that 'shortage of money' was a major problem, and that this was related to instability in the foreign exchanges. Currency upheavals in Germany, linked to the outbreak of the Thirty Years War, could plausibly be seen as the reason why exports fell so rapidly from 1618 to 1620.

The Balance-of-Trade Doctrine

The traditional explanation of the crisis was put forward by Gerard Malynes (*fl.* 1586–1641), a merchant and government official. He claimed that silver had left England because the English coin was undervalued. Foreign-exchange dealers could force the value of English coin below its par value, the value set by the Mint. If the par value reflected the world price of gold and silver, this would cause English coin to be exported, for it would be worth more as precious metal than as coin. This would account for the shortage of money in England. The low exchange rate explained both why English goods were sold cheaply and why imports were dear. The remedy, he argued, was to restore the Royal Exchange and to regulate foreign-exchange transactions in order to restore the exchange rate to its proper level.

Against this were ranged the arguments of the so-called balance-of-trade theorists, notably Edward Misselden (fl. 1608–54, a member of the Merchant Adventurers) and Thomas Mun (1571–1641, a member of the East India Company). They argued that it was flows of goods that governed the exchange rate and flows of bullion, not the other way round. To stem the outflow of treasure it was necessary to increase the balance of trade – to reduce imports, especially of unnecessary items, and to increase exports. This required a low exchange rate, not a high one. More significantly, it was the 'balance of trade' that determined flows of money, not the other way round.

It can be shown that if exports and imports do not respond at all to prices Malynes was right in wanting a higher exchange rate, but that if exports and imports are very responsive to prices Misselden and Mun were right. However, their differences involved more than different assumptions about the responsiveness of trade flows to prices. They agreed that money was the 'soul' of commerce and that England's losses of money abroad had to be stopped, but behind this agreement lay two different views as to how the economy worked. In Malynes's world view, coins had an intrinsic value, dependent on their gold or silver content, which it was the sovereign's prerogative to establish. The Royal Exchange was thus necessary to provide merchants with information on the true value of the coinage, so that exchange transactions could reflect this value. In contrast, for Misselden and Mun the buying and selling of goods was fundamental: supply and demand, not the sovereign, determined values, including the value of the currency.

The work of the balance-of-trade theorists was important for establishing a link between money and economic activity. They viewed money not as wealth to be accumulated but as working capital. For Mun, the clearest exponent of this view, money was needed to drive trade. The way to accumulate treasure was to allow it to be used in trade. In his posthumously published *England's Treasure by Forraign Trade* (1664), in a chapter entitled 'The Exportation of our Moneys in

Trade of Merchandize is a means to encrease our Treasure', Mun argued that the purpose of exporting money is

to enlarge our trade by enabling us to bring in more forraign wares, which being sent out again will in due time much encrease our Treasure. For although in this manner wee do yearly multiply our importations to the maintenance of more Shipping and Mariners, improvment of His Majesties Customs and other benefits: yet our consumption of those forraign wares is no more than it was before; so that all the said encrease of commodities . . . doth in the end become an exportation unto us of a far greater value.[6]

Mun's theory of the balance of trade was important for several reasons. It was a theory of growth centred on foreign trade: as such, it embodied a particular conception of economic activity, increasingly challenged in the seventeenth century, in which production was fundamental. In the passage just quoted, Mun states explicitly that consumption of foreign commodities will not increase. England's entrepôt trade will grow. In addition, Mun's theory provided a justification for the East India Company, of which he was a director, being allowed to export bullion to India. This was necessary because the Company could not find suitable goods for export.

The Rate of Interest and the Case for Free Trade

From the restoration of Charles II to the end of the seventeenth century a recurring question was whether or not legislation should be passed to lower the rate of interest. In 1668 a bill was introduced into Parliament to lower the maximum legal interest rate from 6 to 4 per cent per annum. The most influential advocate of the proposal was Sir Josiah Child (1630–99), a merchant who had made money through supplying the Royal Navy and who was one of the chief defenders of the East India Company. Child was in many respects a representative of what one scholar has called the 'old style' of doing economics: 'he looks like an advocate rather than theorist, a purveyor of patent remedies, an interested party asserting his objectivity, an imperfect copyist rather than a vigorous innovator, and only an occasional liberal'.[7] (The new style was that of the objective scientist.) His *Brief Observations Concerning Trade and Interest of Money* (1668) opens by asking why the Dutch are so much more successful than the English. He offers fifteen explanations, but claims that the last, a low rate of interest, is the most important, being the cause of the other causes of Dutch wealth. Child supports his case with two types of evidence. The first is that previous reductions in the legal maximum interest rate (from 10 to 8 per cent in the 1620s, and from 8 to 6 per cent in the 1640s) were followed by increases in both the number of merchants and their individual wealth. The second is evidence from comparing different countries. Parts of Italy paid 3 per cent interest and were prosperous; Spain paid between 10 and 12 per cent and was desperately short of money; France, with 7 per cent, was in the middle. According to Child, countries are 'richer or poorer in exact proportion to what they pay, and have usually paid, for the interest of money'.[8] This rule, he claimed, never failed.

Child recognized that such evidence did not establish that a low interest rate was the cause rather than the effect of prosperity. However, he offered almost no arguments to support his claim that it was. He claimed that reducing the interest rate from 6 per cent to 4 per cent or 3 per cent would double the nation's capital stock, but he did not explore this and turned instead to answering other people's objections to lowering the interest rate. In response to the absence of usury laws in the Netherlands, he argued that other Dutch institutions had the same effect: high-quality securities, banks, the use of bills of exchange, and low public spending.

The opposite case was argued by John Locke (1632–1704), secretary to Lord Ashley, then Chancellor of the Exchequer, in a pamphlet entitled *Some Consequences That are Like to Follow upon Lessening of Interest to 4 per cent* (1668). Although Locke is not completely consistent and makes clear mistakes (perhaps not surprising, since it was his first venture into economics), his pamphlet differs from Child's in that its method is to construct tight logical arguments.

Restricting the rate of interest to 4 per cent would, Locke argued, reduce the supply of funds available for lending. Going beyond this, he argued that there was a 'natural' rate of interest determined by the quantity of money in a country relative to the volume of that country's trade: 'By natural use [interest] I mean that rate of money which the present scarcity makes it naturally at.'[9] Unlike Child, who focused exclusively on the rate of interest, Locke saw that if a lower rate of interest was produced by increasing the supply of funds (by banks, the use of bills and so on) its effects were very different from the effects of imposing a statutory maximum interest rate.

If interest depended on the amount of money needed for trade, how much money was required by a nation? Petty's calculations, discussed above, could be seen as an attempt to provide a definite answer to this question. Locke's answer introduced the idea of 'quickness of circulation':

Because it depends, not barely on the quantity of money, but the quickness of its circulation – which since it cannot easily be traced [observed] ... to make some probable guess we are to consider how much money it is necessary to suppose must rest constantly in each man's hands as requisite to the carrying on of trade.[10]

Such arguments took Locke away from the rate of interest into the broader questions of monetary economics, such as the relationship between the money supply and the price level. Echoing sixteenth-century writers such as Navarrus and Bodin, he argued that the value of money (or equivalently the value of commodities) depended on the quantity of money in relation to trade. Plenty of money would mean that money would be cheap and commodities dear. If the economy were isolated, this would mean that the quantity of money would not matter: if the quantity of money were lower, prices would be lower and more trade could take place.

On the other hand, in a country open to world trade and that used the same money as its neighbours, there must be a particular ratio of money to trade. The reason is that, if a country has less money (relative to trade) than its neighbours, then either prices must be lower or else goods must remain unsold, there being insufficient money to buy them at the prices prevailing abroad. If home prices were lower than foreign prices, the country would lose through paying more for its imports than it received for its exports. In addition, the country would risk having workers migrate to countries with higher wages.

Locke was not alone in insisting that low interest was the result of wealth, not its cause. Another writer to argue this was Dudley North (1641–91), who made a fortune trading with Turkey, before returning to England to become a commissioner for the customs and then the Treasury. His *Discourses upon Trade* (1691) was stimulated by renewed moves to lower the legal maximum rate of interest. It was published with a preface in which his brother Roger North (1653–1734), an accomplished political writer, emphasized the importance of abstraction and of reasoning being based on 'clear and evident truths'. Knowledge arrived at in this way had become 'mechanical'. This Cartesian method of reasoning, Roger North argued, was characteristic of his brother Dudley's work: 'He begins at the quick, from principles indisputably true; and so proceeding with great care, comes to a judgement of the nicest disputes concerning trade . . . he reduceth things to their extreams, wherein all discriminations are most gross and sensible, and then shows them.'[11]

Dudley North's starting point was that trade was 'a commutation of superfluities'.[12] Those men who are most diligent, grow the most crops or produce the most goods will be wealthy even if no one has any gold or silver. However, in order to get the goods they require, such people have to exchange their surplus produce for goods that other people have produced. It is differences between people that lead to trade.

North then applied this argument to interest. Some men, he argued, will have much stock (capital) but lack the skill to use it; while others will have the required skills but no stock. Those who have too much stock will lend it to those who have too little, in return for interest. It is exactly the same as with land. Those with too much land allow others to use it in return for rent. Interest and rent are essentially the same. It follows, North continued, that if stock and land are plentiful, interest and rent will be low; if they are scarce, interest and rent will be high. Dutch interest rates were, he claimed, low because stock was plentiful, not the other way round.

If interest were lowered by legislation, North continued, the supply of loans would be reduced. Many lenders would be unwilling to accept a lower rate of interest, for it would not compensate them for the risk involved. They would prefer to hoard their wealth or turn it into plate. Alternatively, people might resort to 'underhand bargains' to avoid the law. A notable feature of North's argument here, consistent with his underlying premisses, is that not all borrowers and lenders are the same, so the same interest rate will not be appropriate for all transactions. Lenders and borrowers should be free to make their own bargains. Take away interest, North contended, and you take away borrowing and lending.

North's analysis of money followed the same lines. It rested on the premiss that wealth arises not from having money but from 'land at farm, money at interest, or goods in trade'.[13] Gold and silver are 'nothing but the weights and measures, by which traffick is more conveniently carried on than could be done without them; and also a proper fund for a surplusage of stock to be deposited in'.[14] Thus, if someone cannot sell their goods, the reason must be that too much is being offered for sale, overseas sales are wanting, or poverty is keeping down domestic sales. The reason could not be a shortage of coin, for a rich nation could obtain the money it needed through trade.

A consequence of this view was a favourable attitude towards luxury spending. The 'mercantilist' view was that luxury spending should be curbed by restrictions on imports or by sumptuary laws. Imported luxuries, it was argued, caused money to leave the kingdom unnecessarily. North, on the other hand, saw that spending was necessary if goods were to be sold and if people were to be employed. Perhaps equally important, luxury consumption provided an incentive to work: 'The main spur to trade, or rather to industry and ingenuity, is the exorbitant appetites of men, which they will take pains to gratifie, and so be disposed to work, when nothing else will incline them to it; for did men content themselves with bare necessaries, we should have a poor world.'[15]

Though Dudley North did not take his arguments so far, in his preface Roger North argued that any trade that profited individuals was beneficial to the public, and that regulations on trade were always harmful:

That there can be no trade unprofitable to the publick; for if any prove so, men leave it off; and wherever the traders thrive, the publick, of which they are a part, thrives also . . . That no laws can set prices in trade, the rates of which, must and will make themselves: but when such laws do happen to lay any hold, it is so much impediment to trade, and therefore prejudicial . . . That all favour to one trade or interest against another, is an abuse, and cuts so much of profit from the public.[16]

The Recoinage Crisis of the 1690s

North's pamphlet and Locke's writing on interest illustrate the great change that had taken place in economic thinking since the early seventeenth century. The reason for most writing was still to influence policy, and pamphlets were still written by men actively engaged in trade or with interests to defend. There had, however, been an enormous change in the arguments used. In the writing of Mun and most of his contemporaries, economic thinking was mixed together with advice on how to be a successful merchant: *England's Treasure by Forraign Trade* was primarily a manual on good business practice. In contrast, though Locke and North certainly had interests to defend, they were attempting to stand back – to distance themselves from their material and to analyse it in what they understood to be a scientific way. The influence of thinkers such as Bacon, Descartes and even Hobbes is evident.

Equally important was a profound change that had taken place in attitudes towards economic growth. At the beginning of the seventeenth century the idea that the role of government was to maintain a stable, established order was still strong. Malynes's advocacy of the Royal Exchange followed naturally from such a perspective. This view was challenged by merchants who used the doctrine of the balance of trade as an argument in favour of greater freedom. They promoted a view of the economy in which the objective was growth, fuelled by the money brought in by a balance-of-trade surplus. Resources were to be developed in order to promote exports, and government policy was to be subordinated to this end. Economic growth was seen purely from the producers' and merchants' point of view – it was not based on the goal of increasing consumption.

The merchants' perspective on growth was radically different from the Tudor and early Stuart emphasis on the importance of preserving an established social order. It was, however, unable to explain England's increasing wealth after the Restoration in 1660 – something remarked on by numerous writers, including Petty. London was magnificently rebuilt after the Great Fire of 1666, and the city's prosperity attracted comment from both critics and admirers. There was also, especially from the 1670s, controversy over Indian cottons and silks, imports of which had increased dramatically since the freeing of trade in bullion in 1663. English clothiers began to use the balance-of-trade doctrine to criticize the activities of the East India Company in promoting Indian manufacturing and trade.

The response to this was the emergence, in the works of many writers, including Dudley North, of new ways of thinking about wealth and economic growth. Instead of seeing trade through the eyes of producers, they focused on the role of trade in satisfying consumers' demands. Consumption rather than production came to be seen as the aim of economic activity. It was linked to growth because the only way in which people could satisfy their desires was by increasing their purchasing power. They could do this only by selling more goods in impersonal markets where supply and demand ruled, which meant that producers had to lower their costs and become more competitive. The outcome was a literature in which self-interest was assumed to rule human affairs. This challenged long-established conceptions of society (one reason why Hobbes's ideas were thought so scandalous was his assumption that men formed governments solely because of self-interest) and had potentially radical political implications in its view that the market provided a way of holding society together.

However, not everyone accepted this new view of the market. As trade expanded and commercial relations increasingly dominated economic life, some sectors fell behind. Clothiers and landowners found their incomes rising less rapidly than those of merchants, and they also faced the burden of the rising taxes (levied locally) needed to support those without any means of supporting themselves. Pointing to the problems faced by the poor, such men denied that individual and public interests coincided. Indian manufactures, with which English woollens could not hope to compete, were seen as wrecking businesses, causing unemployment and producing poverty. The solutions offered were to encourage investment and to restrict imports. Whereas in the 1620s the balance-of-trade doctrine had been used as an argument against traditional regulation of the economy, in the 1690s it came to be used to defend manufacturing and landed interests against the threat presented by free trade and commercial expansion.

This conflict came to a head in the recoinage crisis of the 1690s. Since the Restoration, English silver coins had fallen significantly in weight, owing to their edges being clipped as well as to normal wear and tear. It was widely accepted that a recoinage was essential, especially now that milled edges could be used to prevent further clipping. The controversial issue was how much silver should be in the new shillings (the main silver coins in circulation). If their original silver content were restored, there would be fewer coins in circulation and the result would be deflation. So men who emphasized the importance of expanding demand wanted the recoinage to reflect the decline in the shilling's silver content that had taken place during the preceding decades. In contrast, creditors wanted deflation and the restoration of the currency's original silver content. Unlike men in the City of London, where the subject was widely debated, many landowners probably failed to grasp the issues involved in the recoinage crisis, even though they may have understood the balance-of-trade doctrine and the link between trade and employment.

The scheme adopted by the government (and advocated by Locke) involved recoining shillings at their full value. Not only was this in itself deflationary, but the government agreed to accept old shillings at their face value for the first six months. The result was that Gresham's Law went into effect. This law – named after Sir Thomas Gresham (1519–79), a financier under Elizabeth I, though it was known to medieval writers – is usually summarized as 'Bad money drives out good.' If someone has a coin containing the full weight of silver and also a badly worn, clipped coin with the same face value, he will choose to spend the bad one and keep the good one. Good coins will therefore be hoarded and bad ones will circulate. In the 1690s this meant that, as old shillings went into the Mint for recoining, the new full-weight coins were largely melted down and exported. Estimates suggest that the value of silver coins in circulation may have fallen from £12 million in December 1695 to only £4.2 million in June 1696. Though there was no corresponding fall in the circulation of either gold coins or banknotes (usable only for large transactions), there was a sharp deflation. Prices fell, and landlords and creditors reaped the benefit. The long-term effect was that England went on to a de-facto gold standard, as silver, now overvalued, began to disappear from circulation. The theory underlying this transition was Locke's. This held that it was gold and silver that were the instruments of commerce. They had an intrinsic value, determined by common consent. The only thing that was different about money was that it contained a stamp confirming its weight and fineness.

Against this, men such as Nicholas Barbon (d. 1698) claimed that it was money (coins), not the silver in them, that drove trade. This meant that when the government coined more (or fewer) shillings from a certain weight of silver it raised (or lowered) the money supply. It was money, not silver, to which people attached value. However, it was Locke's natural-law theory, supported by the self-interest of landowners and creditors, that triumphed. The price established for gold in 1717 – £3 17s. 10½d. per ounce – came to be regarded as an almost magical figure, and was not finally abandoned until 1925. The arguments of the free-traders such as North were able to explain England's prosperity since the Restoration. However, the balance-of-trade doctrine proved better able to serve the needs of the dominant political class.

Economics in Seventeenth-Century England

Seventeenth-century England falls squarely into the so-called 'mercantilist' era. It produced the balance-of-trade doctrine – arguably the hallmark of mercantilism – and Mun's *England's Treasure by Forraign Trade* was the book that Adam Smith was later to attack as representative of mercantilist thinking. However, it is clear that such a simple characterization of this period's economic thought is grossly misleading. Even the balance-of-trade doctrine, used to justify protection late in the century, was used by its inventors, Misselden and Mun, to defend economic freedom.

During the seventeenth century, England experienced numerous economic problems that provided merchants and government advisers with an incentive to advocate policies that were in their own interests. In an environment largely free of censorship, and in a political system where reasoned argument might influence policy, they did this in an unprecedented number of pamphlets on economic questions. The manner in which they argued their case was strongly influenced by science, a subject in which men were also passionately interested. At the same time, the century's political turmoil raised fundamental questions about what held society together. Though Hobbes's work fell squarely in the realm of political philosophy rather than economics, the challenge he posed related to the whole of society and was taken up, especially in the eighteenth century, by many writers whose work counts unambiguously as economics.

5

Absolutism and Enlightenment in Eighteenth-Century France

Problems of the Absolute State

The conditions that led to the proliferation of writing on economic questions in seventeenth-century England had no parallel in France. Many more feudal institutions remained than in England (although some feudal obligations had effectively become marketable commodities), and the king possessed absolute power. Throughout the seventeenth and eighteenth centuries it was frequently dangerous to express opinions that the state might view as subversive. Of the writers discussed in this chapter, Boisguilbert suffered exile and Mirabeau imprisonment for their economic opinions. In private, however, radical opinions could be, and were, expressed even in salons patronized by the royal family. Political and social criticism could also be left implicit by formulating it as general principles or by directing it against practices found in other countries. Thus, while French writing on economic questions was sparse during the seventeenth century, it grew substantially during the eighteenth, and by the 1750s and 1760s Paris had become the centre of European economic thinking, to which most of the leading figures came.

The structure of French government policy was laid down in the seventeenth century by Jean Baptiste Colbert (1619–83), finance minister under Louis XIV (r. 1643–1715) from 1661. Colbert was not an economist. He did not write on economic questions, and he is not even known to have read widely on the subject. His policies, however, characterize an important type of mercantilism during this period. His primary aim was not to raise the welfare of the population but to increase the power of the King. Internally, he wanted to unify the country, economically as well as politically, so that, for example, famine in one region could not coexist with plenty in another. Externally, the volume of trade was taken as fixed, so that one country's gain had to be matched by a corresponding loss elsewhere. If France were to gain, it could only be at the expense of England or the Netherlands.

Colbert's policies followed logically from these beliefs. He sought to increase exports and reduce imports, thereby both achieving national self-sufficiency and accumulating the treasure which would drive trade. Attempts were made to increase the population and to keep wages low, thus forcing people to work hard. Immigration of skilled workers was encouraged through subsidies, and Colbert tried to stop emigration. Trade was carefully regulated and new industries were set up, sometimes with foreign workers.

France had long faced severe financial and economic problems, and Colbert's policies failed to solve them. It was not until much later that deaths from famine became a thing of the past. Throughout the century, shortages of food, sometimes occurring alongside surpluses in other parts of the country, were common. Such shortages were particularly acute in towns, for these were beginning to outgrow the resources of their traditional hinterlands. The government resorted to numerous measures in order to deal with the problem, including price-fixing, prohibiting speculation in grain, and direct coercion of producers. However, it did not remove the taxes and barriers to the internal movement of food that lay at the problem's heart. The government also faced chronic financial difficulties, these being due in large part to military expenditures incurred both by Louis XIV and his successors. The state was continually on the verge of bankruptcy. The clergy and the nobility, who owned most of the nation's wealth, were largely exempt from direct taxation, and among those who were liable the burden of such taxes was very uneven. Collection of taxes was arbitrary and inequitable. A major reason for this was that the state did not have the administrative apparatus to collect them itself, but farmed the job out to private companies. These would pay an agreed sum to the exchequer in return for the right to collect certain levies. This process was inefficient, and unjust methods of collection were often used. On top of this, in 1738 the *corvée*, or system of forced labour, was extended from specific regions to the whole country.

Early-Eighteenth-Century Critics of Mercantilism

One of the early critics of Louis XIV's economic policies was Pierre de Boisguilbert (1646–1714). In *Détail de la France* (published in 1695, but possibly written some years earlier), and in a series of other publications during the following two decades, Boisguilbert sought to explain what he saw as the disastrous decline in the French economy under Louis XIV. Income had, he claimed, halved during the previous thirty years. The starting point of his analysis was the necessity of exchange. As economic development took place, exchange became more and more complex, making it necessary to use money. However, money did not in itself create wealth. It had to circulate actively if it were to be effective. If money could circulate rapidly – perhaps being augmented by money substitutes such as bills of exchange – this would be as efficient as having a larger money supply. Paper money could perform the functions of metallic money, and had the advantage of costing nothing to produce.

What kept money circulating, Boisguilbert argued, was consumption, for one man's spending is another man's income. Consumption and income were therefore equivalent. Thus the decline in French income could be attributed to a decline in consumption. What had caused this? Boisguilbert's answers included the burden of taxation; the distribution of income away from the poor, who spent money quickly, to the rich, who were more likely to hoard it; and the uncertainty that made the propertied class less willing to invest. More fundamentally, however, Boisguilbert linked prosperity to the price system: prosperity requires that there be a balance or equilibrium between different goods and that 'prices are kept in proportion with one another and with the costs necessary for creating the goods'.[1]

This perspective led Boisguilbert to conclude that nature alone, not the state, can maintain order and peace – *laissez faire la nature*. Though buyers and sellers are both motivated by profit, the balance between the needs to buy and to sell forces both sides to listen to reason.

Thus, although individuals are concerned only with their own interests, provided the state does not interfere they will contribute to the general good. The state's role is to establish security and justice.

However, although Boisguilbert saw markets as establishing order, they would sometimes fail. Uncertainty and incorrect expectations meant that output prices would fluctuate. This was particularly noticeable in the market for grain, where prices fluctuated violently. High prices would mean that even the worst land could profitably be cultivated, leading to a glut that pushed prices so low that all farmers made a loss. Boisguilbert thus proposed an exception to his rule of laissez-faire: the government should intervene to stabilize the price of grain, holding stocks that could be bought and sold to achieve this.

The idea proposed by Boisguilbert that paper money could fulfil the functions of gold and silver at lower cost was taken even further by a Scotsman, John Law (1671–1729), in *Money and Trade Considered: A Proposal for Supplying the Nation with Money* (1705). Like Boisguilbert, Law started from the premises that the value of goods depended not on the quantity of money but on the ratio of the quantity of goods to the demand for them, and that the role of money was to facilitate trade. An increase in the quantity of money would therefore raise employment, cause more land to be cultivated, and increase output and trade. Law worked on the assumption that there were normally unemployed resources that could be brought into use when activity increased. However, whereas the mercantilist response was to argue for measures to accumulate bullion, Law argued for an expansion of paper currency. Apart from being cheaper, a paper currency would have the advantage that its supply could be regulated so as to stabilize its value and the level of economic activity. Security would be provided by the titles to land against which loans would be issued. By being linked to the value of land, which Law claimed was more stable than the value of silver, the value of the currency could be assured.

Law's proposal was designed to revive the Scottish economy, and he submitted it, unsuccessfully, to the Scottish parliament in 1705. In 1706, however, he was forced to flee Scotland to avoid being arrested for murder. The reason was that in 1694 he had killed a man in a duel and, after being arrested, had escaped from prison with the connivance (and possibly the assistance) of the authorities. Union with England in 1707 raised the prospect that he would be rearrested. He settled in France, where he persuaded the Regent under Louis XV to put some of his ideas into effect as a way of solving France's financial problems.

In 1716, in Paris, Law formed the Banque Générale, which in 1718 was nationalized as the Banque Royale. Notes issued by the bank were to be accepted in payment of taxes. In return Law offered to put the French finances, severely weakened by Louis XIV's wars, into order through reducing the rate of interest to 2 per cent. However, the bank's capital was only 825,000 livres, in comparison with a total government debt of around 450 million livres. The result was that the bank had little control over interest rates. As a result Law became drawn into debt management. The Compagnie d'Occident (Company of the West), established by Law in 1717, was given exclusive trading rights in Louisiana in return for taking over a large quantity of government debt, and tax farms were also centralized within the company. To pay for the government debt, shares were issued. Law used numerous marketing devices to sell shares in the Compagnie d'Occident, and through 1719 they rose in value, supported by lending from the Banque Royale. In May 1719 shares were selling for less than their nominal value of 500 livres, but by December they sold for as much as 10,025 livres per share. In January 1720 Law was appointed Controller-General of Finances, the highest administrative post in France, and from January to March plans were made for the demonetization of gold and silver.

In May 1720, however, Law realized that the financial situation still needed to be brought under control and he proposed a plan gradually to reduce the price of shares from their unsustainable value of 9,000 livres per share to 5,000 livres per share by the end of the year. This outraged the public, who had counted on shares rising in value (there was a highly developed forward market, with some trades taking place on the basis that shares would rise as high as 15,000 livres), and by September the price had fallen to only 4,367 livres per share. This conceals the extent of the collapse, for during this period overissue of banknotes had reduced the shares' value substantially. Valued in sterling, tied to gold, the value had fallen from £302 per share to £47 per share. Much of the public's financial wealth had been destroyed, though the government benefited through having its debts substantially reduced. Despite the collapse in the company's share price, Law persisted in believing that it could have survived had it not been for the arrival of plague in Marseilles in 1720. This caused people to demand coins instead of banknotes and created a liquidity crisis for the bank.

Cantillon on the Nature of Commerce in General

One of those who saw the flaws in Law's scheme and got out in time to save his fortune was Richard Cantillon (c. 1680/90–?1734). Cantillon was an Irish merchant banker who spent most of his life in France. He is surrounded in mystery. His home burned down, and for a long time it was assumed either that he was killed in the fire or that the fire was started by an aggrieved servant to cover up his murder. A year later, some of his papers were taken by an unknown traveller to Surinam, leading to the idea that the fire might have been a ruse by Cantillon to cover his disappearance. The motive may have been to escape the lawsuits against which he still had to defend the fortune he had acquired through his activities with Law in the 1720s. The fire, however, had destroyed most of his papers. He published one book, *An Essay on the Nature of Commerce in General*, probably written in 1730, but not published until 1755. It appeared in French, purporting to be a translation from English in order to get round the French censorship laws. Some scholars have seen this book as so significant as to mark the birth of the subject of economics.

Cantillon's *Essay* opens with the statement that land is the source of wealth: 'The land is the source or matter from whence all wealth is produced. The labour of man is the form which produces it: and wealth is nothing but the maintenance, conveniences and superfluities of life.'[2] Labour, regarded by many economists as the source of wealth, simply adjusts to demand. If there are too many labourers in a country, they will emigrate or become poor and starve. In an implicit criticism of Colbert's policy, Cantillon argues that it is impossible to raise wealth by training more craftsmen. He likens this to training more seamen without building more ships. It is land that determines wealth, and the number of labourers will adjust automatically.

Cantillon attaches particular importance, however, to one type of labour – that of the entrepreneur. Entrepreneurs are people who buy goods either to engage in production or to trade them, without any assurance that they will profit from their activities. For example, the farmer, who is an agricultural entrepreneur employing people to work for him, cultivates land without knowing whether corn will be cheap or dear, or whether the harvest will be good or bad. Merchants buy goods in bulk without knowing whether demand from consumers will be high or low, or how many sales will be lost to competitors. However, although entrepreneurs perform an important function in undertaking risky activities, they are still, like labourers who work for a wage, dependent on the proprietors of land.

Two implications follow from this view of land as the source of wealth. The first is that land is the source of value. Cantillon's analysis is based on the concept of 'intrinsic value'. This is not the same as market price. It is the amount of land and labour that enters into the production of a commodity. If labour is valued according to the amount of land needed to maintain the labourers, this reduces to a land theory of value. To produce corn, for example, requires land on which to grow it plus the land necessary to produce the labourers' subsistence. In contrast, market price depends on supply and demand and may fluctuate above or below the intrinsic value of a commodity.

The second implication that Cantillon draws from his view of land as the source of wealth is that all other classes are maintained at the expense of the landowners. Only the landowners are 'naturally independent', for it is their spending that determines how resources are allocated between different uses and, as a result, the values of different goods. To quote one of Cantillon's chapter titles, 'The fancies, the fashions, and the modes of living of the prince, and especially of the landowners, determine the use to which land is put in a state and cause the variations in the market price of all things'.[3] He gives the example of a large self-sufficient estate that is initially cultivated by the owner himself, who directs overseers to manage it so as to produce the goods that he requires. The division of the estate into pasture, arable, parkland, orchards, gardens and so on will be determined entirely by the owner's tastes (though he will of course have to allocate sufficient land to produce the goods that his labourers consume). Cantillon then considers what would happen if the owner decentralized decision-making, setting up his overseers as independent producers, equipped with the relevant amounts of land, and linked to him and to each other through markets. His conclusion is that everyone on the estate would live in exactly the same way as before. Only if the owner changes his consumption pattern will economic activity change:

For if some of the farmers sowed more corn than usual they must feed fewer sheep, and have less wool and mutton to sell. Then there will be too much corn and too little wool for the consumption of the inhabitants. Wool will therefore be dear, which will force the inhabitants to wear their clothes longer than usual, and there will be too much corn and a surplus for the next year. And as we suppose that the landowner has stipulated for the payment in silver of the third of the produce of the farm to be paid to him, the farmers who have too much corn and too little wool, will not be able to pay him rent . . . So a farmer who has arrived at about the proportion of consumption will have part of his farm in grass, for hay, another for corn, wool and so on, and he will not change his plan unless he sees some considerable change in the demand; but in this example we have supposed that all the people live in the same way as when the landowner cultivated the land for himself, and consequently the farmers will employ the land for the same purposes as before.[4]

If the landowner were, for example, to dismiss some of his domestic servants and to increase the number of horses on his estate, corn would become cheap (for demand would be less) and hay dear (demand having increased). Farmers would then turn corn fields into grassland.

Throughout this discussion, as in his discussion of value, Cantillon makes it clear that he is dealing only with long-run equilibrium: 'I do not consider here the variation in market prices which may arise from the good or bad harvest of the year, or the extraordinary consumption which may occur from foreign troops or other accidents, so as not to complicate my subject, considering only a state in its natural and uniform condition.'[5]

After considering production and wealth, Cantillon turns to money. Here his ideas owe much to Locke, for he focuses on the circulation of money, accepting the link between the price level and the money supply. However, he criticizes Locke on the grounds that, while 'he has clearly seen that the abundance of money makes everything dear, . . . he has not considered how it does so'.[6] To resolve this, Cantillon considers the way in which money enters the economy and the channels through which it flows. He considers three main sources from which an increase in the money supply might arise: gold and silver mines, the balance of trade, and subsidies paid by foreign powers.

If money comes from mines, the first people to be affected will be the mine owners and workers in the mining industry. Their incomes will rise and they will spend more, which will raise the prices of the goods they buy. This will increase the incomes of the farmers and manufacturers from whom the goods are bought, who will in turn increase their spending, raising other prices and incomes. Money will gradually spread out throughout the country, raising prices as it goes. Classes on fixed incomes, such as landowners whose rents are fixed by long-term agreements, will be worse off until their leases can be renegotiated. As prices rise, producers will find that their costs have risen, forcing them to raise prices further. As prices continue to rise, people will be encouraged to buy abroad, where goods are still cheap. This will ruin manufacturers. When the inflow of new money ceases – perhaps because the mines are exhausted – incomes will fall and people will have to cut back their spending. Money will become scarce, and poverty and misery will follow. Because much of the gold and silver will have gone abroad to pay for the increased imports, the state will not end up with any more money than its neighbours. This, Cantillon argued, was roughly what had happened in Spain after the discovery of America.

In contrast, if the inflow of money arises from a favourable balance of trade, it will first accrue to merchants. This will in turn raise the incomes of those who produce the goods being exported. The prices of land and labour will in turn also be raised. However, because the money will accrue to industrious people who are keen to acquire property, they will not raise their consumption but will save money until they have sufficient to invest it at interest or to buy land. Only then will they raise their consumption. The rise in prices will cause goods to be imported, but such a situation, Cantillon argues, can continue for many years. The effects will be different from those of an increase in money from mines, because the money will be received by different classes of people, whose spending behaviour will be different.

The effects of subsidies from foreign powers will depend on whether the monies are hoarded or spent. Only in the latter case will they have any effect, raising prices.

Cantillon recognized what has come to be termed the price–specie–flow mechanism – the notion that a rise in the money supply will raise prices, resulting in a trade deficit that causes money to flow out of the country. In its pure form, this mechanism implies that attempts to increase the money supply are self-defeating. Cantillon could thus write that when a state's money supply, and hence its wealth, is at its greatest, the state 'will inevitably fall into poverty by the ordinary course of things'.[7] This would appear to undermine the 'mercantilist' notion that increases in the money supply bring prosperity. However, Cantillon could also write that 'It is clear that every state which has more money in circulation than its neighbours has an advantage over them so long as it maintains an abundance of money.'[8] Higher domestic prices will mean that the same quantity of goods exported will purchase more imports. In addition, plenty of money makes it easier for the ruler to raise taxes. For prices to rise in this way it is necessary that the money be retained within the state. This is more likely if it were obtained from trade than if it were obtained from mines, for the incomes would be received by those more likely to invest it rather than engage in luxury consumption.

Having discussed money, Cantillon could move on to finance. The issues he covered included foreign exchange, variations in the relative values of different metals used as money, debasement of the currency, and, finally, banks. Like Law, he saw that banks could be of value to a nation, this value being measured by the paper currency that entered into circulation. He estimated that the Bank of England kept reserves equal to around 1 million ounces of silver, but its notes amounted, on average, to 4 million ounces of silver. When the circulation of money needed to be speeded up, this situation was, he claimed, of great benefit to England. Banks were of particular benefit to small states where silver was scarce. However, given the experiences of the early 1720s, when both England and France had experienced major speculative bubbles which had burst dramatically, Cantillon pointed out the dangers of insolvency should a bank increase its note issue too far. The example of Law's scheme, from which he had managed to get out in time, was one that he could never have forgotten.

The Enlightenment

Some of the most important ideas underlying the Enlightenment can be traced to seventeenth-century England – to Locke and to the scientific revolution associated above all with Bacon and Newton. The Enlightenment involved a belief in reason, progress, liberty and toleration. Reason was believed to be man's central capacity, which enabled him to think and act correctly. Because all men were equal by virtue of their having reason, it followed that everyone should be free to act and think as his reason directed. The Enlightenment was therefore a revolt against the alleged unreason of earlier ages – reason was to replace religious authorities, sacred texts and traditions as the criterion by which all things were to be judged. Above all, however, the Enlightenment was characterized by a belief in progress. Replacing superstition by reason would enable man to progress without any divine assistance. Newton had shown that the physical world could be understood in terms of a system of laws, comprehensible through reason, and Locke had shown that the human mind could build complex ideas from the basic data of sensory experience. Innate or externally supplied ideas were not needed: reason was sufficient. In the same spirit, Locke had also offered a utilitarian framework for morality, and provided a theoretical basis for representative government.

Such challenges to traditional ideas were suppressed in France under Louis XIV. Censorship still persisted under Louis XV (r. 1715–74), though less rigorously. Printing was still controlled for many years, with the result that unorthodox ideas, circulating only in manuscript form, could not spread as rapidly as if they were printed. However, the relaxation was sufficient to release a pent-up flood of criticism of established ideas and institutions. In the mid 1740s censorship was significantly decreased, and the following decade saw a profusion of new ideas from men such as Diderot (1713–84), on the relativity of knowledge and morals, Montesquieu (1689–1755), on the rule of law, and Condillac (1715–80), who developed Locke's psychology. The optimism of the movement was captured by Diderot and d'Alembert (1717–83), who edited an encyclopedia that would bring together all human knowledge and serve to propagate the new ideas. Between 1751 and 1772, despite periodic attempts by the authorities to suppress it, twenty-eight volumes were published. Covering practical as well as theoretical knowledge, the *Encyclopédie* included articles on economic questions.

Physiocracy

The Physiocrats, or *Les Économistes*, were the first organized group of economists. Physiocratic ideas were developed between 1756 and 1763 by two men, François Quesnay (1694–1774) and Victor Riqueti, Marquis de Mirabeau (1715–89), at a time when the Seven Years War with England was putting great strain on French finances. They held regular meetings to discuss Physiocratic ideas, they had a journal, *Éphémerides*, that published their ideas between 1767 and 1772, and their *La Philosophie rurale* (1763) could be regarded as a textbook in Physiocratic economics. Physiocracy attracted devoted followers, including Du Pont de Nemours (1739–1817) and Mercier de la Rivière (1720–93). There were also economists such as Turgot (see pp. 104–7) who were sympathetic towards Physiocracy, though not in complete agreement with its ideas. Physiocratic ideas underlay some of Turgot's reforms during his term as Controller-General of Finances from 1774 to 1776.

By the time Quesnay turned to economics, he had acquired a considerable reputation as a doctor, first as a surgeon and then as a physician (at the time regarded as having significantly higher status, in England as well as in France). His position in the French court was as physician to Madame de Pompadour, mistress of Louis XV, and it was for his medical services that he received a title and considerable wealth. His medical background is important, as it influenced his perspective on economics. In turning to economics, Quesnay sought to analyse the pathology of society and to propose remedies. Influenced strongly by Boisguilbert and Cantillon (on whose work Mirabeau drew heavily), he focused on the circulation of money – a clear analogy with the circulation of blood within the body, discovered over a century earlier. It is tempting to suggest that the term 'Physiocracy', meaning the rule of nature, reflected the attitude of an experienced physician who knew the importance of working with nature in effecting a cure. Equally significant, the Physiocratic system rested on a clear analysis of the structure of French society.

To understand society, Quesnay and Mirabeau claimed in *La Philosophie rurale*, it is necessary to understand the means by which it obtains its subsistence. Politics and law both rest on this. They outlined the evolution of society, culminating in the commercial societies that had grown up alongside agricultural ones. Trade was essential, which meant that it afforded a secure means of obtaining subsistence, but agriculture remained fundamental. The main reason for this was that it alone, the Physiocrats argued, yielded net revenue – a surplus over the necessary costs of production (see p. 102). They expressed this by describing agriculture as productive and other sectors (trade and manufacturing) as sterile.

The Physiocrats' assumptions about different classes were developed from Quesnay's observations on agriculture, first published in an article in Diderot's *Encyclopédie*. Most land was cultivated by share-croppers, who paid a fraction (usually one half) of their produce to the landowner in return for the use of the land and the loan of seed and livestock. Their methods were hardly more productive than those employed by peasant proprietors who cultivated their lands with minimal capital. In contrast, there had developed in parts of northern France, as in England, a new class of farmers – agricultural entrepreneurs. These were able to improve the lands they rented from their proprietors (usually the nobility or the Church) and produce large surpluses. The crucial difference between them and the share-croppers was that they had access to capital, for it was this that made it possible for them to employ more productive techniques. In contrast, though it was essential in order to produce goods that people needed, industry produced no surplus. It simply covered its costs. Agricultural capital was therefore the key to economic growth.

The relationship between agricultural capital and economic growth was explained by Quesnay in several versions of his *Tableau économique*, the first of which was published in 1758. This was a diagram that showed the circulation of money and goods between the three classes in society (proprietors, farmers and artisans) on the assumption that policies were ideal for agricultural development. In different versions of the *Tableau*, Quesnay listed up to twenty-four conditions that had to be satisfied in order for the economy to operate in the way he outlined. These included the following. (1) The entire revenue enters into circulation. (2) People are not led by insecurity to hoard money. (3) Taxes do not destroy the nation's revenue. (4) Farmers have sufficient capital to achieve a net revenue (surplus) of at least 100 per cent. (5) There is free external trade in raw produce. (6) The needs of the state are met only through the prosperity of the nation, not through raising credit from financiers. (7) People are free to cultivate their land as they think best. Given that none of these conditions was satisfied, obtaining them would amount to a very substantial policy agenda.

The starting point for the *Tableau* is a situation in which farmers have capital, or an 'annual advance', of £2 million (in corn) and proprietors have a stock of money of £2 million. Agriculture produces a surplus of 100 per cent, which accrues to the proprietors as rent. Consider first the circulation of money. Proprietors spend half their revenue (£2 million) on food and half on manufactured goods, so £1 million flows to each sector. This generates incomes which are spent, again half on food and half on manufactures. Each sector thus gains a further £0.5 million from the other. When successive rounds of income are added up, they come to £2 million for each sector (£1 million + £0.5 million + £0.25 million + £0.125 million + . . .). Each sector thus receives an income of £2 million and spends £1 million on buying consumption goods from the other sector. There is, however, an important difference between the two sectors. Manufacturing uses its remaining £1 million to purchase raw materials from agriculture, with the result that it generates no surplus. The entire stock of money (£2 million) thus ends up in the agricultural sector. Agriculture ends up with a financial surplus of £2 million, which is paid to the proprietors as rent.

The reason why agriculture can generate this financial surplus is that, unlike manufacturing, it produces a surplus of goods. The 'advance' of £2 million in corn is used to produce output worth £5 million. Of this, £1 million is sold as food to the proprietors, and £2 million is sold to the manufacturing sector, half as food and half as raw materials. This leaves £2 million worth of corn to replenish agriculture's capital stock for the following year. The accounts balance.

This numerical example is discussed in detail to make an important point. Although the fundamental insight about the circulation of income came from Boisguilbert and Cantillon, Quesnay tried to develop his argument with a degree of rigour that was absent from their work. Quesnay's numbers may seem arbitrary, but they were not. They reflected such statistics as were available about the French economy of his day. The figure of 100 per cent for the surplus, for example, reflected Quesnay's belief about what could be achieved in capitalist farming if sufficient capital were available to employ the most efficient techniques (using horses). These techniques were used on large farms in southern England and parts of northern France, but many French farmers could not afford them. Such numerical examples also enabled Quesnay, in successive versions of the *Tableau*, to explore the sensitivity of the economic system to various changes. For example, he showed that if a tax of £25,000 were imposed on both sectors, the result would be a decline in the annual advance in agriculture from £2 million to £1,950,000. Agriculture would lose £25,000 directly and £25,000 indirectly through reduced sales to the manufacturing sector. The result would be economic decline, for less output would be produced the following year. Similarly, he could show that a fall in productivity (perhaps due to government intervention or keeping the price of corn low) or the diversion of spending from agriculture to manufacturing would reduce output.

The Physiocratic system, centred on the *Tableau économique*, was used to defend a clear and controversial political agenda. The state was needed to maintain markets and the circular flow of income. Quesnay performed exercises with the *Tableau* to show how output would be reduced if his initial assumptions were not satisfied. Taxation, interference with agriculture, artificial stimulation of manufacturing, keeping food prices low – all policies pursued by the governments of Louis XIV and Louis XV – were all harmful and should be abandoned. The laws of nature provided constraints on what the state could undertake without undermining the prosperity on which it depended. However, this did not rule out all state activity. The surplus accruing to the proprietors could be taxed (as was necessary to raise the funds needed to support the market), but taxation could not rise too far. The reason was that the proprietors' spending was necessary to maintain the annual flow of income and spending.

Turgot

Not all reformers belonged to the Physiocratic school. One group that stood apart from the Physiocrats, though it supported them on economic policy, was centred on Vincent de Gournay (1712–59). Gournay was a businessman who made himself a public servant by purchasing the office of Intendant of Commerce, a position he held from 1751 to 1759. His work involved visiting different parts of France to investigate trade and manufacturing there. Gournay popularized the phrase '*laissez faire, laissez passer*', and he probably arranged for the publication of Cantillon's *Essay*. He wrote little, but exerted an important influence on others – including Turgot.

Anne Robert Jacques Turgot (1727–81), in a eulogy written in 1759, argued that Gournay saw himself not as a systematizer but as someone who offered common-sense maxims. Mercantilist regulations that allowed one city in France to treat citizens of other cities as foreigners, preventing them from working within its precincts, or that ruined a weaver because his cloth was inferior to that produced by a guild, did not make sense. Turgot claimed that, though Gournay saw matters as common sense, there was a principle underlying them: that 'in general every man knows his own interest better than another to whom it is of no concern'. Gournay, he argued, reached the conclusion that when the interest of individuals is precisely the same as the general interest, every man ought best to be left at liberty to do what he likes. Now in the case of unrestrained commerce, M. de Gournay thought it impossible for the individual interest not to concur with the general interest.[9]

The government should therefore restore liberty to all branches of commerce – removing barriers to trade, simplifying taxes, and giving everyone the right to work. This would 'excite the greatest competition in the market, which will infallibly produce the greatest perfection in manufacturing, and the most advantageous price to buyers'.[10]

Turgot's first contribution to economics was a critique of Law's monetary theory in 1749. In the 1750s, however, he met Gournay and worked with him, translating a book by the English economist Josiah Tucker (1712–99), and accompanying Gournay on tours of inspection in the provinces. In 1761 he was appointed intendant in the Limousin, a backward region in France, where he engaged in a process of reform. Areas affected included taxation, the system of forced labour during the harvest, and the road system. It was during this period that his main contributions to economics were written. His commitments as a government official meant that these were mostly letters and reports. The two exceptions were *Reflections on the Formation and Distribution of Wealth* (1766) and an unfinished essay, 'Value and Money' (1769).

In 1774 Turgot was promoted to Controller-General of Finances and moved to Paris. Here, too, he engaged in reform. His response to the perennial problem of food shortages was to free the grain trade, though he still prohibited the export of corn and made special provision for the supply of grain to Paris. He replaced the inefficient private company that held the monopoly of saltpetre (needed in the manufacture of gunpowder) with a state-owned firm, run by the chemist Lavoisier. Postal services were also transferred to a government department, and further similar reforms were projected. In 1776 Turgot sought to liberalize the corn trade still further, to abolish the guilds that restricted access to many industries, and to fund road building through a tax on landowners instead of through forced labour. He also spoke up in favour of tolerating Protestants. These measures, however, trampled on numerous vested interests. As a result, Turgot lost the support of other ministers and was attacked in the *parlements*, restored by his predecessor. He tried to force through his reforms using the King's authority, but his opponents managed to turn Louis XVI against him and he was dismissed. Many of his reforms were abandoned.

Though Turgot's reforms may have been pragmatic, they were consistent with the view of economic phenomena outlined in his two most systematic writings on economics. The early sections of the *Reflections* could have been written by a Physiocrat. They discuss the origins of exchange and the pre-eminence of agriculture – of the husbandman over the artisan – and distinguish between a productive and an unproductive class. Like Quesnay, Turgot discusses different ways in which agriculture can be organized, arguing that farming by tenant-entrepreneurs is most efficient, but that it is possible only if there is sufficient capital. However, he takes the argument in a different direction when he argues that lending money can also contribute to the creation of wealth. This leads into a discussion of the role of money in commerce, and eventually to a very un-Physiocratic perspective on the role of industry in creating wealth.

When people save, they accumulate capital that they can then use in a variety of ways: they can lend it at interest, purchase land (which yields rent), or employ it as an advance in industry (which yields profit). Because people have this choice, Turgot argued, the returns on all three of these uses of capital will be linked. They will not be equal, because the risks are different. If you lend money the borrower may fail to repay you, but if you purchase land you are secure. Land will thus yield a lower return than lending at interest. Similarly, investing in industry is more risky and will carry a higher return. Competition will therefore establish an equilibrium between the returns on these different ways in which capital can be employed. If, for example, the value of land is too high (equivalent to the return being too low) compared with other uses of capital, owners will exchange it for other types of capital and its price will be pushed down.

The equilibrium rate of interest is determined by supply and demand: it 'depends directly on the relation between the demand of the borrowers and the offer of the lenders'.[11] Thrift increases the number of lenders and reduces the number of borrowers, while luxury consumption has the opposite effect. Europe's falling rate of interest, Turgot argued, showed that thrift had prevailed over luxury, producing a rise in the amount of capital. This view led him to insist that the rate of interest was a price like any other and should therefore be determined by 'the course of trade' like the price of any commodity. The rate of interest would determine which lands were sufficiently profitable to cultivate and which industrial activities were sufficiently profitable to be undertaken.

Important features of this view can be found in seventeenth-century writing, notably by Locke on the rate of interest and by Mun on capital. However, Turgot integrated the various elements of this theory better than any of his predecessors. Furthermore, he used the theory to answer more clearly than anyone at that time the question of what constitutes a nation's wealth. His answer was that it comprises, to use modern terminology, the present value of the net revenue from land (the value of the land) plus the stock of movable goods. This, in essence, is the answer any modern economist would give. Turgot pointed out explicitly that to include 'capitals on loan' (financial assets) would involve double counting and that, though money was the object of saving, specie (a movable good and therefore part of wealth) was but a very small component of wealth.

In the course of this argument about the nature of wealth, Turgot explored the nature of value, a theme he developed in his later unfinished work. He started from the assumption that the value, or worth, of a good was unique to each individual. It depended on the fitness of the good to serve the purposes for which it was required, and on the difficulty of obtaining it. This concept of value could be described as 'esteem value', for value depended on the esteem in which a good was held. Turgot argued that there is no natural unit in which to measure value, and that the value of one good has to be measured in terms of another good. It is possible, for example, to say how many armfuls of firewood have the same value as a measure of grain. In practice, given that there are many goods, value is measured in terms of an arbitrary unit given by convention – a *numéraire*. If all goods are measured in terms of the same *numéraire*, then the relative value of any pair of goods can readily be calculated.

Turgot's discussion of 'esteem value' was applicable to an isolated person. From there he proceeded to consider exchange between two people who would generally value goods differently. He assumed that two goods would be exchanged at the average of the two parties' esteem values. If this were not the case, one would benefit less than the other from the exchange and would force the other to come closer to his price. This established what Turgot called 'exchange value'. Though conceptually different from the term 'price', which denotes the sum paid for a good, exchange value and price are numerically the same and can, in many contexts, be used interchangeably. Finally, Turgot introduced a second pair of traders, so that he had four people in communication with each other, two selling wood and two selling corn. He outlined how competition would force both sellers of each good to accept the same price.

Turgot was not alone in developing a subjective theory of value. On the contrary, there was a long tradition of such theories, going back through natural-law philosophers such as Samuel Pufendorf (1632–94) and Hugo Grotius (1583–1645) to the scholastics and Aristotle. In the eighteenth century, however, the clearest statements of subjective-value theories came from Italian economists, of whom Ferdinando Galiani (1728–87) is perhaps the outstanding representative. In 1751 Galiani published *Della Moneta*, one of the few works cited by Turgot in his essay on value. In 1759 he was appointed to the Neapolitan Embassy in Paris, where he stayed for ten years. This decade was precisely the time when, due to Quesnay, political economy had become fashionable. Galiani, however, was not a Physiocrat, and criticized the policy of allowing free export of corn while there were still extensive barriers to internal trade. *Della Moneta* clearly states the doctrine, taken up by Turgot, that value is subjective and measurable only in relation to the value of other goods. Utility and scarcity are the main factors explaining value. Galiani's argument that man is the common measure of value was, Turgot claimed, 'one of the newest and most profound truths which the general theory of value contains'.[12]

Economic Thought under the *Ancien Régime*

When the once-strict French censorship laws were relaxed sufficiently to allow the publication of writings that could be used against the government, the main issue driving economic thought was reform. Taxes and regulations were seen by many to be stifling trade. Against this background it is not surprising that the doctrine of laissez-faire was developed by a wide variety of writers, from Boisguilbert at the start of the century to Turgot on the eve of the French Revolution. The effects of government restrictions on agriculture no doubt provide part of the reason (though not the whole reason) why the Physiocrats emphasized the productivity of agriculture so strongly. They needed to counter the assumption, underlying Colbertism, that resources had to be shifted into manufacturing.

However, though economic thought was largely stimulated by urgent policy questions, many abstract ideas were developed. Cantillon's main work was on the nature of commerce *in general*. The Physiocrats went even further, developing an abstract numerical model of economic activity. Turgot, even while involved in the running of the French state, and trying to reform it, probed into the meaning of abstract concepts such as wealth and value. The result was that the French economists of this period produced ideas that proved able to be taken up and used in very different contexts in the following century. French ideas fed into English classical economics through Adam Smith, who was strongly influenced by Quesnay and Turgot, as well as through writers working after the Revolution, such as Jean Baptiste Say (see p. 142). Though his economic views could hardly be more different, the *Tableau économique* inspired Karl Marx (see pp. 156–63).

6

The Scottish Enlightenment of the Eighteenth Century

Background

The Scottish Enlightenment is the name given to the remarkable flourishing of intellectual activity in what, at the time, was a very backward part of Europe. It was sufficiently remarkable that even contemporaries were aware of it. David Hume was not alone in observing, in 1757, that it 'really is admirable how many Men of Genius this Country produces at present'.[1] The universities in Edinburgh, Glasgow and Aberdeen were central to this activity, out of which arose some of the eighteenth century's most notable contributions to economic thought (and to social thought more generally).

The social thought associated with the Scottish Enlightenment had several features which, if not unique, were taken further in Scotland than by thinkers in other countries. It was secular. It did not deny the tenets of established religion (such denial was still dangerous at this time, especially for people in university positions and in the early decades of the century), but it focused on the mundane, everyday aspects of reality. It was also committed to detachment and scientific objectivity rather than to orthodoxy. The thinkers of the Scottish Enlightenment were consciously the heirs of Bacon, Newton and the scientists of the seventeenth century, as well as inheriting important elements of natural-law philosophy. In addition, and more distinctively, the Scottish Enlightenment had a clear social and above all historical focus. Its writers were aware that different societies had different customs, and they sought to discover the causes of these. In this they were following Montesquieu's *Spirit of the Laws* (1748), a work Hume was responsible for translating into English. However, the Scottish writers – in particular Adam Smith – went further than Montesquieu in that they also sought to explain how human societies changed. They sought to provide an account of the history of civil society.

A major theme in these studies was that human nature was the same at all times. History, Hume argued very clearly, could be used to discover what these 'constant and universal principles of human nature' were.[2] The writers of the Scottish Enlightenment, however, also sought to examine the changing environment in which human nature operated. Man's action could change the environment and produce a new situation in which behaviour was different, even though the underlying human nature had not changed. The Scottish writers were led to the view that society had progressed through several historical stages. Primitive society was based on hunting and gathering the fruits of nature, without any antecedent social organization. Pasture followed from the domestication of animals and, because property could now be appropriated, led to inequality and differences in social status. This was followed by the agrarian stage, in which land became regarded as property that could be appropriated. This was the stage in which inheritance became important. The legal system developed accordingly. Finally there was the exchange economy, in which society became divided into classes who gained their livelihoods in different ways. Division of labour raised productivity and also made people more dependent on each other. This was an evolutionary theory of social organization in which economics, politics and law were all bound up together.

The fact of social evolution led both to a belief in progress and to a historical relativism. Adam Ferguson (1723–1816), a historian prominent in the Scottish Enlightenment, could write that 'the present age is perfecting what a former age began; or is now beginning what a future age is to perfect'.[3] Such an outlook had clear political implications. The Jacobite rising of 1745, which attempted to restore the Stuarts to the throne, was backward-looking; the future lay elsewhere. At the same time, however, the writers of the Scottish Enlightenment became convinced that it was important to judge societies according to the customs of each society's own age. It was inappropriate to judge them according to the customs of modern society.

One factor behind the Scottish Enlightenment was an awareness that Scotland was backward in comparison with the south and east of England. The Scottish supporters of the 1707 Act of Union had hoped that the act would stimulate their economy. They were also confronted with the dramatic contrast between the relatively developed Lowlands and the very backward Highland regions. However, despite union with England, Scotland remained different in key respects. The Church of Scotland was Presbyterian, with a Calvinist emphasis on decisions made by the individual. More importantly, the Scottish legal system was, unlike the English, based on Roman law. Natural law, not common law, was fundamental. Feudal elements had survived (as was still the case in the twentieth century). There was thus great interest in comparisons with England, where Roman law was not recognized.

Hutcheson

Francis Hutcheson (1694–1746), who held the chair of Moral Philosophy at Edinburgh from 1729 until his death, is generally regarded as the originator of the Scottish Enlightenment. However, he owed much to his predecessor Gershom Carmichael (1672–1729). It was Carmichael who had introduced the German natural-law philosopher Samuel Pufendorf to Scotland, publishing an edition of one of his most important works together with a set of substantial and influential notes. The link from Aristotle to Adam Smith came through Pufendorf and Carmichael. Carmichael's doctrine that the value of a commodity depended both on the commodity's scarcity and on the difficulty of acquiring it, and that a good could be of value only if it was either useful or imagined to be useful, was very squarely in the Aristotelian tradition.

The significance of Hutcheson's view of human nature is made clear in his criticism of Mandeville. Bernard Mandeville (1670?–1733), was a Dutchman who settled in England in 1699 and became notorious for *The Grumbling Hive: or Knaves Turned Honest* (1705), a twenty-six-page poem that was later expanded into *The Fable of the Bees: or Private Vices turned Public Benefits* (1714). This aroused a public outcry for, not only did it argue for free markets and competition, it was also a forthright attack on puritan morality according to which abstinence was a virtue and luxury consumption a vice. Mandeville challenged the notion that Christian morality was what held society together.

Mandeville's *Fable* was about a large, prosperous hive, well stocked with bees. Vice abounded, in that all the bees were driven by lust and vanity. Wealth was unequally distributed, but all the bees, even the poorest, were better off than they would otherwise have been. The reason was that high consumption created employment. Every bee was kept busy attempting to satisfy another's demands. Even crime and fraud provided opportunities for honest employment – burglars provided employment for locksmiths. Despite prosperity and economic growth, however, the bees felt insecure. Then one day a puritan moral revolution broke out. Crime and military spending ceased, and luxury was spurned. The result was unemployment and the collapse of entire industries. Many bees fled the hive.

The moral of the tale was clear. People are naturally selfish, but in a well-ordered society they will be induced voluntarily to do what is best. Private vices produce public benefits. Vices should not be encouraged, but they should be recognized and turned to good effect. Mandeville did not advocate laissez-faire, however. The market could be allowed to coordinate much economic activity, but he still favoured regulation of foreign trade in order to create employment and to stock the nation with money. There were also many projects that the government could undertake to provide employment for the poor. Mercantilist ideas thus coexisted with his recognition of the importance of the market.

Hutcheson's criticism of Mandeville challenged the assumption that men were purely self-interested. Men were, Hutcheson claimed, altruistic and cared for their fellows. This meant that Mandeville was wrong to argue that luxury spending was needed for nations to prosper. Men would seek to ensure that other people had the goods they needed, and so there would be no need for luxury spending till all demands for necessary goods were satisfied. Whereas Mandeville had assumed that people were selfish, Hutcheson, like many of his fellow Scots, viewed people as driven by a variety of motives. These included the desire to look after oneself, feeling for others, and the desire to better one's condition. As one might expect from someone influenced by Pufendorf and Carmichael, Hutcheson had a supply-and-demand theory of value, and this was taken up a few years later by Sir James Steuart (see pp. 117–21). Hutcheson also emphasized the importance of the division of labour, so important to Adam Smith (see pp. 121–9), combining this with a labour theory of property derived from Locke.

Hume

David Hume (1711–76) is now best known for his philosophical writing, but to his contemporaries he was known as a historian, for his *History of England* (1754–62). A historical perspective permeates his approach to economics, contained in a series of nine essays published in 1752 as part of a volume of *Political Discourses*. In view of contemporary scepticism about the value of abstract reasoning in economics, it is interesting to note that Hume opens this group of essays with a defence of applying what he calls 'refined and subtile' reasonings to such 'vulgar' subjects as commerce, money, interest, taxes and public credit. He appeals to his readers not to be prejudiced against what he has to say merely because his ideas are 'out of the common road'.[4] The public good, Hume argues, depends on a multitude of causes, not on chance and the caprices of a few individuals. This means that the type of historical account that one might give to explain, say, foreign policy, is inappropriate to this subject matter, and that more general reasoning, that may yield unfamiliar conclusions, is required.

Hume's concern in these essays is with the greatness of a state. He starts by distinguishing between this and the happiness of the state's subjects. The latter will be increased by luxury consumption and will thus be reduced if the state diverts resources from this into defence and foreign ventures. In this sense, there is a trade-off between the happiness of the people and the power and influence of the state. However, luxury spending is important to the state, for it is necessary to persuade people to work. This is why manufacturing is needed – the manufacture of luxury goods provides husbandmen (farmers) with an incentive to work more than the minimum amount required to subsist. Without such an incentive, they would prefer to be idle for much of the time. This desire for luxury goods benefits the state because, if husbandmen are producing a surplus over what they need for their subsistence, resources are available to which the sovereign can lay claim in order to raise fleets and armies. In a society of self-sufficient farmers, there would be no surplus available to be appropriated. Hume supports this claim with evidence from ancient Greek and Roman history.

The basis for Hume's argument about commerce and wealth is the theory that labour is the basis for wealth and that labour will be supplied only if people have an incentive to do so. He writes, 'Every thing in the world is purchased by labour; and our passions are the only causes of labour.'[5] Manufacturing is valuable because it enables labour to be stored up, available for use in times of need:

[M]anufactures encrease the power of the state only as they store up so much labour, and that of a kind to which the public may lay claim, without depriving anyone of the necessaries of life. The more labour, therefore, is employed beyond mere necessaries, the more powerful is any state; since the persons engaged in that labour may easily be converted to the public service. In a state without manufactures, there may be the same number of hands; but there is not the same quantity of labour, nor of the same kind. All the labour is there bestowed upon necessaries, which can admit of little or no abatement.[6]

For much the same reason, foreign commerce is valuable. It increases the stock of labour in a nation.

Having established that the strength of a state depends on labour and commerce, Hume proceeds to demolish the argument that money is wealth. Money, he claims, is simply 'the oil which renders the motions of the wheels [of trade] more smooth and easy'.[7] There is no benefit to be had from having a greater quantity of money, for prices will be higher in the same proportion. The only exception to this is that, if gold and silver are plentiful, the sovereign will have more resources that can be drawn upon in times of war. In other respects, a large quantity of money is a disadvantage – higher prices will cause manufacturing industries to shift abroad, where costs will be lower. Labour will be lost to the state. Hume was thus opposed to the use of paper money, for this harmed manufacturing without the offsetting benefit of raising the state's stock of gold and silver.

However, although the quantity of money was of no importance, a rising money supply did make a difference – inflation could be beneficial. 'Accordingly we find, that, in every kingdom, into which money begins to flow in greater abundance than formerly, every thing takes a new face: labour and industry gain life; the merchant becomes more enterprising, the manufacturer more diligent and skilful, and even the farmer follows his plough with greater alacrity and attention.'[8] The explanation was that, although money raises prices, it does not do so immediately. There is thus an interval during which the money supply has increased by more than prices, and during this interval industry will be stimulated. Conversely, a falling money supply will have damaging effects on industry – a conclusion that Hume was able to support with much historical evidence.

Hume concluded that the best policy was to keep the money supply continually increasing. However, he was strongly opposed to trying to do this through 'mercantilist' policies. Attempting to maintain a balance-of-payments surplus would be self-defeating, for the inflow of money would raise prices, causing manufacturing to go abroad, thus undermining the policy. He likened money to water in the sea: it is possible to raise the water level in one region only if it is cut off from the rest of the sea. If there is communication between different regions, money will, like water, find its own level. The only effect of mercantilist policies, therefore, was to interfere with trade. Furthermore, if one wanted to increase reserves of gold and silver for use in wartime, the right method was to hoard it, not to spend it. If money disappeared from circulation into hoards, it would no longer affect prices. This was in contrast with the mercantilist view, exemplified by Mun, that the purpose of increasing the money supply was to increase the circulation.

Sir James Steuart

Many themes from the work of Hutcheson and Hume can be found in
the book that has been described as the first systematic treatise on
economics in the English language, the full title of which was *An Inquiry
into the Principles of Political Oeconomy: Being an Essay on the Science
of Domestic Policy in Free Nations, in which are Particularly Considered
Population, Agriculture, Trade, Industry, Money, Coin, Interest, Circulation, Banks, Exchange, Public Credit and Taxes* (1767). The title
introduced into English the term 'political economy', a translation of
the term '*œconomie politique*' used by Antoyne Monchrétien (*c.* 1575–
1621) in the title of a book published in 1615. This was to become the
standard name for economics as the subject began to achieve a separate
identity during the nineteenth century. The English book was also the
first work to use the phrase 'supply and demand' to explain how prices
were determined:

The nature of demand is to encourage industry; and when it is regularly made,
the effect of it is, that the supply for the most part is to be found in proportion
to it . . . And when it is irregular, that is, unexpected, or when the usual supply
fails, . . . [this] occasions a competition among the buyers and raises the current,
that is, the ordinary prices.[9]

This explanation of prices was followed up with a detailed account
of competition. Particular attention was paid to what the author called
'double competition', in which there was competition both between
buyers and between sellers. This was important because it set upper
and lower limits to price and caused the interests of different individuals
to balance each other. This balance, however, vibrated, with the result
that buyers and sellers could not observe it exactly. Their decisions had
to be based on the price for which they expected to be able to resell the
goods. The conclusion was drawn that forestalling (buying goods in
order to resell them when there was a shortage) was a crime because it
diminished the competition that ought to take place and that would
ensure that goods sold for their real value.

The author of the book was Sir James Steuart (1712–80). He was part of the Scottish Enlightenment, but stood apart from other writers in that he was a Jacobite, and supported the 1745 rebellion. Sent by Charles Edward Stewart, the Young Pretender, as an ambassador to France, Steuart remained in exile after the defeat of the Jacobites at Culloden, not returning to Scotland until 1763. During this period he travelled widely in Europe.

Steuart's experience during his exile influenced his book. He became very sceptical about general rules concerning political matters, on the grounds that everything needed to be considered in relation to the circumstances of the country in question. Different countries had different customs, and these needed to be taken into account. He thus wrote that the merit of his book, in so far as it had any merit, arose from 'divesting myself of English notions, so far as to be able to expose in a fair light, the sentiments and policy of foreign nations, relatively to their own situation'.[10] Continental influences account for Steuart's emphasis on the role of the statesman (used as a shorthand for the king, Parliament, or whoever was ruling a nation). His book was, as he put it, 'addressed to a statesman', even though its object was 'to influence the spirit of those whom he governs'.[11] This went against the prevailing mood, which was in favour of liberty and playing down the importance of state action.

Steuart's historical perspective echoed that of Hutcheson, though he distinguished only three stages in history: hunting and gathering, agriculture, and exchange. Growth was seen in terms of an increase in population, this being limited by the supply of food. In the first stage of history, population was limited by the spontaneous fruits of the earth, but, when 'labour and industry' were applied to the soil, a further quantity of food could be produced, enabling a larger population to be supported. However, if farmers were to be induced to produce more than they needed for their own consumption, there had to be a market for their produce – the third stage. This led Steuart to state two principles:

[1] Agriculture among a free people will augment population, in proportion only as the necessitous are put in a situation to purchase subsistence with their

labour . . . [2] That agriculture, when encouraged for the sake of multiplying inhabitants, must keep pace with the progress of industry; or else an outlet must be found for all superfluity.[12]

These principles, he claimed, were confirmed by experience. We can see him here arguing for a balance between the more extreme views of mercantilist support for industry and Physiocratic support for agriculture – views that he would obviously have encountered during his stay in Europe.

Like Hume, Steuart saw a close link between labour and wealth. However, in line with the trend in English economic thought from the late seventeenth century, he placed much greater emphasis on the need to keep people employed. He recognized that employment would fail from time to time, and he believed that the state should seek to mitigate this as much as possible. Maintaining employment required that there should be a balance between supply and demand: 'The greatest care must be taken to support a perfect balance between the hands in work and the demand for their labour.'[13] Demand must be neither too high nor too low, and it was the statesman's duty to see that this was achieved.

Steuart had what has come to be called a 'Malthusian' view of population growth. Procreation was not the same as multiplication of the population, for, if the birth rate were too high, fewer children would survive. It followed that population could grow in response to the demand for labour, but only if agriculture could produce more food. There were, however, limits to what agriculture could provide, the main one being rising agricultural costs. Rising food prices would raise the price of subsistence and hence wage costs. The statesman would then be caught in a dilemma between encouraging 'expensive improvements of the soil' (which require high food prices) and cheap imports which enable wages costs to be kept low. This dilemma could be resolved, Steuart argued, only by 'right application of public money'.[14] This is one example of the ways in which Steuart believed that the state might have to use government spending or alterations to the money supply in order to achieve a balance between supply and demand. Public money could be used to raise demand and reduce unemployment, but care had to be taken not to lean too far the other way.

Given such an attitude, it is not surprising that Steuart did not accept the quantity theory of money. The theory of the relationship between money and prices proposed by Montesquieu and Hume, he conceded, was 'so simple, and so extensive, that it is no wonder to see it adopted by almost everyone who has written after them'. However, he argued that 'in this, as in every other part of the science of political economy, there is hardly such a thing as a general rule to be laid down'.[15] The reasons he gave for this were that demand and competition determined prices, and that these depended on wealth and on the circumstances of the economy, not on how much coin people happened to have:

Let the specie of a country, therefore, be augmented or diminished, in ever so great a proportion, commodities will still rise and fall according to the principles of demand and competition; and these will constantly depend upon the inclinations of those who have *property* or any kind of *equivalent* whatsoever to give; but never on the quantity of *coin* they are possessed of.[16]

Throughout his *Principles*, Steuart emphasized the role of the states-man. It would, however, be a mistake to see him either as a totalitarian planner or as someone who was simply looking back to a pre-market era. Not only did he assume people to be self-interested, he regarded this as essential if government policy were to be effective:

The principle of self-interest will serve as a general key to this inquiry; and it may, in one sense, be considered as the ruling principle of my subject . . . This is the main spring, and only motive which a statesman should make use of, to engage a free people to concur in the plans which he lays down for their government . . . [W]ere every one to act for the public, and neglect himself, the statesman would be bewildered, and the supposition is ridiculous.[17]

One can see from this passage that Steuart lies firmly in the approach to politics that goes back, through Hobbes and Locke, to Machiavelli.

For a few years, Steuart's *Principles* was well received. Hume welcomed the book, and Steuart's advice was sought by the British government. However, the book rapidly fell into oblivion, at least in Britain. The main reason was clearly the publication of Adam Smith's *Wealth of Nations* only a few years later. Smith's work caught the public imagination far more effectively than Steuart's, and Smith adopted the effective rhetorical strategy of completely ignoring the earlier book. Part of the reason, however, may have been Steuart's rambling style, which did not always make his message clear. In Germany, however, where Steuart's mercantilist ideas found a more receptive audience, the book continued to be read, and his discussion of supply and demand received considerable attention in the early nineteenth century (see p. 146).

Adam Smith

Adam Smith (1723–90), who came from an influential Scottish family, was a student of Hutcheson's and, after a year holding the chair of Logic, held the chair of Moral Philosophy at Glasgow from 1752 to 1764. During this time he lectured on rhetoric and belles-lettres, jurisprudence and moral philosophy. His work on economics arose out of this, and formed part of a broader inquiry into the science of society. This inquiry was squarely in the tradition of the Scottish Enlightenment, with its focus on history and on the foundations of civil society. The book that sustained Smith's reputation for subsequent generations, dominating nineteenth-century economics as did the work of no other economist, was *An Inquiry into the Nature and Causes of the Wealth of Nations*, first published in 1776, the year of the American Declaration of Independence. In Smith's lifetime, however, his reputation was based not on this book, but on *The Theory of Moral Sentiments*, published in six editions between 1759 and 1790. Smith regarded both books as part of his broader inquiry into social science. The relationship between the two books was described at the beginning of the sixth edition of *The Theory of Moral Sentiments*:

In the . . . first Edition of the present work, I said, that I should in another discourse endeavour to give an account of the general principles of law and government, and of the different revolutions which they had undergone in the different ages and periods of society; not only in what concerns justice, but in what concerns police, revenue and arms, and whatever else is the object of law. In the *Inquiry concerning the Nature and Causes of the Wealth of Nations*, I have partly executed this promise; at least so far as concerns police, revenue and arms. What remains [is] the theory of jurisprudence.[18]

This last part of his project was never completed.

The main concern of *The Theory of Moral Sentiments* was with the criteria on which moral judgements can be based. Smith thus explored the basis for the sense of propriety, the sense of approbation, and judgements of merit and virtue. A key element in his approach was provided by the concept of sympathy – the ability to see things from someone else's point of view, and to see our own behaviour from the perspective of an impartial spectator. The reason why this is relevant to social science is that, in undertaking this inquiry, Smith was exploring the question of what makes it possible for men to live in society. How is it that selfish desires can be restrained in order to prevent men from injuring one another? The simplest answer is the desire to please others – a desire for the approbation of other people. We view our own behaviour from the point of view of the impartial spectator, and act accordingly. This motive, however, will not be strong enough. When we contemplate our actions before we act, 'eagerness of passion' – the desire to do things – will bias our judgement. After an action has been taken, on the other hand, the desire not to think badly of ourselves will lead to bias. Neither beforehand nor afterwards, therefore, can we take an unbiased view of our actions. Further guidance is needed. This is provided by moral rules – generalizations from our experience of what types of action are approved of and disapproved of. However, moral rules are in themselves insufficient and need to be backed up, in some cases, by positive laws.

If people are held together by mutual affection and give each other the support that they need 'from gratitude, from friendship, and esteem', society can flourish. However, Smith argued that such motives are not necessary:

Society may subsist among different men, as among different merchants, from a sense of its utility, without any mutual love or affection; and though no man in it should owe any obligation, or be bound in gratitude to any other, it may still be upheld by a mercenary exchange of good offices according to an agreed valuation.[19]

A commercial society can flourish even though people do not have strong affections for each other. On the other hand, this is emphatically not the same as saying that a society can flourish if there are no limits to behaviour:

Society, however, cannot subsist among those who are at all times ready to hurt and injure one another . . . If there is any society among robbers and murderers, they must at least . . . abstain from robbing and murdering one another. Benefi-cence, therefore, is less essential to the existence of society than justice. Society may subsist, though not in the most comfortable state, without beneficence; but the prevalence of injustice must utterly destroy it.[20]

This is the context for the *Wealth of Nations*. Smith is exploring how a commercial society can prosper, even though men are pursuing their own interests. He is, however, assuming a framework of justice, without which society would be destroyed. The society he is talking about differs from a Hobbesian state of nature in that men are assumed to be guided by morality and restrained by a just legal system. Within this framework Smith explains the benefits that arise from a system of liberty.

Division of Labour and the Market

More clearly than any previous writer, Smith was concerned with the process of economic growth. Of the five 'Books' that make up the *Wealth of Nations*, the first discusses 'the causes of improvement in the productive powers of labour' and how produce is distributed among the different classes of society. Book 2 considers capital accumulation, and Book 3 what Smith calls 'the different progress of opulence in different nations'. He then turns to government policy, offering in Book 4 critiques of both the 'mercantile system' and the 'agricultural system' (Physiocracy), and in Book 5 a discussion of government revenue and taxation. Taken as a whole, the work is a vast compendium of theory, economic history and policy advice. Its variety and range provide part of the explanation of why economists have been able to interpret it in very different ways.

The most important cause of economic growth, Smith claimed, is the division of labour. On introducing the idea, he illustrated it with a 'very trifling manufacture' – pin making. He pointed out that, without being trained in the industry and without the assistance of the right machinery (and both training and machinery were the result of division of labour), a worker could probably make no more than one pin per day and certainly no more than twenty. In contrast, in the modern industry, where the task of making a pin was divided into eighteen different operations (drawing the wire, straightening it, cutting it, grinding it, putting the head on, whitening the pin, putting the pins into paper, and so on), a team of ten men could make upward of 48,000 pins per day. Division of labour was, Smith claimed, carried furthest in the most advanced countries.

However, although Smith introduced the division of labour by considering its application within a single factory, just as important for his case was the social division of labour, where different people perform different tasks, obtaining what they need through exchange. The division of labour, he argued, was 'the necessary, though very slow and gradual consequence of a certain propensity in human nature . . . to truck, barter, and exchange one thing for another'.[21] This led him to the proposition that the division of labour was limited by the extent of the market. In a village, people had to perform for themselves many of the tasks that, in a city, would be performed by specialists. A country carpenter, Smith observed, was not only a carpenter, but a joiner, a cabinetmaker, a wood carver and a wagon maker, each of which would be a separate trade in a larger market. The development of water transport, Smith observed, was crucial to this process of opening up more extensive markets.

Having established the link between economic growth and the expansion of markets, Smith then turned to the question of how markets operated. This took him into the fields of value and the distribution of income. Three concepts are particularly important to his analysis of these problems. The first is the distinction between the real and the nominal prices of commodities. In an exchange economy it is more convenient to use money than to engage in barter and, as a result, prices are measured in terms of money (the nominal price). However, the real price of a commodity is 'the toil and trouble of acquiring it'. This is a quantity of labour, not a quantity of money – though, given the problems involved in measuring labour, it might best be measured in terms of other commodities. Variations in the value of gold and silver would cause the nominal and real prices of commodities to differ from each other. It is the real price that matters and that his theory of value sought to explain.

The second important concept in Smith's value theory is the breaking down of the prices of commodities into their component parts – wages, profits and rents, the returns to labour, capital and land. This is the basis for the third key concept: the distinction between the market price and the natural price of commodities. The market price of a commodity is the price it fetches in the market, which will depend on supply and demand. If supply is insufficient to meet demand at the going price, the market price will rise; if there is a surplus of goods, the market price will fall. Because prices can be broken down into their component parts, it follows that, if the market price rises, so too must at least one of the components of price. The natural price of a commodity is thus defined as the price at which labour, capital and land are all receiving their natural prices. It is, Smith argued, 'the central price, to which the prices of all commodities are continually gravitating'.[22] The mechanism that causes this to happen is competition. If, for example, the rate of profit in producing hats is higher than the natural rate of profits, and if capitalists are free to move their capital from one industry to another, they will move into hat-making. This will increase the supply of hats and bring the price of hats down to the natural price. Alternatively, if workers in mining are earning more than the natural rate of wages, other workers will become miners, pushing wages downward.

This mechanism is the basis for Smith's conclusion that the market can work like an invisible hand, causing people to produce what other members of society want, even when individuals have no intention to do anything for anyone else. It is the reason why self-interest can produce an outcome that is in the interests of society – why a commercial society can prosper even though people have no affection for each other. Its crucial element is what Smith called 'liberty', the freedom of individuals to move their capital and labour from one activity to another as they choose. It was a concern to promote liberty that led Smith to denounce mercantilist restrictions on industry and trade. Such restrictions would benefit particular individuals but would hinder the operation of competition.

Capital Accumulation

Book 1 of the *Wealth of Nations*, with its emphasis on division of labour and the link between labour and wealth, falls squarely within the Scottish Enlightenment tradition. In Book 2, on the other hand, Smith emphasizes the role of capital in a way that makes him much closer to Turgot than to Hutcheson or Hume. A precondition for the division of labour, Smith contended, is the accumulation of what he called 'stock'. This includes both the tools that workmen need and also the provisions that they need while they are working. If growth is to occur, stock has to be increased, and to achieve this it is necessary to employ labour productively. This leads to Smith's distinction between productive and unproductive labour.

The basic idea underlying this distinction is that productive labour 'adds to the value of the subject on which it is bestowed'. It 'fixes' itself 'in a permanent subject or vendible commodity' that is there when the labour is finished, and which can then be sold to obtain more labour.[23] Unproductive labour, however, does not add to the value of anything. Thus the labour of a manufacturer who adds to the value of the materials with which he works, or of the farmer who produces a tangible output at the end of the year, is productive. In contrast, the labour of the menial servant or even of the sovereign or judges or the army is unproductive. Given that all labour has to be maintained by annual produce, the accumulation of capital depends on the proportion of labour employed productively. Consider the extreme cases. If the entire labour force were employed unproductively, there would be no produce at all the following year. At the other extreme, if labour were all employed productively, produce must be higher.

The need for capital accumulation is the reason why Smith sees a link between saving and economic growth. 'Capitals are increased by parsimony, and diminished by prodigality and misconduct.'[24] He argues forcefully that there is no need for luxury spending to maintain demand, for savings are spent just as much as is expenditure on consumption goods:

What is annually saved is as regularly consumed as what is annually spent, and in nearly the same time too; but it is consumed by a different set of people. That portion of his revenue which a rich man annually spends, is in most cases consumed by idle guests, and menial servants, who leave nothing behind them in return for their consumption. That portion which he annually saves, as for the sake of profit it is immediately employed as capital, is consumed in the same manner, and nearly in the same time too, but by a different set of people, by labourers, manufacturers, and artificers, who re-produce with a profit the value of their annual consumption . . . The consumption is the same, but the consumers are different.[25]

In other words, saving (which for Smith means investment, for otherwise savers could not earn a profit, which is their objective) is employing productive labour, whereas consumption is employing unproductive labour.

Smith and Laissez-Faire

Smith advocated what he described as the system of 'natural liberty', to be contrasted with the other two systems of political economy that he discussed: the mercantile system and the system of agriculture (Physiocracy). The main characteristic of this was the freedom of any individual to bring his capital into competition with that of any other man. He opposed monopoly, which in his day was normally the result of privileges granted by the government: 'Monopoly . . . is a great enemy to good management, which can never be universally established but in consequence of that free and universal competition which forces every body to have recourse to it for the sake of self-defence.'[26] Free competition would result in resources being moved into those activities where they were most needed. The individual would be 'led by an invisible hand to promote an end which was no part of his intention'.[27] Though Smith made little use of the phrase 'the invisible hand' (it appears once in each of his major books), this can be seen as his contribution to the debate on what holds society together, opened up by Hobbes over a century earlier. However, Smith was not arguing for complete laissez-faire, for he saw an important role for government.

The main reason why government was needed was that the arguments of the *Wealth of Nations* presupposed a system of justice. Without justice, the system of natural liberty would be unable to function. Men would be insecure, continually being damaged by each other. Spending on the legal system and on the armed forces might be classified as unproductive, but it was nonetheless essential for the system to work. For Smith, to maintain law and order was therefore the first duty of the sovereign. It is worth noting that this involved some significant exceptions to the principle of laissez-faire. In particular, Smith supported the Navigation Acts (which severely restricted competition in shipping), on the grounds that they contributed to the strength of the Royal Navy.

Defence and justice, however, were not the only exceptions Smith saw to the principle of laissez-faire. The third duty of the sovereign was that of

erecting and maintaining those publick institutions and those publick works, which, though they may be in the highest degree advantageous to a great society, are, however, of such a nature, that the profit could never repay the expence to any individual or small number of individuals, and which it, therefore, cannot be expected that any individual or small number of individuals should erect or maintain.[28]

His main examples concerned transport (bridges, roads and canals) and primary education. However, although he argued the case for intervention, he sought to make use of tolls and fees wherever possible. This was for two reasons. He wanted users (for example of roads) to pay as much as possible, and he wanted employees (such as teachers) to have an incentive to do their work properly. Thus, immediately after saying that the cost of education might 'without injustice' be met out of public funds, he declared that it would be better for it to be paid by those who benefited from schooling. His view was that privately provided education was, in his day, better than public education. He was scathing in his criticism of universities, in which teachers failed to teach and students failed to learn.

One area where Smith saw no role whatsoever for the government was in maintaining the level of employment. Writers from Misselden (in the early seventeenth century) to Steuart (writing only a few years before Smith) had seen the disruption that fluctuations in trade could produce and had sought to design policies that would mitigate the resulting underemployment. Mercantilist policies can be seen, at least in part, as attempts to reduce unemployment by increasing the circulation of money. The defence of luxury consumption by numerous writers in the seventeenth and eighteenth centuries was also a response to periods when demand was seen to be inadequate. Smith, on the other hand, with his doctrine that saving constituted spending, denied that there was a problem. If there were perfect liberty, men would move into an occupation where there was a demand for their services. Monetary economics thus played a minor role in Smith's system. This separation of monetary economics from problems of value, income distribution and growth stood in clear contrast with mercantilist ideas, and was to dominate economic thinking throughout the nineteenth century.

Economic Thought at the End of the Eighteenth Century

For contemporaries, as much as for subsequent generations of economists, the crowning achievement of eighteenth-century economic thought was Smith's *Wealth of Nations*. This arose out of the long-standing controversy over the role of Christian morality in holding society together to which Hobbes and Mandeville had made such dramatic contributions. Smith approached the question from the perspective of moral philosophy. He combined this with a focus on the interdependence of the various sectors of the economy. This was a pervasive theme in eighteenth-century thought, in both Britain and France, and it can even be found as far back as the sixteenth century (as in the *Discourse on the Common Weal*), but it was Smith's version of it that caught the imagination of his contemporaries. Over time, however, the origins of the *Wealth of Nations* in this debate over the morality of commercial society became forgotten, resulting in Smith's work being seen in a different light. He became seen as the advocate of laissez-faire – a perspective that would have surprised his contemporaries, who would have been aware how much further he was from such a position than, for example, many French authors.

Smith's debts to his predecessors and contemporaries are so great that some commentators have gone so far as to argue that the *Wealth of Nations* contains not a single original idea. Supply and demand as the explanation of value has a history too long to summarize briefly. Elements of the labour theory of value can be traced to Petty and to some scholastic writers. The phrase 'division of labour' was coined by Hutcheson, and the concept was widely understood in Xenophon's day. The importance of capital was recognized by Turgot. The notion of a spontaneous order can be found in Mandeville and Cantillon. And so on. It was, however, Smith's interpretation of these themes that found its way into nineteenth-century economics, especially in Britain. This neglect of the past had significant costs. For example, subjective-value theory, though it remained strong in France and Germany, was pushed aside by Smith and most of his English followers, who minimized the role of demand in determining prices. The seeds were sown for what has come to be known as classical political economy and, within that, the Ricardian 'detour'.

7

Classical Political Economy, 1790–1870

From Moral Philosophy to Political Economy

Smith's *Wealth of Nations* was part of a much broader inquiry into the foundations of society. It was inseparable from moral philosophy – from the project of seeking to find a basis on which people could live together when the Church no longer provided an unquestioned set of answers to questions about how society should be organized. Smith's economics should therefore be seen as a response to Mandeville, and before him Hobbes, as much as to the Physiocrats or the mercantilist writers. In the half-century or so after Smith's death, however, political economy, though dominated by the framework set out in the *Wealth of Nations*, became independent of moral philosophy. It acquired a more 'scientific' character that appealed to a class of radicals, many of whom wanted to explain social phenomena without reference to a deity.

To understand this transition, it is important to remember that the discipline was thoroughly involved with politics, and that the political context changed dramatically during this period. Among the political-economic issues facing Smith were the relationship between Britain and the American colonies (especially trade and tax policies), restrictions on both domestic and foreign trade caused by the creation of monopolies, and the appropriateness of intervention in the market for food in order to prevent famine. In the 1780s and 1790s, as the growth rate of the population increased, the problem of poverty and its alleviation increased, with the phrase 'the labouring poor' coming into widespread use to describe a supposedly new category of workers who were unable to achieve a decent standard of living even though they were able-bodied and had work. (The need for public support for the old, the sick and children was never questioned.) The 'Speenhamland System', introduced in the 1790s, involved the payment of allowances linked to the price of bread to men earning low wages. These payments were financed from local taxation, and aroused great controversy. Some people argued that the system depressed wages, exacerbating the position of the poor instead of relieving it.

The French Revolution in 1789 and the ensuing wars (1793–1815) had a profound effect on economic thought. The Revolution raised the spectre of republicanism, and popular unrest was a constant worry for the ruling classes in Britain, especially after the outbreak of war in 1793. The war also created acute economic problems. A financial crisis in 1797 led to the suspension of the convertibility of sterling into gold, and Britain remained on a paper currency until 1819. During the decade and a half after the suspension, the number of banknotes issued by the Bank of England increased and prices rose. A particular problem was the rise in the price of grain, which raised agricultural rents and caused an expansion in the amount of cultivated land. Farmers and landlords prospered. At the same time, people were becoming aware that the 'manufacturing system' was growing rapidly. Steam power, though still used only on a small scale, was spreading, and mechanization was rapidly transforming the long-established woollen industry and making possible the dramatic growth of the newer cotton industry. The mix of social unrest caused by high food prices and the social dislocation caused by industrial change was a potent one, especially when combined with fear of French republicanism.

A key figure in the transition from the moral philosophy of Hume and Smith to classical political economy was Thomas Robert Malthus (1766–1834). In the 1790s, radicals, of whom William Godwin (1756–1836) and the Marquis de Condorcet (1743–94) were most prominent, argued that private property was the root of social ills and that resources should be distributed more equally so as to provide everyone with a decent standard of living. Given Condorcet's links with the policies that developed in France, under Robespierre, into the Terror (in which Condorcet was killed), this was regarded as a seditious doctrine by much of the British Establishment. Malthus, a clergyman in the Church of England, responded to such arguments with his *Essay on the Principle of Population*. This was published as a small, anonymous, tract in 1798, then considerably expanded and published under his name in the second edition of 1803. In it, Malthus offered a series of related arguments against utopian views, focusing in particular on Godwin. Far from being a source of harm, Malthus argued, private property was essential, for otherwise self-love would fail to have the beneficial effects that Smith had pointed out. Giving money to the poor would not improve their condition unless someone else was prepared to consume less, for it would have no effect on the quantity of resources available. Furthermore, any extension of poor relief would increase the dependence of the poor on the state – something Malthus viewed with apprehension. Under the Poor Laws, the poor were 'subjected to a set of grating, inconvenient, and tyrannical laws, totally inconsistent with the genuine spirit of the constitution . . . utterly contradictory to all ideas of freedom . . . [and adding] to the difficulty of those struggling to support themselves without assistance'.[1]

Though it was only one among many ideas presented in the *Essay*, Malthus has become most widely associated with the argument that there is a continual tendency for population to outstrip resources. He expressed this by claiming that, if unchecked, population would grow according to a geometric progression (1, 2, 4, 8, 16, . . .), whereas food supply could grow only in an arithmetic progression (1, 2, 3, 4, 5, . . .). Population was held down by two types of check: preventive checks, which served to lower the birth rate, and positive checks, which raised the death rate. These two types of check fell into two categories: misery (war, famine) and vice (war, infanticide, prostitution, contraception). In the second edition of the *Essay* he added a third category, moral restraint, which covered postponement of marriage not accompanied by 'irregular gratification'. This third category enabled him to reconcile his theory with the evidence he had collected, between 1798 and 1803, that his original theory was not supported by the facts. Moral restraint was very important because it opened up the possibility of progress. However, although Malthus softened the hard line taken in the original *Essay*, he never shared Godwin's or Condorcet's optimism, for he did not share their belief in the goodness of human nature. Men required moral guidance, and Malthus sought to provide it. The term 'moral' restraint was carefully chosen.

Malthus, therefore, was operating within the sphere of eighteenth-century moral philosophy. He based his case against the utopians on laws of society – the security of property and the institution of marriage. Socialism was at fault because it violated natural laws. In arguing along these lines, Malthus was arguing that Christianity, properly interpreted, was consistent with the Enlightenment – indeed, that it was the highest form of enlightenment. Though he disagreed with Godwin's and Condorcet's conclusions, he shared with them a belief in reason, presenting himself as applying Newtonian principles to the art of politics. He criticized them for endangering the enlightened, Newtonian, view of science by fostering hopes of progress that could never be realized.

This belief in the power of reason was not shared by Malthus's 'Romantic' critics, Robert Southey (1774–1843), Samuel Taylor Coleridge (1772–1834) and the other 'Lake poets'. During his own lifetime, the term 'Malthusian' came to be used as a term of abuse, referring to the materialistic, spiritually impoverished outlook of what was also called 'modern political economy'. This was a reaction that continued throughout the nineteenth century, notably with Thomas Carlyle (1795–1881), who coined the phrase 'the Dismal Science', and John Ruskin (1819–1900). The term 'economist' came to denote someone with an identifiable approach to politics and a congenitally hard heart.

The *Wealth of Nations*, with its optimism about the prospects for growth, offered little guidance to politicians facing the problems of wartime. Malthus reoriented political economy so as to respond to these problems, and in doing this he helped lay the foundations for classical political economy. However, he continued to work within the eighteenth-century tradition in which political economy was closely linked to the science of morals and politics. Other economists, though they acknowledged an equally great debt to the *Wealth of Nations*, did not share this perspective and sought to turn political economy into a secular science.

Utilitarianism and the Philosophic Radicals

After Adam Smith, the main influence on the classical economists was Jeremy Bentham (1748–1832), a man idolized by his followers. His utilitarianism arose out of the natural-law tradition, though Bentham rejected the idea of natural law. Moral codes did not reflect natural laws, but arose to serve the needs of society. Civil laws, needed to provide rules by which conduct was to be governed, should be based on moral codes, but both might become outdated and need to be changed. The standard by which moral rules and civil laws should be judged was 'the principle of utility' – the maximization of the sum of the happiness of the individuals that make up a society. This was also the standard that should be used to judge government actions.

Bentham's interpretation of utilitarianism rested on some clear-cut value judgements. (1) Society's interest is the sum of the interests of the members of society. (2) Every man is the best judge of his own interests. (3) Every man's capacity for happiness is as great as any other's. These resulted in a philosophy that was both egalitarian and individualist and served as the foundation for Bentham's elaborate schemes for legal and penal reform. For Bentham, however, the principle of utility did not reduce policy-making to a simple rule. Utility had several dimensions (intensity, duration, certainty, and nearness), and it was necessary to balance these against each other. The utilitarian principle nonetheless provided a rough guide that policy-makers could follow.

Bentham wrote on economic questions, acknowledging his debt to Smith, but his major influence was indirect, through his followers, the Philosophic Radicals. Among these, the most eminent were James Mill (1773–1836), Mill's intellectual protégé, David Ricardo (1772–1823), and John Stuart Mill (1806–73). James Mill studied divinity in Edinburgh and briefly became a Presbyterian preacher before turning to teaching. In 1802 he moved to London to pursue a career as a journalist and writer. His major work was *A History of British India* (1818), after which he obtained a post in the India Office, rising to the position of Chief Examiner, the senior permanent post in the government of India. In London he became a close associate of Bentham. Ricardo, the son of a stockbroker, came from a Jewish family. He married a Quaker and was subsequently disowned by his father. At Mill's instigation, he became a Member of Parliament. John Stuart Mill was the son of James Mill and received a very rigorous education from his father. At three he started Greek, and at eight Latin, algebra, geometry and differential calculus. Political economy and logic came at twelve. He spent many years working at the India Office, rising to the same position as his father, and in 1865 he became a Member of Parliament.

The Philosophic Radicals were actively engaged in politics, using utilitarianism as the basis for criticizing the institutions of society and advocating policies of reform. By the standards of the day they were genuine radicals, even though their schemes were far removed from the socialism of Godwin and Condorcet or of some of their contemporaries such as Robert Owen (1771–1858), author of the New Lanark socialist experiment. They remained, like Malthus, Whigs. However, though James Mill and Ricardo were close to Malthus on many issues (Ricardo and Malthus were close friends, constantly debating economic issues), they did not share his commitment to economics remaining a moral science. For them economics was *political* economy, but they sought to make it a rigorous discipline offering conclusions as certain as those offered by Euclidean geometry. This resulted in the subject becoming, in Ricardo's hands, more abstract and less inductive than in the hands of either Smith or Malthus.

Ricardian Economics

Ricardian economics was a response to the situation in Britain during the Napoleonic Wars (1804–15), when the price of corn (wheat) and agricultural rents rose dramatically and the margin of cultivation was extended. Ricardo sought to demonstrate two propositions: that, contrary to what Smith had argued, the interests of the landlords were opposed to the interests of the rest of society, and that the *only* cause of a declining rate of profit was a shortage of cultivable land. It is easy to see how such a perspective arose from Britain's wartime experience. Influenced by James Mill, with his desire to make political economy as rigorous as Euclidean geometry, in his *Principles of Political Economy and Taxation* (published in three editions, 1817–23) Ricardo constructed a system that was unprecedented in the analytical rigour with which it was developed.

Ricardo's system rested on three pillars: a Smithian perspective on the link between capital accumulation and growth, the Malthusian theory of population, and the theory of differential rent. The last of these was worked out, apparently independently, by Malthus, Ricardo, Edward West (1782–1828) and Robert Torrens (1780–1864), in 1815. The theory rested on two assumptions: that different plots of land were of different fertility, with the result that applying the same labour and capital to them would yield different quantities of corn, and that agricultural land had no alternative use. Competition would ensure that the least fertile plots of land under cultivation would earn no rent: the corn produced would sell for just enough revenue to cover production costs, with the result that there would be nothing left for the landlord. If there were a surplus, more land would be brought under cultivation; if costs were not covered, the land would not be cultivated. All other plots of land, however, because they must by definition be more fertile, would yield a surplus. Being the owner of the land, the landlord would be able to demand this surplus as rent. The result was that rent emerged as the surplus earned by land that was more fertile than the least fertile land under cultivation.

The theory of differential rent explained the share of national income that was received by landlords. The Malthusian population theory was then used to explain the share of income received by workers. While wages might rise above or fall below this level if the population were growing or declining, they were linked, in the long run, to the subsistence wage rate. The residual after deducting rent and wages was profit, the share of income accruing to capitalists. From there it was a short step to a theory of economic growth. High profits would encourage capitalists to invest, raising the capital stock. This would raise the demand for labour, keeping wages high and causing population growth. However, as the population grew, so too would the price of corn, the result being that the margin of cultivation would be extended: more land would be cultivated, and plots already under cultivation would be cultivated more intensively. As this happened, rents would rise, eating away at profits (wages could not fall, at least for very long, below subsistence, so could not be reduced). This fall in profits would cause the rate of capital accumulation, and hence the rate of growth, to fall.

It was thus apparently a short step to Ricardo's two key propositions. As capital accumulated, rents rose but profits fell. Given that capital created employment, this was bad for the workers too. In addition, Ricardo had shown that falling productivity in agriculture, caused by the need to bring decreasingly fertile land into cultivation, was the cause of a declining profit rate. There were complications, however. The first was that, as growth took place and demand for food increased, it might be possible to import food, thus removing the necessity to extend the margin of cultivation. These imports would have to be paid for through exports of manufactured goods. In itself this caused no analytical problems: capitalists would invest in either agriculture or manufacturing, depending on the rate of profit available in each, so, if agriculture could not be expanded without lower profits, capital would move into manufacturing, creating the necessary exports.

However, the introduction of a manufacturing sector into Ricardo's model raised major theoretical problems. The first was that, if there were two goods (food and manufactures), Ricardo needed to explain their relative price: he needed a theory of value. For this he turned to the labour theory of value – the theory that prices of commodities will be proportional to the labour required to produce them. The problem here, cutting through an immensely technical issue, is that, under competition, prices will be proportional to production costs and production costs will depend on the amount of capital used, not just the quantity of labour. It follows that the ratio of price to labour cost will vary according to the ratio of capital to labour in an industry. The labour theory of value will not hold. Ricardo struggled to find a way out of this problem, but in the end he had to resort to an act of faith – he used a numerical example to argue that, in practice, variations in labour time explained virtually all variations in relative prices (93 per cent in his example).

The existence of manufactured goods also created problems for Ricardo's claim that diminishing agricultural productivity was the *only* cause of a declining profit rate. If workers consumed only corn, this would be true. Agriculture would be self-contained (corn would be the only output and the only input), and the rate of profit would not depend on conditions in manufacturing. Competition would ensure that the rate of profit earned in manufacturing, and hence in the whole economy, would equal that earned in agriculture. On the other hand, if workers' subsistence were to include, say, clothing as well as food, then the subsistence wage would depend on the cost of producing clothing as well as the cost of producing food. Agriculture would not be self-contained. The result would be that the rate of profit would depend on conditions in manufacturing as well as on those in agriculture. Ricardo's theorem that agricultural productivity was the *only* determinant of the profit rate would be undermined.

It is clear, even from this account, that in Ricardo's economics we are dealing with a level of analytical rigour that is to be found in few, if any, of his predecessors. Ricardo simplified the world he was analysing to the point where he was able to show with strict logic that his conclusions followed. When account is taken of the aspects of his system that are not discussed here (notably his theories of international trade and money) these remarks apply *a fortiori*.

Ricardo's two propositions, though rooted in wartime conditions, had clear political implications in the nineteenth-century post-war world. After the war, corn prices remained high because of the Corn Laws, which prevented a price fall by severely restricting imports. His message that the interests of the landlords were opposed to the interests of the rest of society resonated with many political agitators: workers wanted cheaper corn so that their wages would buy more, and manufacturers wanted cheaper corn in the belief that it would reduce wages. Furthermore, Ricardo's theory argued that, unless the Corn Laws were repealed, profits would fall and growth would come to a halt. However, even if the Corn Laws were repealed, there would still be problems, the reason being that, if Ricardo's theory were correct, growth would involve the progressive expansion of manufacturing relative to agriculture. Britain would become the workshop of the world, exporting manufactured goods and importing corn. This was unacceptable to conservatives such as Malthus.

One of the most significant points about Ricardo's predictions is that they were based on a fallacy in his reasoning. He argued that it would not be in the interest of landlords to undertake improvements. Rises in productivity would simply cause the margin of cultivation to contract, with the result that rents would not rise. This, however, refers to rents in the economy as a whole. What Ricardo failed to see is that, even if aggregate rents do not rise, it will still be in the interests of individual producers to make improvements. This means that improvements will be introduced. If improvements are made, his predictions about the falling rate of profit and class conflict are undermined. The reason why this apparently small technical detail is so important is that Ricardo's mistake followed directly from his method. He theorized about aggregates, viewing agriculture as one giant farm. This approach allowed him to reach striking conclusions, but was potentially misleading.

Alternatives to Ricardian Economics

Ricardian economics made a deep impression. In the words of one commentator, it 'burnt deep scars on to the classical-economic consciousness'.[2] It was also the origin of Marx's economic theory and of many concepts that were used in more orthodox economics in the nineteenth and twentieth centuries. The idea that the rate of profit depended on the marginal cost of growing corn (the cost of growing an additional unit of corn, which would typically be higher than the unit cost of the corn that was already being grown) – arguably the defining theme in Ricardian economics – persisted throughout English economics up to the 1880s. In this sense, Ricardo had a lasting influence. However, Ricardian economics in its purest form (including the labour theory of value, Ricardo's deductive method and the theory of population) dominated the subject for only a brief period in the early 1820s.

The labour theory of value was strongly criticized by Samuel Bailey (1791–1870) in 1825. Bailey argued for a subjective theory of value in which value depended, not on costs, but on 'the esteem in which an object is held'.[3] Nassau Senior (1790–1864), appointed to the first chair of Political Economy at Oxford, moved away from both the Malthusian population doctrine and the labour theory of value. He introduced the idea that profits were not a surplus but a reward to capitalists for abstaining from consuming their wealth. He also formulated the idea that the value of an additional unit of a good (the concept that, in the 1870s, came to be called marginal utility) declined as more of the good was consumed. John Ramsay McCulloch (1789–1864), Professor of Political Economy at University College London from 1828 to 1837 and the most prolific economic writer in the Whig *Edinburgh Review*, was at one time a staunch Ricardian. However, he substantially modified his views, placing a much greater emphasis on history and inductive research than did Ricardo. He rejected Ricardo's view of class conflict. He considered it fallacious on the grounds that individual landlords would always have an incentive to introduce improvements. This would raise the productivity of land and would offset the tendency of the rate of profit to fall.

In short, English classical economics was not purely Ricardian. It reflected the work of a variety of individuals, and encompassed a plurality of views on most questions. If one work dominated, it was not Ricardo's *Principles* but Smith's *Wealth of Nations*, with its more catholic blending of theory and history. Even in 1900 there were still textbooks organized on Smithian lines.

Outside England, the influence of Ricardian economics was even less strong. In France, Smith's main interpreter was Jean Baptiste Say (1767–1832), a member of the Tribunate under Napoleon, and later an academic economist. Say was widely considered the leading French economist of his generation. Though a supporter of Smithian ideas, he advocated a subjective theory of value, consistent with a long-standing French tradition going back at least to Condillac. He also developed the law of markets. This was the proposition, previously put forward by Bentham and James Mill, and accepted by Ricardo, that there could never be a shortage of demand in general: that supply creates its own demand. Depressions arise not from a shortage of demand in the aggregate, but from shortages of demand for particular commodities.

Equally important, there developed in France a long tradition of applying mathematical analysis to economic problems. Condorcet had paved the way with his analysis of voting theory. He had shown, for example, that if there were three or more candidates in an election, majority voting might result in the election of a candidate who would lose in all two-candidate contests. However, the person who made what to modern economists is the most remarkable contribution was Antoine Augustin Cournot (1801–77). Cournot was briefly Professor of Mathematics at Lyon, but spent most of his career as a university administrator. Making the assumption that each producer maximized profit, and that sales in the market were constrained by demand, he derived equations to describe the output that would result if there were different numbers of firms in an industry. Starting with a single producer (a monopolist) he showed how output would change as the number of firms rose, first to two, and then towards infinity. For Cournot, competition was the limiting situation as the number of firms approached infinity. In a competitive market, no firm could affect the price it received for its product.

Cournot is also considered to have been the first economist to use a diagram to explain how supply and demand determine price in a competitive market. The demand curve (MN in Cournot's diagram below) shows that the amount that people wish to buy falls as price rises. The supply curve (PQ) shows that the amount that producers wish to sell increases as price rises. The market price (OT) is the price at which supply and demand are equal. Cournot went on to show how the diagram could be used to show how market price would change in response to events such as the imposition of a tax on the commodity.

An emphasis on demand for goods was also characteristic of the work undertaken by engineers at the École des Ponts et Chaussées (School of Bridges and Highways). Their work was prompted by the need to find a basis for deciding the merits of civil-engineering projects. In the 1820s, the conventional view was that such projects should be self-liquidating – that they should completely cover their costs. Claude Louis Marie Henri Navier (1785–1836), well known to engineers for his work on mechanics, challenged this in an article, published in 1830 in *Le Génie civil* (a civil-engineering journal) and in 1832 in the *Annales des ponts et chaussées*. His argument was that a public work, such as a canal or a bridge, could raise public welfare. Taxpayers would get goods more cheaply, and the expansion in trade caused by the

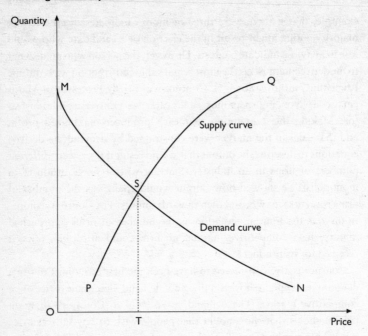

Fig. 1 Supply and demand curves

project would increase tax revenues in general. He estimated benefits derived from a project by multiplying the quantity of goods carried using the canal or bridge by the reduction in transport cost produced. If these benefits were greater than the ongoing annual cost of the project, the construction cost should be financed out of taxation. Navier thought that tolls should be zero, but if they had to be levied they should cover only interest payments and regular maintenance. He extended these ideas in later articles and in his lectures at the École des Ponts et Chaussées, taking account of such things as the relation between costs and the length of a railway line. He also considered whether public works should be provided by the state or franchised to private firms, and the type of regulation that should be imposed.

These problems were also tackled, independently of Navier, by

Joseph Minard (1781–1870), another engineer, who wrote what he viewed as a practical manual to guide civil engineers involved in public-works projects. He used the idea of a downward-sloping demand curve to argue that Navier's method (quantity of goods carried times the cost saving) would overstate the benefit derived from a project. The reason is that some of the people using the canal or bridge would not have made their journeys had it not been built, which means that the benefit they get from it will be less than the cost saving. He used arguments about the distribution of income between those who use the canal and those who do not to propose that tolls should be charged to cover annual costs. He also produced a formula (involving interest and inflation rates) to calculate the benefits from a project that took time to build, would not last for ever, and had an annual maintenance cost. However, though Minard wrote his manuscript in 1831, the course for which he planned to use it was not approved for many years, with the result that he did not publish his work until 1850. By that time, other articles on the subject had appeared.

Jules Dupuit (1804–66), another engineer concerned with methods by which the benefits of public-works projects could be estimated, also argued, in a series of articles in the 1840s and 1850s, that Navier's method overestimated the benefits. First, what mattered was not the reduction in transport costs but the reduction in the price of products. When production rose following the construction of a new bridge or canal, goods would be transported over longer distances. The result was that production costs would not fall as much as the cost of transport over a given distance. Second (and here he was making a point similar to Minard's) Dupuit argued that the utility of an additional unit of a good could be measured by the price the consumer was willing to pay for it. This price would fall as consumption rose. Dupuit went on to argue that the benefit obtained from building a canal or bridge could be measured by subtracting the cost of the project from the area under the demand curve. The demand curve, used by Cournot simply to analyse behaviour, could be used as a measure of welfare.

The three engineers discussed here form part of a long, well-established tradition at the École des Ponts et Chaussées in the middle decades of the nineteenth century. Starting with the practical problem of evaluating civil-engineering projects, they developed an alternative to the orthodox theory of value associated with Smith and Say. Some of Dupuit's later articles were published in the *Journal des économistes*, but much of the engineers' work was published in journals where economists would not see it. Say did express an interest in Minard's work in 1831, but he died a year later.

Another tradition, owing little to Ricardo, is found in the writers of economics textbooks in Germany, notably Karl Heinrich Rau (1792–1870), Friedrich Hermann (1795–1868), Hans von Mangoldt (1824–68) and Wilhelm Roscher (1817–94). These were Smithian in that they accepted Smith's ideas about the importance of saving and division of labour for economic growth. However, they rejected the labour theory of value. Instead, they took from Steuart the idea that prices are determined by supply and demand. Unlike most of the English classical economists, they attached great importance to demand. Hermann, for example, wrote explicitly about how changes in demand can cause changes in costs. Their textbooks discussed demand before supply, and explored the connections between demand and human needs. The result was a subjective theory of value in which the value of a good depended on what other goods people were prepared to forgo in order to obtain it – subsequently known as an opportunity-cost theory.

As in the French engineering tradition, supply and demand were represented graphically. Independently of Cournot, Rau used a supply-and-demand diagram in the fourth edition (1841) of his textbook. (He began the convention, followed in most of the modern literature, of putting quantity on the horizontal axis and price on the vertical axis.) Unlike Cournot, he analysed not only the equilibrium (where demand and supply are equal) but also the stability of this equilibrium. If price were too high, supply would exceed demand, pushing price down; if price were too low, demand would exceed supply, pushing price up. These ideas were taken further by Mangoldt in his textbook (1863). He argued that the shape of the supply curve would depend on the behaviour of costs as output increased and he used his curves to see how prices would change in response to changes in supply or demand.

For most of the nineteenth century, Germany was not a single country but a mosaic of small states. It is thus not surprising that different approaches to economics could coexist alongside each other. One such tradition is represented by Johann Heinrich von Thünen (1783–1850). Thünen was a farmer who became, by 1827, an internationally known authority on agriculture. His main work, *Der isolierte Staat* (*The Isolated State*), was published in three instalments between 1826 and 1863. It is best known for its analysis of location, in which the profitability of agriculture (and hence the level of rent and the type of agriculture that will be undertaken) depends on how far farms are from the city. He took as his starting point a city located in the centre of a large, fertile plain in which there were no rivers or other natural factors affecting transport costs. On such a plain, farming would be organized in a series of concentric circles. Closest to the city would be horticulture and market gardening, the produce of which cannot be transported far. Furthest away would be hunting, for which large tracts of land were needed and where transport costs were not a problem. In between would be various types of forestry, arable farming and pasture.

Perhaps as significant as Thünen's theory of location was his method. He tackled the question of how much capital and labour to use by regarding it as a maximization problem. Farmers use the quantities of capital and labour that will maximize their profits. Thünen formulated this problem using algebra, and solved it using differential calculus. By these methods he obtained the result that the wage paid will equal the contribution to output made by the last worker to be employed – the marginal-productivity theory of distribution. These methods also led him to see the problem of forest management as one involving time and the rate of interest. If the essence of capital is seen as being that it allows production to take place over time (a view later developed by Austrian economists), this can be seen as a marginal-productivity theory of the rate of interest.

Government Policy and the Role of the State

The British classical economists wrote during the period when economics was only just beginning to become institutionalized as an academic discipline. They were linked by organizations such as the Political

Economy Club (a group, founded in 1821, that met each month to discuss economic questions), the Royal Society, the Royal Statistical Society and the British Association. The journals in which their ideas were published did not specialize in economics, but addressed the educated classes in general and were frequently identified by their political leanings, not by their disciplinary coverage. The *Edinburgh Review* was Whig, the *Westminster Review* was Benthamite, and the *Quarterly Review* was Tory. Some economists held academic posts (often for short periods, not as a lifelong career), but most did not. For example, Ricardo was a stockbroker; Torrens had served in the army and was a newspaper proprietor, West and Mountifort Longfield (1802–84) were lawyers, and McCulloch (a professor for a brief period) was a civil servant and for a short time editor of the *Scotsman*. Many had a legal training, and many held government appointments at some stage in their careers. However, though abstract issues were discussed, political economy was never far from questions of economic policy. Many economists and many members of the Political Economy Club were Members of Parliament. Even when they were not involved in policy-making, however, almost all the economists formed part of the circles in which policy-makers moved, and they played an active role in discussions of economic policy. In the 1830s, after the Reform Act of 1832 (which extended the franchise to most of the propertied classes), the Philosophic Radicals formed an identifiable group in Parliament.

Though there were enormous differences between economists, it is a fairly safe generalization to say that they were in general pragmatic reformers. Like Smith, they opposed mercantilism. In so far as there was an ideological dimension to this, it stemmed from opposition to the corruption associated with mercantilism rather than any commitment to non-intervention. It was generally accepted that government had an important but limited role to play in economic life. Even the Philosophic Radicals, who favoured more radical reforms than most economists, were utilitarian – adhering to a philosophy that placed utility above freedom. They were quite willing to see the government regulate, provided that legislation did not undermine the security of private property, an institution they regarded as crucial in stimulating economic growth. Their attitudes and the changes that took place in the political context are best illustrated by considering some of the major questions that arose in the first three-quarters of the century: trade policy, poor relief, and labour-market policies.

The classical economists were basically free-traders, and produced a wide range of arguments to support their stance. Not only was there the 'invisible hand' argument found in the *Wealth of Nations*, they also pointed to the opportunities that protection provided for corruption and the distortion of domestic industry in favour of powerful groups. There were debates over whether free trade should be imposed unilaterally or on the basis of commercial treaties, but on the whole they supported unilateral free trade. The most contentious issue in trade policy, however, concerned the Corn Laws. Ricardo's theory was aimed at precisely this issue and provided a strong case for repeal, but this was not the ground on which most economists argued. They were influenced more by Smith. Thus McCulloch and Senior rejected Ricardo's arguments that the interests of the landlords differed from those of other classes in society. Some economists even supported the levying of tariffs to raise revenue, provided that these were not sufficiently high to distort trade flows.

The Poor Law was an issue for which the Malthusian theory had direct implications. Malthus and Ricardo favoured the abolition of the Poor Law, though both wanted this to be done gradually. Others thought this solution impracticable and favoured radical reform. Senior, for example, argued for the policy embodied in the Poor Law Amendment Act (1834), under which relief for the able-bodied poor was confined to those living in workhouses and which tried, in vain, to enforce the principle of less eligibility (that those out of work should be worse off than anyone in work). Most of the classical economists, however, were more relaxed about the provision of poor relief, being sceptical about the Malthusian argument that it would inevitably stimulate growth in the number of paupers. They wanted to continue 'outdoor' relief, and were not insistent on enforcing the principle of less eligibility.

Industrialization was changing dramatically the conditions under which an increasing proportion of people worked, and there was pressure for government regulation. In addition, trade unions began to be formed after the repeal of the Combination Laws (under which the formation of unions was illegal) in 1824. On neither issue did the economists adopt a doctrinaire position. The first act regulating factory conditions had been passed in 1802, and during the following decades a series of acts was passed increasing the degree of regulation. In much of this legislation the main target was children's and women's hours and conditions of work, but legislation here inevitably affected men too. There was a tendency to refrain from regulating adult men's hours, on the grounds that this would interfere with the principle of freedom of contract, but in general the economists were pragmatic and responded to events. They kept up with public opinion rather than leading it. On trade unions, the economists' position was generally to favour high wages and to view unions as counterbalancing employers' higher bargaining power.

The classical economists accepted the Smithian case for free enterprise, and many of them viewed the encroachments of the state on individual liberty with great suspicion. On neither, however, were they doctrinaire. They judged particular cases according to the principle of utility. The result was a pragmatic outlook in which the role for laissez-faire was severely circumscribed.

Money

Monetary policy was a major concern of the classical economists from the 1790s onwards. In 1793 and 1797 serious financial crises took place against the background of a banking system that had changed significantly since Hume's work on the subject. These formed the background to *An Inquiry into the Nature and Effects of the Paper Credit of Great Britain* (1802) by a banker, Henry Thornton (1760–1815). Thornton viewed banknotes and bills of exchange as assets that people hold, with the result that he placed great emphasis on confidence. If people became uncertain about the value of the assets they were holding (whether bills of exchange or notes issued by banks outside London), they would increase their holdings of the more secure asset. In Thornton's day this meant notes issued by the Bank of England.

Thornton thus perceived that there was a hierarchy within the banking system. In times of crisis, when they experienced a run on their reserves, the country banks (outside London and generally small) would turn to their correspondents in London for support. These in turn would turn to the Bank of England for liquidity. The Bank of England thus stood at the apex of a pyramid of credit.

This had enormous implications for the policy that the Bank of England should pursue. The normal practice for a bank facing a loss of reserves was to cut back on its lending. However, Thornton argued that this was exactly the wrong policy for the Bank of England, which should increase its lending when it experienced a loss of reserves to the country banks. The reason was that, if there were a crisis of confidence, an increase in the availability of credit from the Bank of England would serve to restore confidence and provide reserves that the rest of the banking system required. This was different from the case of the country banks – an increase in their note issue would reduce confidence in their ability to redeem their notes. In other words, the Bank of England, Thornton argued, should be acting as a central bank, taking responsibility for the financial system as a whole.

After 1804 the price of gold bullion rose significantly above its par value, established by Newton at £3 17s. 10½d. per ounce. In other words, the value of the Bank of England's notes had fallen. Ricardo, in 1810, argued that the rise in the price of bullion reflected the overissue of notes by the Bank of England. He argued that the directors of the Bank could not be trusted to manage the issue of notes, and that convertibility should be restored – albeit gradually. This was the strict bullionist position – that notes should be convertible into bullion. This was also Thornton's position, though unlike Ricardo he accepted that the link between note issue and the price of bullion might be weak in the short run. In the short run it was possible for factors that affected the balance of payments – such as bad harvests (which caused an increase in imports of corn), subsidies to foreign governments, or overseas military expenditure – to raise the price of bullion independently of the note issue.

The anti-bullionist position can be found in the writings of the directors of the Bank of England. They denied that the quantity of banknotes in circulation bore any relationship to the price of bullion. Their argument was the so-called 'real-bills doctrine'. This was the theory that, provided a bank lent money against 'real bills' (bills issued to finance genuine commercial transactions, not to finance speculation), the bills would automatically be repaid when the transaction was complete. The amount of currency in circulation would therefore exactly equal the demand for it. It was assumed that no one would borrow money and pay interest if they did not need to. The answer to this was offered in Thornton's *Paper Credit*. Thornton pointed out that the decision on whether to borrow money from a bank would depend on how the interest rate on the loan compared with the rate of profit that could be obtained through investing the money. If the interest rate were below the profit rate, people would have an incentive to increase their borrowing, the circulation of banknotes would increase, and prices would rise. This process would continue for as long as the interest rate was below the profit rate. Conversely, if the interest rate exceeded the profit rate, the quantity of notes issued and the price level would fall. The real-bills doctrine, with its assumption that no one would borrow money unnecessarily if interest had to be paid on it, was thus flawed.

A parliamentary report into the currency in 1810, largely drafted by Thornton, supported the bullionist case, and as a result the government took the decision to return to convertibility, this being achieved in 1819. However, this did not end discussions of monetary policy. The period after 1815 was one of severe deflation – of depression and falling prices. Although the policy of maintaining convertibility of sterling into gold was not questioned, it became clear that this in itself was not enough. The Bank of England's policy had to be organized so as to ensure that its bullion reserves were always sufficient for convertibility to be maintained. This led into a debate over what would nowadays be termed counter-cyclical policy: economists debated the merits of alternative ways of coping with fluctuations in the demand for credit.

The banking school argued that monetary policy should be conducted according to the needs of the domestic economy. In a depression there was a shortage of credit, and so the note issue should be expanded. If too many notes were issued, they would be returned to the Bank – the so-called 'doctrine of reflux'. It stressed that notes were merely one among many forms of credit. One of the main supporters of the banking school, Thomas Tooke (1774–1858), countered Thornton's argument that low interest rates led to inflation with extensive statistical evidence to show that inflation typically occurred when interest rates were high. In opposition to this view, the currency school, of which Lord Overstone (1796–1883) was the leading member, advocated the so-called 'currency principle', or 'principle of metallic fluctuation'. This was the principle that a paper currency should be made to behave in the same way as a metallic currency would behave. This meant that, if the Bank of England lost gold, it should reduce its note issue pound for pound. The money supply would thus be linked to the balance of payments. This was, like the banking school's proposal to meet the needs of trade, a counter-cyclical policy, for it was designed to ensure that corrective policies would be implemented before an expansion had gone too far. Without the currency principle, the currency school argued, action would be taken too late. Thus, whereas the banking school focused on policy to alleviate depressions, the currency school sought to design a policy that would make them less likely to occur.

John Stuart Mill

That Ricardian economics exerted an influence beyond the 1820s is due to two people, both major figures in nineteenth-century intellectual history. The first of these was John Stuart Mill. Mill was educated by his father to be a strict disciple of Bentham. In the 1820s and 1830s he was a member of the Philosophic Radicals. Around 1830 he wrote a series of essays on economics in which he built upon the Ricardian approach to economics, but he had problems in finding a publisher and they were not published till 1844, after the great success of his *System of Logic* (1843). After his father's death in 1836, and influenced by Harriet Taylor (1807–58), whom he married in 1851, Mill moved away from a narrow utilitarian position and became much more sympathetic to socialism – albeit a form of socialism very different from what is now meant by the term, in that he did not advocate state ownership of the means of production. His main contribution to economics was his

Principles of Political Economy, published in several editions between 1848 and 1873. This served as the point of departure for most British and many American economists until the publication of Alfred Marshall's *Principles of Economics* in 1890.

Mill's achievement in the *Principles* was to retain the Ricardian framework but at the same time to take into account the many points made by Ricardo's critics. Given that Mill did not lay claim to originality and that he claimed to be doing little more than updating Smith's *Wealth of Nations*, the result was a book that has been dismissed as eclectic. This, however, is to understate Mill's originality and creativity. The basic theory of value, income distribution and growth was Ricardian, but Mill modified it in important ways. He placed much greater emphasis on demand in explaining value, and the way in which he conceived demand (as a schedule of prices and quantities) marked a significant change from the Smithian and Ricardian concept. When applied to international trade (in his theory of reciprocal demand), the result was a theory that went far beyond Ricardo in two ways. It allowed for the possibility that costs might change with output, and it explained the volume of goods traded. He followed Senior in accepting that profits might be necessary to induce capitalists to save.

Perhaps the main significance of Mill's *Principles*, however, was that, although it retained the basic Ricardian framework, it embodied a radically different social philosophy. Mill wrote of seeking to emancipate political economy from the old school, making it less doctrinaire than it had become in many quarters. In this he was strongly influenced by socialist writers, notably a group known as the Saint-Simonians, named after Claude Henri Saint-Simon (1760–1825), who advocated a form of socialism in which the class structure of society was changed but in which production was controlled by industralists. Mill reconciled his adherence to Ricardian theory with a social outlook that verged on socialism through introducing, at the start of the *Principles*, a distinction between the laws of production and the laws of distribution. After a survey of the evolution of societies, reminiscent of the Scottish Enlightenment, he argued that the production of wealth depended on factors beyond human control:

The production of wealth ... is evidently not an arbitrary thing. It has its necessary conditions. Of these, some are physical, depending on the properties of matter, and on the amount of knowledge of those properties possessed at the particular place and time ... Combining these facts of outward nature with truths relating to human nature it [political economy] attempts to trace the secondary or derivative laws, by which the production of wealth is determined.[4]

These laws of production were based on the physical world, knowledge of that world, and human nature. In contrast, the laws governing the distribution of wealth depended on human institutions:

Unlike the laws of production, those of distribution are partly of human institution: since the manner in which wealth is distributed in any given society, depends on the statutes or usages therein obtaining.

He added, however, the qualification that

though governments have the power of deciding what institutions shall exist, they cannot arbitrarily determine how these institutions shall work.[5]

Political economy could discern the laws governing economic behaviour, enabling governments to create appropriate institutions. Social reform therefore involved redesigning the institutions of capitalism.

The institutions through which Mill sought to improve society were ones that gave individuals control over their own lives. He supported peasant proprietorship, giving small farmers the incentive to improve their own land and raise their incomes. He advocated producers' cooperatives and industrial partnerships (involving profit-sharing) as institutions that would enable workers to share responsibility for the successful conduct of business. These schemes all had the characteristic that they maintained incentives. He described such schemes as socialist – the difference between socialism and communism, as he used the terms, being that socialism preserved incentives whereas communism destroyed them. He still accepted the Malthusian theory of population growth, but he believed that education of the working classes (including education about birth control) would lead them to see the advantages of limiting family size and that living standards would then be able to rise. This outlook also affected his view of the stationary state. Growth might slow down, but if workers turned to self-improvement there would be no cause for concern.

As his book *On Liberty* (1859) makes clear, Mill was a liberal in the classical nineteenth-century sense. He believed in individual freedom. He was even prepared to argue that there should be a general presumption in favour of laissez-faire. However, he was far from an unqualified supporter of laissez-faire, going so far as to describe the exceptions as 'large'. He listed five classes of actions that had to be performed by the state, ranging from cases where individuals were not the best judges of their own interests (including education) to those where individuals would have to take action for the benefit of others (including poor relief) if the state were not involved. He argued that anything that had to be done by joint-stock organizations, where delegated management was required, would often be done as well, if not better, by the state. Even more radically, Mill argued that there might be circumstances in which it became desirable for the state to undertake almost any activity: 'In the particular circumstances of a given age or nation, there is scarcely anything, really important to the general interest, which it may not be desirable, or necessary, that the government should take upon itself, not because private individuals cannot effectually perform it, but because they will not.'[6] Having made the case for laissez-faire, Mill thus qualified it so heavily as to leave open the possibility of a level of state activity that many would regard as socialist.

Karl Marx

The other major mid-nineteenth-century economist to build on Ricardo's economics was Karl Marx (1818–83). However, whereas Mill remained within the classical framework laid down by Smith and Ricardo, Marx sought to provide a radical critique of orthodox 'bourgeois' political economy. His starting point was the study of ancient philosophy at the University of Berlin, then dominated by the ideas of

Georg Wilhelm Friedrich Hegel (1770–1831). Central to Hegel's work was the idea of dialectics, according to which ideas progressed through the opposition of a thesis and an antithesis, out of which a synthesis emerged. However, whereas Hegelian dialectics applied to the realm of ideas, Marx offered a dialectical analysis of the material world and the evolution of society (historical materialism). Each stage of history produced tensions within itself, the outcome of which was a move to a new, higher, stage of society. Feudalism gave way to capitalism, which in turn would give way to socialism and eventually to communism, the highest stage of society. This dialectical analysis of the material world is Marx's historical dialectics.

Marx's writings fall into several distinct stages. In the early 1840s Marx worked as a journalist in the Rhineland, where he had to tackle economic issues such as free trade and legislation on the theft of wood. The theoretical framework that underlies his later work was completely absent – he considered the notion of surplus value (an idea central to his later work) an 'economic fantasy'. In 1844, however, Friedrich Engels (1820–95), a cotton manufacturer with interests in Britain and Germany, who became Marx's lifelong friend, supporter and collaborator, introduced him to English classical economics. In an article published the previous year, Engels had argued that the intensity of competition among workers impoverished them. Capitalists could combine to protect their own interests and could augment their industrial incomes with rents and interest, whereas workers could do neither. Marx, in 1844, went on to explain low wages in terms taken straight from Smith. If demand for a product falls, at least one component of price (rent, profits or wages) must fall below its natural rate. He argued that, with division of labour, workers became more specialized and therefore found it harder to move from one occupation to another. The result was that when prices fell it was the workers whose incomes were reduced below the natural rate. Capitalists were able to keep the competitive price of their product above the natural price – to charge more than the value of their produce, and hence to extract a surplus.

In the next three years Marx studied Ricardo further and adopted the labour theory of value. However, whereas Ricardo had used the term 'value' to mean the price of a commodity, Marx defined value as something that lay beneath price: the labour time required to produce a commodity. Value and price were distinct. The significance of this was that it provided him with a rigorous explanation of how exploitation could arise, even in equilibrium. Exploitation was inherent in the basic relationships of capitalist production.

The year 1848 saw publication of *The Communist Manifesto* and Marx's involvement in the revolutions that took place (especially the one in Paris), followed by his exile to Britain. In London he turned again to economics and started work on a more systematic, scientific treatment of the subject. The main manuscript dating from this period, the *Grundrisse*, was never finished for publication (though it was published many years later). By the end of the 1850s all he had published was a short introduction to the subject, *A Contribution to the Critique of Political Economy* (1859), his first major economic work. In correspondence with Engels, he outlined a project involving six volumes, dealing with capital, landed property, wage labour, the state, international trade, and the world market. His major work, *Capital*, was thus conceived as the first volume of a much larger study. *Capital* itself grew to three volumes, only one of which was published in Marx's lifetime, in 1867; the remaining two volumes were published by Engels in 1885 and 1894. (Marx also wrote the material on the history of economic thought later published as *Theories of Surplus Value*, planned as the fourth volume of *Capital*.)

Capital is characterized by the method of inquiry (discussed in more detail in the *Grundrisse*) that some scholars have termed 'systematic' dialectics. In this method, ideas are criticized from within (as Marx was analysing capitalism from within a capitalist society) in a series of stages that lead from the abstract to the concrete. Because the analysis started with very abstract categories, it could explain only very general phenomena in its early stages. At each stage, it failed to explain more complex empirical phenomena. However, this failure carried the analysis forward to more complex and concrete categories. This movement from the abstract to the concrete is reflected in the organization of the three volumes of *Capital*. Volume 1 starts with the concept of a commodity and the process of capitalist production. It discusses value and the production of surplus value (explained in the next paragraph), and analyses the antagonism between capital and labour. Volume 2 discusses the circulation of capital and the various forms that capital can take. Volume 3 investigates competition and the antagonism between capitalists. Whereas Marx dealt with capital and surplus value as very abstract concepts in Volume 1, by Volume 3 these categories have become much more complex. The result is that he is able to explain many more empirical features of capitalism, such as the division between interest payments and entrepreneurial profits, and the tendency of the rate of profit to fall.

Marx's argument about exploitation rested on the distinction between labour and labour power. The value of an individual's labour power was, like the value of anything else, its cost of production (measured in labour time). If it took, for example, six hours' labour to produce the goods a worker needed in order to subsist and reproduce, the value of his labour power was six hours. However, it might be possible to force the worker to work for ten hours – his labour. The worker produced goods to the value of ten hours' labour, but his wages would be only six hours' labour, for this was the value of his labour power. The result would be the creation of surplus value equal to four hours' labour. This surplus value, Marx contended, was the source of profit. The reason why capitalists could exploit labour in this way was that they owned the means of production. Because capitalists owned the means of production, workers could not undertake production themselves. They were forced to sell their labour power to the capitalists. Exploitation thus lay at the heart of the capitalist system: it was not an accidental feature that could be removed without affecting the entire structure of the system.

The surplus value created by extracting unpaid labour from workers and fixing it in commodities was realized by the capitalist as a sum of money. Capital, however, was not simply money. To function as capital, it had to be transformed first into means of production and labour power, then into capital in the production process, then into stocks of commodities, and finally, once the commodities were sold, into money again. The simplest form of this circuit was summarized by Marx as M–C–M' (money–commodities–more money). He analysed this in two stages. The first was 'simple reproduction', in which an economy reproduced itself on an unchanged scale. The second was 'extended reproduction', where capital was increasing. He agreed with Smith that capital accumulated not because capitalists hoarded money but because they used money to employ labour productively.

In Volume 2, after an extensive discussion of the circulation of capital and the different forms that capital took in the process of circulation, Marx illustrated the process with some numerical examples – his reproduction schemes – inspired by Quesnay's *Tableau*. These were based on a division of the economy into two 'departments' or sectors. Department 1 produced capital goods, and Department 2 produced consumption goods that might be consumed by either capitalists or workers. He also distinguished two of the forms that capital could take: constant capital (machinery etc.) and variable capital (used to employ labour). The economy started with given stocks of constant and variable capital. Simple reproduction occurred when, after capitalists had used their surplus value to purchase consumption goods, the produce of the two departments was exactly sufficient to reproduce the capital used up in production. Extended reproduction occurred when stocks of capital at the end of the process were larger than at the beginning, with capitalists turning part of their surplus into constant and variable capital. Marx was using what would nowadays be called a 'two-sector' model to analyse the process of capital accumulation.

Volumes 1 and 2 remained at a very abstract level, analysing the movement of capital as a whole. In Volume 3 Marx considered the concrete forms taken by capital – notably costs of production, prices and profits. He analysed the way in which surplus value was converted into various forms of profit and rent. Here he addressed the problems that Ricardo had encountered when working out his labour theory of value. Prices would be higher than values in industries that employed a high proportion of fixed capital, and lower in industries where little fixed capital was used. Prices, therefore, would not be proportional to labour values. For Marx, this arose as the transformation problem – the problem of how values were transformed into prices. As he defined values in terms of labour time, this problem did not undermine his labour theory of value as it did Ricardo's.

Marx's analysis of the dynamics of capitalism went far beyond his reproduction schemes. It is not possible to cover all the details, but several points need to be made. The first is that Marx predicted that capitalist production would become more mechanized and more centralized. Increased mechanization led to what Marx called a rising 'organic composition of capital' – a rising proportion of capital would take the form of constant (fixed) capital, and a lower proportion would take the form of variable capital. Because surplus value was produced by variable capital (by exploiting living labour), this meant that surplus value per unit of capital would fall and with it the rate of profit. Capitalists would attempt to offset this by increasing the exploitation of workers by means such as increasing the length of the working day and forcing workers to work more intensively.

Marx was also led into analysing economic crises and the business cycle. Capitalists, he argued, were forever striving to accumulate capital. From time to time capital would accumulate so rapidly that they would be unable to sell all the output that they were producing. The result would be a crisis in which they failed to realize their profits. Capital would be liquidated as some businesses failed and others simply failed to replace the capital that was wearing out. Eventually the rate of profit would rise to the point where new investments were started and the system would move from depression into a new period of expansion. Marx therefore saw capitalism as undergoing successive periods of depression, medium activity, rapid expansion, and crisis. There would be a cycle, the period of which depended on the turnover rate or life cycle of capital goods. He assumed that this had increased, and that by the time he was writing it was around ten years in the 'essential branches of modern industry'.[7]

It is also important to note that Marx saw capitalism as containing the forces that would lead to its downfall. The main force was the concentration of capitalistic production:

This expropriation is accomplished by the action of the immanent laws of capitalistic production itself, by the centralization of capital. One capitalist always kills many. Hand in hand with this centralization, or this expropriation of many capitalists by few, develop, on an ever-extending scale, the cooperative form of the labour process, the conscious technical application of science, the methodical cultivation of the soil, the transformation of the instruments of labour into instruments of labour only usable in common, the economizing of all means of production by their use as the means of production of combined, socialized labour, the entanglement of all peoples in the net of the world-market, and with this the international character of the capitalistic regime.[8]

This centralization would at the same time increase the misery of the working class and cause it to become more organized:

Along with the constantly diminishing number of the magnates of capital, who usurp and monopolize all advantages of this process of transformation, grows the mass of misery, oppression, slavery, degradation, exploitation; but with this too grows the revolt of the working class, a class always increasing in numbers, and disciplined, united, organized by the very mechanism of capitalist production itself.[9]

Eventually capitalism, which up to that point had been a progressive force, would become an impediment to further development and would be overthrown:

The monopoly of capital becomes a fetter upon the mode of production, which has sprung up and flourished along with, and under it. Centralization of the means of production and socialization of labour at last reach a point where they become incompatible with their capitalist integument. This integument is burst asunder. The knell of capitalist private property sounds. The expropriators are expropriated.[10]

Marx never finished *Capital*, let alone the other books that would have filled out his analysis of the capitalist system. After his death, Volumes 2 and 3 of *Capital* were edited by Engels from his unfinished manuscripts. There were further delays of around twenty years before these volumes were translated into English. His early writings were not published in German until 1932, and the *Grundrisse* not until 1953, with English translations of these appearing only during the 1970s. The result of the delay in publication was that for many years his work was virtually unknown. Though written much earlier, and reflecting the situation of the 1860s and 1870s, Marx's economics became widely known only in the 1880s and 1890s. During the twentieth century, interpretations of his work changed as new evidence became available. Given that Marx's writings extended far beyond economics, into philosophy and social science, any interpretation of Marx offered here is inevitably very limited: it is one among many different possibilities.

The first point to make about Marx is that his economics is classical in that he built upon the economics of Smith and Ricardo. Marx's labour theory of value clearly owes much to his reading of Ricardo. It is therefore possible to view Marx as a Ricardian. To do this, however, is to miss the point that, though he started with the classical analysis, he transformed it and produced a radically different type of economics. For the classical economists, the laws of production were laws of nature. For Marx, on the other hand, the laws of production were based on the laws and institutions of capitalism, a specific historical stage in history. Capital could exist only because people had the right to own the produce of other people's labour. Wage labour – common in British industry, but in Marx's time far less widespread than it is today – was another institution central to the process of exploitation. Exploitation, the circulation of money and goods, capital, and the institutions of capitalism were therefore intertwined.

Despite its roots in classical economics, Marxist economics developed largely independently of the mainstream in economic thought. Its other roots in Hegelian philosophy were foreign to the Anglo-Saxon traditions that increasingly dominated the economics profession. The association of Marxian economics with socialist political movements – and, after 1917, with Russia and the Soviet Union – provided a further barrier. As economics distanced itself from other branches of social thought, the Marxian amalgam of economic and sociological analysis became remote from the concerns of most economists.

Marx's economics was, however, important even for non-Marxian economists. The obvious reason is that attempts were made by non-Marxian economists to rebut Marx, and Marxists responded. The most notable example was perhaps the debate between the Austrian economist Eugen von Böhm-Bawerk (see p. 211) and the Marxist Rudolf Hilferding (1877–1941) following the publication of Volume 3 of

Capital. Much more importantly, however, Marxian ideas fed into non-Marxian thinking – sometimes directly, sometimes indirectly. Marx's analysis of the business cycle in terms of fixed-capital accumulation fed, via the work of the Russian economist Mikhail Ivanovich Tugan-Baranovsky (1865–1919), into twentieth-century business-cycle theory, which came to focus on relations between saving and investment (see Chapter 10). His analysis of the waste caused by competition between capitalist producers was a crucial input into the debates over the possibility of rational socialist calculation in the inter-war period (see pp. 275–9). Marx's vision of the future of capitalism stimulated economists to offer their own alternatives, as in Joseph Alois Schumpeter's *Capitalism, Socialism and Democracy* (1943) (see p. 209).

Conclusions

Classical political economy comprised a great variety of theories and ideas. These ideas were held together by their roots in Smith's *Wealth of Nations*. Ricardo had created a far more rigorous system based on much more abstract reasoning, but his deductive style of argumentation did not win widespread support. Even Mill – responsible for sustaining the Ricardian tradition after interest in it waned in the 1820s – reverted in his *Principles* to the combination of inductive, historical analysis and deductive reasoning that characterized the *Wealth of Nations*.

Classical economics was never far from issues of economic policy: academics formed part of the same intellectual community as politicians, journalists and men of letters. At one end of the political spectrum were supporters of doctrinaire laissez-faire, and at the other were the Ricardian socialists. Most economists, however, fell between these two extremes. They succeeded in using the framework laid down by Smith to address first the policy problems arising during the revolutionary and Napoleonic wars, and later those arising from industrialization and the immense social changes that accompanied this. In Smith's day Britain was ruled by a narrow oligarchy, whereas by the 1870s, although corruption had not been eliminated, its scope had been very much reduced by reforms such as the extension of the franchise, secret voting and competitive examinations for the civil service. The extension of the franchise to include the working classes – a process started in the 1867 Reform Act and extended in 1884 – placed socialism much higher on the political agenda than it could ever have been in the days of Smith and Bentham. Mill and Marx, in radically different ways, showed that the Smithian structure, modified by Ricardo, could still be used in this changed environment.

However, although classical theory proved adaptable, it was becoming outdated. Even Mill had no analytical tools suitable for tackling problems of monopoly. Towards the end of the nineteenth century, problems of big business became more and more prominent, especially in Germany and the United States. Competition between industrial nations meant that free trade could not be taken for granted in the way that it had been as late as the middle of the century. Above all, real wages had, at least since the 1850s, risen substantially, with the result that the Malthusian population theory, which underlay the whole of classical economics, was becoming hard to defend. On top of this, Romantic critics of economics, such as Ruskin, were questioning the value judgements on which the subject was based. Thus by the 1860s the confidence in the subject that had enabled Senior to describe the Great Exhibition of 1851 as a triumph of political economy had dissipated.

8

The Split between History and Theory in Europe, 1870–1914

The Professionalization of Economics

In the closing decades of the nineteenth century, economics, like many other disciplines, became professionalized. It came to be dominated by men (there were few women) who specialized in the subject. Most of them were full-time academics. This marked a dramatic contrast with the world of Smith, Malthus, Ricardo and their contemporaries. This change took place in both Britain and the United States. In addition, research began to be published in specialist journals, such as the *Quarterly Journal of Economics*, established in 1886, the *Economic Journal* (1890) and the *Journal of Political Economy* (1892).

In continental Europe these changes had taken place earlier. In Germany, with a long tradition of *Cameralwissenschaft* (the science of economic administration), centred on the training of public servants, academics had dominated economics for much of the century. The Humboldt University of Berlin, as it later came to be known, founded in 1849, had established a strong research tradition on the basis of providing professors with security and freedom from pressure to teach particular doctrines. This freedom was later extended to other German universities by Bismarck. Specialist academic journals had been established much earlier than in the English-speaking world – the *Zeitschrift für die gesamte Staatswissenschaft* (which has since become the *Journal of Institutional and Theoretical Economics*) in 1844 and the *Jahrbücher für Nationalökonomie und Statistik* (*Yearbook of Economics and Statistics*) in 1863. In France, economic ideas had been developed by university professors such as Say and Cournot, and by engineers in elite colleges such as the École des Ponts et Chaussées.

There were also important changes in the intellectual environment in which economic ideas were developed. Newtonian ideas inspired economists for much of the eighteenth and nineteenth centuries. Smith and Malthus both saw their work as deriving Newtonian laws applicable to the social realm. Even in the seventeenth century, science had influenced the way in which economic questions were tackled. In the nineteenth century, however, the idea of the 'scientist' became established, the term being coined by William Whewell (1794–1866) in 1833. People stopped referring to science as 'natural philosophy', and the gap between science and philosophy widened. This affected economics in several ways. People with backgrounds in natural science turned to economics. They sought to emulate the achievements of science – notably physics, widely regarded as the most successful science. Some sought to strengthen the foundations of economics through basing it on experimental psychology (very different from Bentham's psychology). Others were inspired to apply Darwinian ideas on evolution to economics (the *Origin of Species* was published in 1859).

These developments were associated with changes in the way in which economics was conceived. Though many of the questions tackled by the subject remained the same, economics moved, or at least appeared to move, away from its origins in political philosophy. By 1900 the term 'economics' was beginning to displace 'political economy' as the generally preferred label for the discipline. The use of mathematics was becoming more common (although it remained a minority activity), and the idea that students should be able to specialize in economics, rather than coming to it through mathematics or philosophy, was gaining ground.

Jevons, Walras and Mathematical Economics

Throughout the nineteenth century there had been French and German economists who had used mathematics. In France this tradition went back to Condorcet's social mathematics and included Cournot and the engineers at the École des Ponts et Chaussées. In Germany there were the examples of Thünen and Hermann Heinrich Gossen (1810–59). The bulk of the subject, however, remained non-mathematical. In Britain, if we leave aside Ricardo's use of numerical examples, none of the classical economists used mathematics. From the 1870s, however, mathematical analysis began to be used much more widely, as economists sought to follow the example set by physics. Along with this came several other changes: there was a greater focus on individual behaviour, and the subject moved away from the classical themes of long-term development to focus on narrower problems. Two people were at the forefront of this process: in Britain, William Stanley Jevons (1835–82) and, at Lausanne, the French economist Léon Walras (1834–1910).

Jevons was a meteorologist, a chemist and the author of *The Principles of Science* (1874), a widely read treatise on scientific method. He was also a utilitarian. These elements in his background had a major influence on his approach to economics. Although his training in economics was (typically for the time) based on Mill's *Principles*, he reacted strongly against Mill and the Ricardian tradition in economics in his *The Theory of Political Economy* (1871). He disagreed with Ricardo over the theory of value. Ricardo, following Smith, had argued that, although a good must have utility if it is to have value, its value is determined by its production cost, not by its utility. Jevons argued that this was wrong, and that value depended entirely on utility. In particular, value depended on the benefit a consumer received from the last unit consumed (the marginal utility or, as Jevons put it, the 'final degree of utility'). There was a link between value and cost of production, but it was indirect. He summarized it as follows:

Cost of production determines supply;
Supply determines final degree of utility;
Final degree of utility determines value.[1]

Jevons started *The Theory of Political Economy* by arguing that economics was inherently mathematical because it dealt with quantities. He was optimistic about the possibilities of measuring economic quantities, pointing out that numerical data abounded – in account books, price lists, bank returns, government data and so on. The problem was not the absence of data but that economists did not know how to use them, and that the data were incomplete. Establishing economics as a science was, for Jevons, closely linked to the exact measurement of economic quantities.

Jevons's starting point was Bentham's theory of utility, in which utility was defined as the ability to increase pleasure or to reduce pain. Though feelings and motives could not be measured directly, Jevons argued that it was possible to measure them indirectly. The goods someone buys or sells will depend on comparisons of the pleasure to be obtained from various goods, which means that comparative pleasures can be measured by observing behaviour in the marketplace. He used an analogy with the measurement of gravity through measuring the movements of a pendulum. Jevons thus devoted much attention to the problem of defining utility and working out how it might be measured, drawing extensively on contemporary psychology. Only then could he use the theory to analyse economic phenomena.

In *The Theory of Political Economy* Jevons used utilitarianism to explain behaviour. This involved assuming that individuals sought to maximize their utility – to increase pleasure and reduce pain as much as possible. He suggested four ways in which this might be accomplished, and analysed each in turn: (1) allocating stocks of a good between different uses in the best possible way; (2) exchanging goods with other people; (3) working to produce goods; and (4) through employing capital. He used differential calculus to express the conditions for utility maximization in each of these four settings. In the context of exchange, for example, he derived the condition that utility would be maximized when the ratio of the marginal utility of two goods was equal to the relative price of the two goods. For example, if an apple costs twice as much as a banana, the pleasure obtained from the last apple purchased must be twice as large as the pleasure of an additional banana. If it were less, the individual would give up an apple to get two extra bananas. With labour, the equivalent result is that a worker works the number of hours such that the pain of an additional hour's work is exactly equal to the pleasure obtained from the additional commodities that that hour's labour enables him or her to purchase.

Walras, too, was concerned to make economics scientific through making it mathematical, and he developed many of the same results as Jevons concerning consumer behaviour and the determination of prices in competitive markets. However, he reached these conclusions by a very different route, and his focus was also very different. Walras was not a utilitarian but instead started from the notion – well established in the French tradition going back through Say to Condillac – that value depended on scarcity. He measured this scarcity in terms of what he called '*rareté*' – the intensity of the last want satisfied. Using this he derived conclusions similar to those worked out by Jevons. However, whereas Jevons analysed markets in terms of exchange between two individuals (allowing for competition with other potential traders), Walras focused on an organized market in which everyone faced a market price. In this situation, an individual would decide how much of each commodity he or she wished to buy or sell. This led Walras to construct demand and supply curves, relating desired purchases or sales to price: as price rose, demand would typically fall and supply would typically rise. The market would be in equilibrium where the two were equal.

Up to this point there were only minor differences in the conclusions reached by Jevons and Walras. The main difference between them was that Walras went on to discuss the problem of multi-market equilibrium – the problem of how prices are established in a large number of markets at the same time. He started by deriving demand and supply curves for the case of two-commodity exchange. People have stocks of two commodities, and exchange them with each other so that they end up with the combination of the two commodities that they prefer, given the relative price of the two commodities. Walras then extended his analysis to the exchange of many commodities. After that he introduced production, assuming that entrepreneurs moved resources from one activity to another until all opportunities for profits were eliminated. Introducing production meant bringing in markets for factor services (markets for renting the labour and machinery used to produce goods). Finally he added a market for credit, in order to explain the rate of interest. This was then used to link the rental rates on capital goods to their purchase price.

The end result was that Walras had a mathematical model – a set of simultaneous equations – describing an entire economy in which everything, in principle, depended on everything else. For example, a change in fashion might reduce the demand for beer and increase demand for tea. This could affect not just the prices of beer and tea but the prices of all other goods, wages, and even the rate of interest. Given the complexity of the set of equations and the very abstract level of his analysis, Walras confined his attention to doing two things. First, he sought to show that his set of equations had a solution: that there was a set of prices and quantities that satisfied all his equations. This is the problem of *existence* of equilibrium. He achieved this by counting the number of equations and showing that it was equal to the number of unknowns (the prices and quantities). Second, he sought to show that the solution to his set of equations was stable in the sense that, if the economy started with any arbitrary set of prices, it would end up with the set of prices that satisfied his equations. This is the problem of *stability* of equilibrium. Walras's method was to postulate that if supply of a commodity exceeded the demand the price of the commodity would fall, and vice versa. This was the *tâtonnement* process, through which an economy 'groped' its way towards the equilibrium.

Walras knew that real economies did not solve sets of simultaneous equations. He claimed that the *tâtonnement* described the trial-and-error process through which real-world economies determined prices, but argued that the economist could reach the same solution by solving the simultaneous equations. Both methods gave the same answer. The theory he had derived was 'pure' economics, and it needed to be applied. However, while Walras applied his ideas to a variety of policy issues, he failed to get much attention for them. His most radical proposal was for a tax on increases in land values or rents. He used his model to argue for the Ricardo-like conclusion that, over time, the share of rents in national income would rise. This meant that, over time, a tax on the increase in rents would yield more and more revenue. Such a tax was consistent with Walras's views on justice. To tax labour income would be unjust, because people were entitled to the fruits of their own labour, whereas the value of land derived from society, which meant that it was legitimate for it to accrue to society in the form of taxation.

Jevons also saw his abstract mathematical theory as comprising only part of economics. His applied economics was statistical and inductive. This was consistent with his view about science being to do with measurement. He became famous for *The Coal Question* (1865), in which he examined the effects of Britain's coal reserves becoming exhausted. When Britain ran out of coal, he concluded, growth would cease. He made this case with detailed statistics, not only on stocks of coal but also on the expansion of British industry. He was, however, wrong, for he failed to appreciate how technological change would transform the situation. In the 1860s he also tackled the question of the effect of the Californian gold discoveries on the price of gold. The main characteristic of this work was his use of index numbers to quantify the rise in prices that had taken place during the 1850s. However, perhaps Jevons's most innovative work was on the trade cycle. He used statistical series to establish the existence of fluctuations in economic activity every ten years. At the time, sunspots were believed to affect the weather, and so he sought to establish a correlation between sunspot activity and the business cycle on the assumption that there were strong links between the weather and the harvest. To test this idea he collected and analysed large quantities of data on prices.

Walras and Jevons came to their ideas about marginal utility and prices independently (Jevons had presented his ideas almost a decade earlier, but no one had taken any notice of them). They discovered each other's work in the mid-1870s, and agreed to cooperate in furthering mathematical economics and opposing Ricardian doctrines. During the following decade, however, the spread of mathematical economics was slow. They were both social reformers, Walras going so far as to call himself a socialist on the basis of his views on land taxation. Jevons, in contrast, used his utilitarianism as the basis for a series of piecemeal, pragmatic suggestions for reform, much in the manner of J. S. Mill.

Economics in Germany and Austria

In the second half of the nineteenth century, German economics was dominated by the historical movement – usually divided into the 'older' historical school, headed by Wilhelm Roscher and the 'younger' historical school, headed by Gustav Schmoller (1838–1917), even though the former was much less of a school than the latter. Classical economics could be found in Germany, but it drew on Smith and French theorists such as Condillac, not on Ricardo. Before the emergence of the historical schools there was no orthodoxy in German economics, merely a variety of groups, such as the so-called 'Romantic' school, having little in common with each other. The term 'Smithianism' was associated with an extreme variety of liberalism.

The historical movement in German economics was established by Roscher with his *Grundriss zu Vorlesungen über die Staatswissenschaft nach geschichtlicher Methode* (*Outline of Lectures on Political Economy According to the Historical Method*) of 1843. In this book, Roscher argued not that classical political economy was wrong, but that it was inappropriate given the political and industrial conditions in the Germany of his day. Economic theories needed to take account of the circumstances in which different countries found themselves. It was, furthermore, important to work out laws and stages of historical development. However, despite such views, the works of the older historical school did not differ markedly from those of Smith or Mill, both of whom mixed extensive empirical and historical material with their theoretical arguments.

The younger historical school was more radical. Schmoller shared the older historical school's attitude towards classical economics, and sought to broaden the subject to include what would now be termed economic sociology. He was sceptical about the idea of laws of history, arguing that they were frequently no more than dubious generalizations or psychological truths – they bore no relationship to the laws of the natural sciences. It was, he argued, important for economic propositions to be based on detailed empirical observation, for only then could proper account be taken of the circumstances of particular times and places. He was not opposed to theory, but he argued for extreme caution in ascertaining the facts of the case before making any generalizations. The method by which the necessary empirical basis would be established consisted of detailed historical studies.

Politically, Schmoller was conservative, a supporter of the Hohenzollern monarchy. However, he was a social reformer committed to the view that economists should be involved in the process of economic and social change. To this end, he organized committees that would work out desirable social policies within the Verein für Sozialpolitik (Union for Social Policy), founded in 1872. The members of this organization became known as academic socialists. They were liberal but were supporters of the existing regime, and were equally opposed both to communists and to ultra-liberals. They were committed to piecemeal studies that could result in social reform on topics such as working hours, social insurance and factory legislation.

In Austria, a different type of theoretical economics was offered by Carl Menger (1840–1921), in his 1871 *Grundsätze der Volkswirtschaftslehre* (translated into English as *Principles of Economics*). Though an Austrian, based in Vienna, he drew on the German tradition of supply-and-demand analysis established by writers such as Rau, Hermann and Roscher. In contrast to Jevons and Walras, Menger was not seeking to make economics scientific according to the standards of contemporary physics. Rather, his approach was closer to Aristotelian philosophy with its desire to uncover the essence of economic phenomena – to discover their real nature. However, despite this radically different perspective, he also argued that value was determined at the margin – by the value of an additional unit of a commodity.

Menger started from the presupposition that the purpose of economic activity was the satisfaction of human needs. Goods were things that contributed to this purpose:

If a thing is to become a good . . . all four of the following propositions must be simultaneously present:

1 A human need.
2 Such properties as render the thing capable of being brought into a causal connection with the satisfaction of this need.

3 Human knowledge of this causal connection.

4 Command over the thing sufficient to direct it to the satisfaction of the need.[2]

To be a good, not only must a thing be able to satisfy human needs, but also people must know about how they can use it to this end, and they must have sufficient control over it.

What about things that appear to satisfy no human needs? Menger's answer is that goods may satisfy needs either directly (he called these low-order goods) or indirectly (higher-order goods). Goods can thus be arranged in a hierarchy, with goods that satisfy needs directly at the bottom and ones that satisfy them extremely indirectly at the top. Bread would be at the bottom, whereas steelworks would be much higher up.

From here, Menger went on to define value as the importance of a good in satisfying needs: it is the satisfaction derived from command over a good. The value of a particular commodity is thus the needs that would not be met if the good were not available. Menger assumed that this value fell as the quantity of the good increased – the concept of diminishing marginal utility. This was a concept that could easily be extended to higher-order goods – to goods that do not satisfy human needs directly: 'The value of a given quantity of a particular good of higher order . . . is equal to the importance of the satisfactions provided for by the portion of the product that would remain unproduced if we were not in a position to command the given quantity of the good of higher order.'[3] What Menger is saying here is that if a higher-order good (for example, a kilogram of wheat) is not available, a certain quantity of lower-order goods (two loaves of bread) will not be produced. The value of the kilogram of wheat is the human needs satisfied by the two loaves of bread.

As defined by Menger, the concept of value does not involve either exchange or price. Price enters only with exchange, and is determined by values. In an exchange between two isolated individuals, all that can be said about price is that it will be between the limits set by the values which the two individuals place on the goods being exchanged, otherwise one of them would opt out. Where there is competition, the level of indeterminacy will be less.

Menger's verbal analysis of price determination can be compared with the mathematical analysis of Jevons and Walras. All three assumed that prices depended on marginal utility and rejected the Ricardo–Marx labour theory of value. However, simply to bracket Menger with the other two is to overlook important points to which his, less formal, analysis drew attention. Menger did not assume that markets were in equilibrium, with individuals maximizing utility. On the contrary, individuals would frequently have limited knowledge of the possibilities available to them. Entrepreneurs emerge as people who seek out and take advantage of opportunities for profit, creating goods that previously did not exist and finding new ways to create existing goods. Competition, therefore, was for Menger a dynamic process that had much more in common with Adam Smith's view of competition than with the static concept found in Walras or Jevons. For Menger, competition was not the absence of monopoly but a process through which monopolies were progressively eliminated: 'the need for competition calls forth competition, provided there are no social or other barriers in the way'.[4]

A further characteristic of Menger's economics was his stress on the way in which institutions arose from the nature of goods. The most important of these institutions was private property itself. Property, he argued, 'is not an arbitrary invention, but rather the only practically possible solution to the problem that is . . . imposed upon us by the disparity between requirements for, and available quantities of, all economic goods'.[5] The legal order, therefore, had an economic origin. However, while institutions might have had economic origins, they had often not been designed by anyone. Rather, they emerged as the unintended consequences of individuals' actions. For example, money, Menger claimed (seemingly overlooking the substantial evidence concerning the role of the state in setting monetary standards), was not planned, but arose unplanned from the actions of individuals seeking to satisfy their needs as best they could.

Menger's *Grundsätze* was dedicated to Roscher, the founder of the historical school. His subjective-value theory continued the earlier German tradition, and met with little resistance. There was no sense of a break with the past. In 1883, however, Menger published a methodological critique of the (younger) historical school as it was developing under Schmoller. He sought to provide a rigid distinction between theoretical and historical economics. Theoretical economics, he argued, dealt with 'exact' laws based on assumptions of pure self-interest, omniscience and freedom of movement. To test the resulting theory involved a misunderstanding, because it was based on abstractions: in the real world, 'pure self-interest' cannot exist any more than can 'pure oxygen'. Menger also objected to mathematical economics, on the grounds that all that mathematics could demonstrate was relationships between quantities: it could not establish the essence of economic phenomena, which was his concern. To analyse interdependence and mutual determination, as did Walras, was to lose sight of causal connections. Menger also put forward two doctrines that, though minor themes in the book, subsequently became very important in Austrian economics. One was methodological individualism (the idea that all analysis must start with the individual, not with aggregate or collective concepts). The other was the idea that there is a spontaneous order underlying social phenomena.

Schmoller reviewed Menger's book very critically, and the outcome was a bitter controversy – the *Methodenstreit*, or Struggle over Method. In the ensuing discussion, many issues were confused. It has been argued that the dispute was as much over policy (Schmoller supporting protection and Menger opposing it) and about jockeying for dominance as about substantive issues. It is arguable that Schmoller and Menger could otherwise have agreed that different methods were needed to answer different questions. The disagreement had, however, the effect of splitting the economics profession in Germany.

Historical Economics and the Marshallian School in Britain

In Britain, historical methods were advocated by Richard Jones (1790–1855), who used them to criticize Ricardo's theory of rent. With Malthus he established the Statistical Society of London, later the Royal Statistical Society. However, the writer who bore most responsibility for stimulating debate on the issue of whether economics should be a historical subject was Thomas Edward Cliffe Leslie (1827–82). In 1870 Leslie took up the point, made by the German historical schools, that economic laws were not universal, but varied from place to place. He also challenged the prevailing conception of Smith's *Wealth of Nations*. Smith, Leslie contended, had adopted an inductive approach (though he had not taken this far enough) and he had not assumed that behaviour was selfish. Leslie called for the replacement of abstract political economy with a more inductive, historical approach that took into account the whole variety of human motivations and the evolution of economic, political and social institutions. Competition and movement of capital were increasing the complexity of the world and also increasing uncertainty, undermining the assumptions of orthodox theory.

These arguments – that economics had become too abstract and that the conclusions of political economy were of limited relevance – were developed by other writers in the following years. The 1880s also saw the appearance of pioneering works on English economic history by J. E. Thorold Rogers (1823–90), William Cunningham (1849–1919) and William James Ashley (1860–1927). One of the most influential (perhaps because he died so young and came to be regarded by many of his generation as a saint) was Arnold Toynbee (1852–83), who popularized the term 'the Industrial Revolution'. Toynbee was committed to social reform, and succeeded in inspiring a generation of Oxford students to take up economics in order to achieve this end. He refused to accept that ethics could be separated from economics, at least on questions of distribution, and he insisted that to understand current economic and social problems it was necessary to consider their history. He argued the case for economic and social history as autonomous from, though dependent on, other types of history.

Though there were sharp differences between the advocates of theoretical and historical economics, British economics avoided being split in the same way as the German profession. One reason for this was the attitude of Alfred Marshall (1842–1924), the economist who, from his position as Professor of Political Economy at Cambridge, dominated the British economics profession from the 1880s until around 1930. Another was the different structure of the British university system, which did not have any centralized process of appointing professors.

Marshall came to economics through translating Mill's doctrines into mathematics, a task he undertook during the late 1860s. This involved mathematical representations of demand and supply. In attempting this, he was strongly influenced by the German writers, notably Rau, Hermann and Thünen. After reading Jevons's *The Theory of Political Economy*, he grafted utility theory on to his theory of supply and demand by using it to explain the demand curve. The result was a system of equations describing a static equilibrium, comparable to those of Jevons or Walras. However, whereas Walras's analysis remained at a very abstract level, Marshall continually sought to be realistic. In particular, he wished to take proper account of time. To do this, he could not analyse general equilibrium, allowing for all the possible instances of interdependence in the economy, but had to deal with one market at a time. He therefore developed the method of partial-equilibrium analysis, in which one part of the economy is analysed on its own.

There was, however, a further reason why Marshall adopted this approach. Like many of his contemporaries, he was very interested in biology, and in particular in evolutionary ideas. Biological metaphors were, he argued, more useful than mechanical ones in dealing with economics. This meant that he was sceptical about the mathematics used by Jevons and Walras, so closely linked with mechanics. This passion for evolutionary ideas came out in several ways. He considered continuous, gradual change as typical of economics, adopting the motto '*Natura non facit saltum*' ('Nature does not make jumps'). He did not take individuals' behaviour as given, but assumed that they would modify this in response to their environment. Thus if workers spent their income on wholesome goods and activities, the result would be an increase in their strength and intelligence, and their productivity would rise. In contrast, if they indulged in ways of living that were unwholesome, both physically and morally, neither efficiency nor character would improve. Evolution also affected Marshall's view of firms, which he saw as progressing through a life cycle analogous to that of the individual. They began young and vigorous, but after a period of maturity they became old and were displaced by newer, more efficient firms. An industry, therefore, was like a forest – it might remain the same when seen as a whole, even though every tree in it was changing.

The foundation of Marshall's economics is the theory of supply and demand. Time is taken into account through the device of distinct periods. These are defined not in terms of calendar time but in terms of what is free to change within each period. The calendar time involved in each period might vary from one problem to another. The shortest possible time period is defined as the market period. There is a certain quantity of goods available, as there is no time to produce more. If the commodity is perishable, such as fish (before the advent of refrigeration), it will be sold for whatever it can fetch. Price will be determined entirely by demand. But if the commodity can be stored without great expense (for example, wheat), price will be governed primarily by the price that sellers expect to prevail in the future: sellers will be reluctant to accept a lower price, even if demand is low. The result is that demand will determine sales, not price.

Marshall's next time period, the short run, is sufficiently long to allow variations in the level of production to take place. In the short run, firms are able to alter the quantity of unskilled labour they employ, but not the amount of skilled labour and machinery, or their production methods. The result is that output can be increased, but only at increasing unit cost. Supply and demand therefore determine price. If demand increases, price will rise, because of rising production costs caused by the limited stock of skilled labour and machinery.

In the long run, Marshall's next longest time period, however, firms have time to change the skilled labour and machinery they use and to organize in different ways. Under these circumstances, Marshall believed, expansion of output will result in falling costs. An increase in demand will therefore result in output increasing and price falling.

Finally, Marshall postulated a very long period, in which 'there are very gradual or *secular* movements of normal price, caused by the gradual growth of knowledge, or population, or capital, and of the changing conditions of demand and supply from one generation to another'.[6]

Like Toynbee and so many others of his generation, Marshall came to economics because he believed it offered a way to improve society.

Social reform was providing a partial replacement for the Christian faith that was being lost. However, Marshall was equally concerned that economics be established as a scientific discipline. This meant that he was extremely reluctant to get involved in public controversy, for he believed that this would undermine the authority of the subject. The role of the economist was not to propound truths about the economy, but to develop an agreed body of economic principles that could be used to tackle economic problems. This was one of the reasons why, in his *Principles of Economics* (first edition 1890, eighth edition 1920) – a book that was still used as a textbook as late as the 1950s – he presented his results verbally in the text. Diagrams were relegated to the footnotes, and algebra was banished to an appendix. In this way, he hoped, the subject could be made accessible to businessmen as well as to professional economists. Such an arrangement also accorded with his suspicion of mathematical arguments.

Marshall was trained as a mathematician, and developed his economics using mathematics. He was an innovative theorist, developing many of the theoretical concepts that have become standard in modern economics. However, he always remained very sceptical about the use of mathematics in economics. He wanted economics to be realistic, but the use of mathematics made it very easy to derive results that had no foundation in reality. If mathematical results could not be translated into English, he was suspicious of them. His papers, for example, contain a mathematical model of economic growth, but, because he was doubtful about the value of the equations, he did not publish it. His methodological pronouncements emphasize the need for quantitative and statistical methods, but, unlike with Jevons, the empirical evidence he used appears anecdotal rather than statistical, and illustrative rather than essential. This is true not only of the *Principles* but also of *Industry and Trade* (1919), a volume that contained an enormous amount of information on the organization of industry. This attitude towards evidence must have arisen, at least in part, from his strong desire to keep theory and reality close together.

A similar ambiguity underlay Marshall's attitude towards history. As a young lecturer, Marshall was enthusiastic about history. In the first edition of the *Principles* he began with economic history. He mixed factual material and history in most chapters of the book, and argued that only one part – on the general relations of supply, demand and value – should be considered 'theory'. However, in later editions the historical element was played down and moved into appendices. When the time came to appoint a successor to the chair at Cambridge, Marshall supported A. C. Pigou (1877–1959), strongly inclined towards theory, in preference to the historian H. S. Foxwell (1849–1936). The historical content of the first edition of the *Principles* had been strongly criticized by Cunningham (his review was entitled 'The perversion of economic history'). Marshall may have decided that it was safer to avoid controversy and to accept a disciplinary division of labour, in which history was left to historians.

European Economic Theory, 1900–1914

By the start of the twentieth century, marginalist economics – economics based on marginal utility and individual maximization – had become well established. Walras's successor in the chair at Lausanne, Vilfredo Pareto (1848–1923), had developed and refined his general-equilibrium system. A fellow Italian, Enrico Barone (1859–1924), had applied general-equilibrium theorizing to the problem of a hypothetical socialist economy. In Sweden, Knut Wicksell (1851–1926) had integrated Walras's general-equilibrium theory with Böhm-Bawerk's capital theory (see pp. 211–12). In their work, marginal-productivity theory displaced classical theories of wages and profits. In England, Marshall had imposed his view of economics on Cambridge and dominated the discipline, promoting a supply-and-demand analysis that built on the French and German traditions as well as on British writers. Economics had ceased to be political economy and was in the process of becoming dominated by an abstract, 'pure' economic theory. At the London School of Economics, established by the historians and socialists Beatrice and Sidney Webb (1858–1943 and 1859–1947), and at Oxford, a slightly more historically minded economics was being pursued, but these institutions were dwarfed by Marshall's Cambridge. Furthermore, because LSE, despite the socialist element in its origins, was committed to free inquiry, it also included economic theorists and supporters of laissez-faire. (By the 1930s, with Lionel Robbins and Friedrich von Hayek – see pp. 239 and 217 – these elements had become very prominent.) Theory and history, despite Marshall's desire to keep them together, had separated. In England (unlike in the United States), historical economics was about to turn into economic history, leaving economics behind. In the German-speaking world, the *Methodenstreit* had split the profession and reduced chances of cooperation.

Not only was mathematics, in particular differential calculus, increasingly used, but economics had almost lost the classical concern with long-run dynamics. Static theory – more amenable to treatment with the mathematical tools economists had begun to use – received more attention. However, some economists were concerned with dynamics. Several economists investigated the business cycle, notably Arthur Spiethoff (1873–1957), a student of Schmoller's, Mikhail Ivanovich Tugan-Baranovsky (1865–1919), a Russian influenced by Marx, and Albert Aftalion (1874–1956), a professor in France, though born in Bulgaria. In 1912 Joseph Alois Schumpeter (1883–1950) – an Austrian working in the tradition of Friedrich von Wieser (1851–1926) and Böhm-Bawerk (Menger's two disciples) – published *Theorie der Wirtschaftlichen Entwicklung* (*The Theory of Economic Development*), in which he argued that technical progress was the motive force underlying the cycle and economic growth. Innovation moves the economy out of equilibrium, creating new opportunities for entrepreneurs to make profits and causing an expansion as these are taken up. When these opportunities are exhausted, slower growth and depression occur as the economy settles down to a new equilibrium before it is disturbed by a new wave of innovations. Such ideas, however, can be regarded as marginal to the pure theory that was becoming increasingly prominent.

This divide between theorists and historians extended to questions of economic policy. Theorists tended to support free trade, whereas historians (in both Germany and England) were more sympathetic towards protection. This was starkly revealed in England in 1903 when fourteen British economists (including Marshall, Francis Ysidro Edgeworth (1845–1926) and Pigou) wrote a letter to *The Times* supporting free trade. This was an attempt to bring the authority of the profession to bear on an urgent political issue. However, its effect was to show that the British profession was split. With two exceptions, the theorists supported free trade and the historians protection.

Most of the economists involved in these developments were social reformers. Though they were far from being Marxists, they were not content with the status quo. If their work was ideologically motivated, their goal was to develop policies that would reduce poverty and improve the condition of the working class. They generally favoured piecemeal reform and were opposed to radical schemes such as those of Marx or the American Henry George (1839–97), whose enormously successful and widely read book *Progress and Poverty* (1879) proposed replacing all taxes with a single tax on rent. But they were by no stretch of the imagination doctrinaire defenders of capitalism. Even the Austrians, who were such strong critics of Marx, wrote of the need for capitalism to be reformed. However, economics had become an academic discipline. Most economists were motivated by strong social concern, but the discipline had become much more clearly separated from politics than was the case in the classical era.

9

The Rise of American Economics, 1870–1939

US Economics in the Late Nineteenth Century

In retrospect, the most significant development towards the end of the nineteenth century was the rapid development of economic thought in the United States. There is still dispute about whether American economics in the mid nineteenth century should be considered entirely derivative of European economics. However, by the 1880s, if not earlier, the profession was expanding rapidly in the United States, and American economists were making original contributions to the subject. Furthermore, the context of US economics was significantly different from that in Europe. With the expansion of the frontier, many states were setting up institutions of higher education, and in many of these a culture where research was important was becoming established. However, American academics were subject to pressures different from those facing their European counterparts. Research was dominant in relatively few institutions, and the quality of different institutions was extremely variable. There was no central control of higher education, and personal and institutional rivalries were strong. Academics were regarded as employees who could be dismissed very easily if what they said was unacceptable to their sponsors, but at the same time they were expected to undertake work that was relevant to the problems facing their society. Though this was an extreme case, in the 1880s the University of Pennsylvania insisted that its economists were not to support free trade. Popular interest in economic and social questions was high, and academic economists were expected to have 'sound' opinions to offer about them. The result was a tendency towards a professional (though not political) conservatism.

For most of the nineteenth century the tariff had been the dominant issue in US economic policy. Manufacturers generally favoured high taxes on imports of manufactured goods, whereas farmers complained that such tariffs raised the prices they had to pay. By the 1890s, however, it had become clear that there was no possibility of protective tariffs being removed and the issue received less attention than money and the control of business.

Money was a perennial issue in American history, but the Civil War, financed by the issue of inconvertible currency (the greenbacks), served to focus attention on the question. Rapid territorial expansion, a weak banking system, the deep depression of the late 1870s and continued depression during the 1880s ensured that monetary problems remained on the agenda. Opinion was divided between those who regarded paper currency as tantamount to fraud and the cause of much speculative activity and those who welcomed the additional purchasing power it created. The former ranged from those who wanted the issuing of paper currency severely curtailed to those who wanted it abolished altogether, or at least wanted all currency to be backed 100 per cent by gold reserves. The latter included farmers and others who wanted higher prices. On top of this there was the silver question, relating to the terms under which silver should enter the currency alongside gold. Given the interests of states that produced the two metals and the uneven distribution of agriculture and manufacturing across the continent, sectional interests were strong.

Control of business was a more important issue than in Britain because of the concentration that had accompanied the growth of railroads. Not only were railroads large organizations in themselves, control of them was also widely used to further the tycoons' interests in other industries. Pools, trusts and other devices were used to counteract the potentially damaging effects of competition. Farmers and industrialists alike complained, with good reason, about high and discriminatory freight rates. Consumers and rival industrialists objected to trusts as raising prices to take advantage of monopoly positions. In response, the operators of cartel arrangements responded that these were essential in industries where unlimited competition would force prices below cost, creating instability in the industry. Competition was thus high on the agenda facing economists.

The expansion of economics in the 1880s saw important developments in the American economics profession. The first independent economics department was established at Harvard in 1879, responsible for the *Quarterly Journal of Economics* a few years later (see p. 166). The American Economic Association was established in 1885. This was soon designed as a broad, inclusive organization, open to anyone sufficiently interested to pay a membership fee, and served as a focus for serious discussion of economic questions. Though the Association did not publish its own journal until 1910, it produced a series of scholarly publications.

The main European influence during this period came from Germany, not Britain. The historical school, with its notion that economic theories needed to be adapted to fit different historical situations, had strong appeal to those who believed that economic conditions in the United States were different from those in Europe. Though postgraduate training developed in the United States, especially after the establishment of Johns Hopkins University in 1876, many economists had gone to Germany for their postgraduate work. The Verein für Sozialpolitik, with its emphasis on social reform, was the model underlying the American Economic Association. Though it expressed a commitment to non-partisan inquiry, the first constitution of the Association expressed opposition to doctrinaire laissez-faire and, as a result, several economists of the 'old school' refused to join. By the 1890s, however, the offending clauses had been removed and most of the 'old school' economists were members.

John Bates Clark

One of the most eminent figures during this period of American economics was John Bates Clark (1847–1938). Like many American economists of his generation, he was educated in Germany, studying in Heidelberg under Karl Knies (1821–98), a member of the older historical school. It is thus not surprising that in his first book, *The Philosophy of Wealth* (1886), he sought to broaden the premises on which economics was based. He wanted to take account of elements in human nature that were more ethical and less mechanical than those taken into account in conventional theory. In addition, he sought to apply to economics an organic concept of society. Thus, although he proposed a theory of marginal utility (which he attributed to what he had learned from Knies, not from Jevons, Menger or Walras), he understood 'effective utility' (his name for marginal utility) somewhat differently from others. The market, he argued, measures the value that society, not just the individual, places on a commodity. This shift of attention from the individual to the social reflected his organic conception of society, and was something that the European marginal-utility theorists would not have considered.

The American context explains Clark's treatment of competition, for he brought in ethical considerations to distinguish between 'conservative' competition – competition in which competitors try to provide a better or cheaper service than each other – and 'cut-throat' competition – in which ethical constraints on behaviour are abandoned. The idea of competition without moral restraints was, for Clark, absurd. To find it we would have to go back to 'the isolated troglodyte, the companion of the cave bear'.[1] Ethics also entered his analysis of what he saw as the dominant problem facing contemporary American society – highly aggressive 'competition' between firms that eventually forced all but one of them out of business, thereby creating a monopoly. The solution, he suggested, lay in cooperative ventures and profit-sharing, with arbitration being available until these were more widely developed. Such institutions would result in a just outcome and, once imposed, society would accept them.

In *The Distribution of Wealth* (1899), based on articles written over the previous decade, Clark proposed a theory of income distribution in which each factor of production (land, labour and capital) received a reward equal to the marginal value of its contribution to output. The wage rate, for example, would be equal to the money that an employer would lose if he had to employ one fewer worker. Clark applied the theory to capital by likening this to a fund: individual capital goods (machines, buildings etc.) come and go, but the fund remains intact. The rate of interest, he argued, was the marginal product of this fund of capital – the additional revenue that could be obtained if capital increased by one dollar. There was no essential difference between land and capital goods: they both yielded a return that was determined by the rate of interest. As in his previous book, he drew ethical conclusions – in this case the conclusion that, if there is competition, each agent of production gets what it is entitled to. This was a potentially conservative doctrine, criticized by radicals for justifying the profits earned by capitalists. It countered socialist claims that capitalists took a share of the produce that rightfully belonged to labour.

Clark defended the use of static theories (in which prices and quantities settled down to values that did not change) by using the analogy of an ocean. Oceans are continually in motion, but provided we are not concerned about fine detail a static theory is adequate:

A static ocean is imaginary, for there was never such a thing: but there has never been a moment in the history of the stormiest seas, when the dominant forces that controlled them were not those which, if left entirely alone, would reduce their waters to a static condition. Gravity, fluidity, pressure, and nothing else, would have the effect of making the sea level and motionless . . . If we take a bird's eye view of the ocean, we are tempted to say that a static philosophy of it is sufficient and that we may treat waves and currents as minor aberrations due to 'disturbing causes'.[2]

This is a clear statement of the view to which Keynes (see p. 222) was later to object when he claimed that it was useless for the economist to say that, when the storm had passed, the sea would be calm again. Clark was concerned not with short-run fluctuations but with what he believed to be the underlying phenomena.

Like his European contemporaries Marshall and Schumpeter, Clark regarded the study of statics as the prelude to studying dynamics. An innovation, he argued, would move the economy out of equilibrium, creating profits for entrepreneurs. In time, wages would respond, reducing profits back to their normal level; but before that could happen another innovation would usually occur, disturbing the equilibrium again.

Clark illustrates very clearly the characteristics of American economics during this period. Ethical considerations permeated his approach, and, although he was a critic of American society, his stance could be described as conservative, not breaking radically with established methods. He was driven by a concern with the problem of big business, and he adopted an approach to competition that was the result of this concern. In his earlier book he, like many of his contemporaries, was alarmed by the problem of monopoly, and he proposed cooperation as the means of tackling it. In his later book he was much less concerned about the problem. 'Latent' or potential competition would prevent firms from raising prices too far, and the growth of capital would lead to new competition. Furthermore, the costs to consumers of higher prices would be offset by the benefits that would accrue from the accumulation of capital. He became distinctly more optimistic about capitalism, and moved away from the Christian socialism of his youth.

Mathematical Economics

Other American economists proposed more mathematical versions of marginalism. Simon Newcomb (1835–1909), an astronomer and mathematician, defended the methods employed by Jevons (though he argued that Cournot was superior) and criticized the old school of American economists for deprecating them. He claimed that these economists criticized mathematical theory because they did not understand it: their own theories were substantially the same, even though they did not use mathematics. His own use of mathematics in economics was prompted by the currency question, in particular the problems after the Bland–Allison Silver Act of 1878, which reintroduced and increased the coinage of silver. He argued that fluctuations in prices were harmful because, when prices changed, people did not realize that the value of the dollar had changed. In a time of falling prices, such as the 1880s, workers would resist cuts in wages because they did not realize that prices had fallen even more than their wages were being cut. If prices fell but wages did not, employment and production would be reduced. Newcomb's remedy was the creation of a dollar whose value was linked to an index number of prices – a novel idea in the United States. This dollar would be a paper currency, and the amount of precious metal it represented would be changed from time to time, to compensate for changes in prices. Contracts in such dollars would be index-linked, reducing the problems that arose from ignorance about what was happening to prices. This was a scheme that had already been proposed in Europe, but Newcomb developed it in more detail.

Newcomb was also responsible for a mathematical formulation of the quantity theory of money. His equation was $V \times R = K \times P$. This stated that, in any period, the quantity of currency in circulation, R, multiplied by its velocity of circulation (the number of times that each dollar is, on average, used to make a transaction), V, equals the amount of business undertaken, K, times the price level, P. (In different statements of the quantity theory, K might be replaced with total transactions or total income. Though the interpretation might differ, the essentials of the theory were the same.) Newcomb used this equation to argue that, if the quantity of currency increased and other things stayed the same, the price level would rise. However, his main interest was astronomy and, although he remained an ardent supporter of mathematical methods, he did not develop his economic ideas or continue publishing in economics after around 1886.

The first American with a rigorous training in mathematics to pursue a full-time career in economics was Irving Fisher (1867–1947). He was influenced by Willard Gibbs (1839–1903), a chemist and physicist, known for his work on statistical mechanics. Fisher's doctoral dissertation, *Mathematical Investigations in the Theory of Value and Prices* (1892), provided a rigorous mathematical treatment of the marginal-utility theory of value. However, although he used the concept of utility in his mathematics, he stripped it of any connection with pleasure and pain: it was merely a way to describe individuals' behaviour and was not based on psychology. The only psychological assumption necessary for the theory was that 'each individual acts as he desires'. Utility meant simply 'intensity of desire', and implied nothing about the psychology underlying desires for different goods. Fisher's greater proficiency in the use of mathematics meant that his theory was more general than that of Jevons or Walras and that he was able to tackle some of the technical problems that they had ignored.

Fisher's mathematical approach to the theory of value had much in common with the approach that came to dominate the subject after the 1930s. At the time, however, it gained little support. Other versions of marginalism, such as those of J. B. Clark or Frank Albert Fetter (1863–1949), which offered ethical or psychological interpretations of utility, and which eschewed the use of mathematics, were more widely used. It was thought that special genius was needed to be able to handle economics mathematically without being led astray into making unjustified speculations. Thus Arthur T. Hadley (1856–1930) suggested that the use of the mathematical method made it possible to frame a hypothesis and then end up treating it as a rigorously verified proposition. Only exceptional men, such as Jevons, Walras or Fisher, could avoid this trap. It is interesting to note how close this objection was to Marshall's reservations about the use of mathematics in economics.

In contrast to his early work on value theory, which was not widely appreciated, Fisher's work on money, capital and interest attracted widespread attention and respect. He developed his ideas in a series of books written after his move from the mathematics department to the economics department at Yale in 1895. They included *Appreciation and Interest* (1896), *The Nature of Capital and Income* (1906), *The Rate of Interest* (1907, later much extended as *The Theory of Interest*, 1930) and *The Purchasing Power of Money* (1911). In them he tackled a series of fundamental conceptual issues in economic theory relating to capital, prices, the rate of interest and money. *Appreciation and Interest* developed the idea of the real rate of interest. If interest is 10 per cent, for example, and the inflation rate is 8 per cent, the real return on the loan is only 2 per cent. Given that it is the real rate of interest that matters to people, if inflation were to change, one would expect the nominal rate to change by the same amount. He then offered a theory of the real rate of interest as the outcome of decisions to save and invest. These depended on two things. The first was individuals' attitudes towards consumption now and in the future. If people were more impatient, they would need a greater inducement to save (i.e. they would have to be paid a higher rate of interest) than they would if they were more content to postpone their consumption. The second was the productivity of capital – how much additional income could be created by postponing consumption in order to invest the resources. Fisher produced a mathematical theory to show how the real rate of interest was determined by these two forces of time preference and productivity.

In *The Purchasing Power of Money* Fisher took up Newcomb's mathematical version of the quantity theory of money, extending it to cover bank deposits as well as currency and providing a more thorough exposition, linking it with his theories of capital and interest. He also attempted to provide a statistical verification of the theory. His central thesis was that changes in the money supply would, in the long run, produce corresponding changes in the price level, but that there would be what he termed 'transition periods' during which everything would change. His theory of the relation between inflation and the rate of interest played an important role in his analysis of these transition periods and the processes that caused the level of production to change.

Fisher approached economics as a mathematician who was concerned to make economics scientific along the lines of physics and mechanics. One effect of this was his ability to use what, for economists of his generation, were advanced mathematical techniques. Possibly more important, however, was his persistent use of mechanical analogies. This is perhaps clearest in his work on money, where he persistently uses two types of analogy. One was the idea of a balance (in the sense of scales) in which money appeared on one side and commodities on the other. (Here, Fisher was simplifying by focusing purely on transactions that involved buying and selling commodities, ignoring the use of money to support transactions in financial assets, property and so on.) The lengths of the arms corresponded to the velocity of circulation and the price level.[3] The other was the levelling of fluids in a

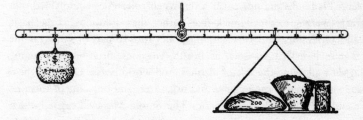

Fig. 2 Fisher's balance model of the quantity theory of money

system of cisterns. In the following diagram, stocks of gold and silver are represented by the levels of liquids in two barrels. Both barrels have leaks (corresponding to losses of metal to non-monetary uses) and inflows (gold and silver entering the circulation). Liquid is free to flow from each of these into the central cistern, in which a movable membrane keeps them separate from each other. The pressure from each liquid will ensure that the level of the liquid is the same in all three cisterns. This illustrates the operation of a bimetallic system. If a model were constructed, it could be used to illustrate changes such as the effects that a silver discovery would have on the equilibrium. This use of diagrams, representing physical models, was also a feature of Fisher's doctoral dissertation.

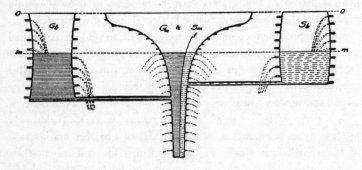

Fig. 3 Fisher's cistern model of bullion flows

Much of Fisher's work dealt with relatively abstract conceptual issues. However, he was also an ardent reformer and felt impelled to offer solutions to the problems his books discussed and to some problems his books did not cover, even when colleagues complained that these were sometimes quick fixes rather than solutions to the basic difficulties. His work on economic policy formed part of a programme that included causes such as health, eugenics, prohibition (arguing *against* allowing the sale of alcohol) and world peace. On all of these he was an active campaigner and organizer, and on some of them he could be regarded as a fanatic. The Stable Money League, which propagated his views on money, was merely one of many such organizations in which he was involved. He worked hard to get his scheme for a 'compensated dollar' implemented. This would have varied the weight of gold in the dollar in order to stabilize an index number of prices.

Thorstein Veblen

Another major figure in American economics in the first half of the twentieth century was Thorstein Bunde Veblen (1857–1929). Like Marx, Veblen was a strong critic of bourgeois society and of orthodox economics. However, whereas the background to Marx's work was the England of the 1840s and 1850s – vividly described in the novels of Charles Dickens – Veblen was concerned with American capitalism at the very end of the nineteenth century. He spent the first sixteen years of his life in an isolated, almost self-sufficient, Norwegian community in Wisconsin. This community was then destroyed by technological change in the flour industry, which caused farmers to switch to producing a single crop and brought railroads and an extension of the money economy. Even after he left the community of his childhood and entered academia, he remained an outsider to the mainstream of American society. This was clearly reflected in his writing. In *The Theory of the Leisure Class* (1899) he satirized the lifestyles and mores of the capitalists of his day, developing the concepts of conspicuous consumption and pecuniary emulation. Consumption had, for the very wealthy, ceased to be undertaken for its own sake but had instead become part of a process whereby people sought to establish their place in society – certain types of consumption were desirable because they were expensive and demonstrated success in acquiring wealth. Such behaviour, he argued, was a relic of a predatory, barbarian past.

This perspective on the wealthy classes in America was part of an attempt to apply Darwinian evolutionary ideas systematically to the analysis of society. Human behaviour developed in response to circumstances, including the prevailing technology. Habits of thought – or 'institutions' as Veblen termed them – could become stuck, remaining even when the circumstances that produced them had disappeared. People become conditioned to accept certain ideas, and these ideas persist – often because of vested interests. A modern example might be attitudes towards the environment and the use of energy. These attitudes, which have their origins in an era when resources appeared plentiful, have become strongly entrenched in the institutions of society and do not change even though they are ill suited to a world in which the environment is threatened. Sometimes, however, technological developments result in the creation of new habits of mind that are strong enough to overthrow existing institutions. But in time these too become entrenched and out of phase with the material environment.

Veblen's analysis of American industrial society as he found it in the 1890s rested on the distinction between two institutions: the machine process and business enterprise. The machine process denoted the entire system of production in which mechanized processes were used. It comprised a set of delicately balanced sub-processes, none of which was self-sufficient. The values it required and which it engendered reflected the instinct of workmanship and included precision and uniformity – mechanical standardization was more important than craftsman-like skill in enabling the machine process to operate efficiently. These values were very different from the pecuniary standards of business enterprise, concerned not with making goods but with making money. Businessmen might gain not by enabling the machine process to run smoothly but by disrupting the system, opening up opportunities for profitable speculation. Depression and the manipulation of markets could make it possible to buy business assets cheaply, enabling their purchasers to make money without undertaking any productive activity. The creation of monopoly power, through acquisition of other businesses or through advertising, would raise profits though contributing nothing to production. Advertising, for example, was competitive, and businesses were forced to undertake it even though it added nothing to the value of the goods produced. Veblen was therefore critical of the emergence of what he called 'parasitic' lines of business that were useless or harmful to the community at large but were profitable for individual businessmen.

It followed that the machine process and business enterprise would engender completely different spiritual attitudes. The machine process, with its enforcement of a standardization of conduct, would engender the habit of explaining things in terms of cause and effect: 'Its metaphysics is materialistic, and its point of view is that of causal sequence.'[4] In contrast, business enterprise is centred on the concepts of ownership and property: 'The spiritual ground of business enterprise . . . is given by the institution of ownership. "Business principles" are corollaries under the main propositions of ownership; they are the principles of property, – pecuniary principles.'[5] In the United States, Veblen contended, business enterprise was dominant, for it provided the mechanism whereby different parts of the machine process were linked. The machine process, though it had a logic of its own, had been extended to meet the objectives of business enterprise – in order to make money. The habits of mind associated with business enterprise had affected American culture, conspicuous consumption by the very wealthy being but one manifestation of this.

However, there was a potentially disruptive element in this process. The machine process inculcates habits of mind that conflict with those of business enterprise. Veblen therefore predicted that two types of people would emerge: one employed in running business and the other in running the machine process. These two groups would have different ways of thinking: the former in terms of natural rights, the latter in terms of cause and effect. The working classes would cease to think in terms of natural rights and would thus be unable to understand the justification for business enterprise. They would turn to socialism, threatening the status quo. In *The Engineers and the Price System* (1921) Veblen saw the possibility that the regime of business might be overthrown not by workers but by the engineers on whom the system depended but whose values were so different from those of the businessmen for whom they worked. He wrote,

And there is the patent fact that such a thing as a general strike of technological specialists in industry need involve no more than a minute fraction of one per cent. of the population; yet it would swiftly bring a collapse of the old order and sweep the timeworn fabric of finance and absentee sabotage [disruption of industry by absentee owners] into the discard for good and all.[6]

Like Marx, Veblen held out the prospect that internal contradictions within capitalism would lead to its overthrow. The nature of these contradictions and the manner of this overthrow, however, were different for Marx and for Veblen.

Veblen's critique of orthodox economics followed naturally from this evolutionary perspective. Orthodox economics – which included both classical and marginalist economics – was pre-Darwinian. It took human nature as given, not as changing in response to material conditions, and it explained society in terms of natural laws. It was hedonistic (individuals were assumed to be motivated solely by the pursuit of pleasure), teleological (changes in society were explained as movement towards an ideal) and taxonomic (involving mere classification without explanation). It had emerged at an earlier stage of industrial development, antedating the emergence of business enterprise, and had become entrenched even though it was no longer appropriate. Orthodox theory might be defended as hypothetical speculation, but it nonetheless influenced the way the world was perceived:

Of course, this perfect competitive system, with its untainted 'economic man' . . . is an expedient of abstract reasoning; and its avowed competency holds . . . only in so far as the abstraction holds. But, as happens in such cases, having been once accepted and assimilated as real . . . it becomes an effective constituent in the inquirer's habits of thought, and goes on to shape his knowledge of facts.[7]

These criticisms applied equally to classical political economy (Smith, Ricardo and Mill) and to modern writers such as Alfred Marshall, for whom Veblen coined the term 'neoclassical'. What was required, Veblen argued, was the replacement of such economics with a Darwinian evolutionary economics that took account of changes in human nature and was based on cause-and-effect reasoning. However, he never managed to specify this method clearly.

John R. Commons

John Rogers Commons (1862–1945) was an ardent social reformer. He was a student of R. T. Ely (1854–1943), who had taken his Ph.D. at Heidelberg with Karl Knies and whose approach to economics was strongly influenced by the German historical school. Because of his radical views, Commons found it hard to find a long-term academic post until, in 1904, Ely managed to create a position for him at Wisconsin, where he remained until his retirement in 1932. In his early work he sought to reconcile Austrian utility theory with the historical school's emphasis on the role of law and the use of statistics.

By the 1920s Commons had come to base his work on the idea that economic activity depended on the underlying legal and institutional relationships, and that these evolved over time. The economist should not take these as given, but must explain them. This led Commons into detailed historical research, notably his four-volume *History of Labor in the United States* (1918–35), a project he took over from Ely, and *The Legal Foundations of Capitalism* (1924). However, although he attached great importance to empirical research, he developed a distinctive theoretical framework, culminating in *Institutional Economics* (1934).

The main feature of Commons's analysis of the legal and institutional foundations of capitalism was that he took transactions as the basic unit of analysis. Transactions involve the transfer of property rights, but do not necessarily take place through the market. In addition to 'bargaining' transactions (ones that do take place through markets), he distinguished 'managerial' transactions (as when a manager orders a subordinate to do something) and 'rationing' transactions (as when the state levies taxes). The main characteristics of bargaining transactions are that, unlike the other two types of transaction, they are between legal equals and that there is a double transfer of ownership. Each side has the legal right not to participate, and each party gives something to the other. This focus on transactions led Commons to analyse not just markets but the whole range of institutions through which transactions are organized. These include 'going concerns', such as the state, corporations, trade unions, families and Churches, each of which has its own 'working rules'. These rules evolve over time in such a way that the organization is enabled to function.

Commons's view was that collective action was necessary to maintain order. Without external sanctions, including the threat of force, individuals would not respect the institutions on which society relied. This immediately put him at odds with conservatives, who rejected the idea that individual freedom had to be controlled, and led to the charge of socialism being applied to his work. However, he denied that his ideas were socialist. Rather, he emphasized that collective action was necessary to preserve individual freedom. Collective action can prevent people from interfering with the liberties of others, and provides a framework within which people can act. Freedom within a market system, for example, is possible only if property rights exist and if it is possible to make contracts that will be honoured.

The main source of external sanction was provided by the legal system. Commons attached particular importance to property rights, and in *The Legal Foundations of Capitalism* he explored in detail the way in which these had evolved as a result of decisions made by the courts. For example, he showed how the United States Supreme Court had, in the late nineteenth century, dramatically changed the notion of property. It had moved from an interpretation of the law that assigned property rights only to physical objects to one that assigned them to the expected earning power of physical objects. He argued that the courts regularly took account of economic effects when reaching their decisions.

Commons was a pragmatist who devoted much of his career to the task of reform. He did not try to find ideal solutions, but looked for solutions that worked. In this he was extremely successful, influencing legislation both in Wisconsin and at the federal level. This included civil-service reform, factory legislation, workmen's compensation, unemployment insurance, interest-rate control, rural credit schemes, inheritance taxation, property-assessment laws, immigration policy, and industrial relations. Through his students, many of whom went into government, in the 1930s he had an indirect influence on Roosevelt's New Deal, the programme of economic measures, including large public-works projects, designed to lift the United States out of the Depression.

Inter-War Pluralism

J. B. Clark, Fisher, Veblen and Commons represent four of the many approaches that were to be found in US economics in the early twentieth century. By the 1920s the subject was genuinely pluralist, in that it was dominated by no single approach. The conventional way to view this pluralism is in terms of a split between 'neoclassicals' and 'institutionalists'. The neoclassicals, including J. B. Clark and Fisher, emphasized individuals' maximizing behaviour and the role of competitive markets. Institutionalists, inspired by Veblen, denounced this approach and argued for a more holistic view in which economy and society could not be separated. Such a characterization is, however, very misleading, for the picture was much more complicated. There was great diversity of approach within both neoclassical and institutional economics. Even more significant, there were many individuals who defy such classifications. Even John Maurice Clark (1884–1963), one of the founders of institutionalism as a self-conscious movement, is best seen as standing on the boundaries between institutionalism and neoclassicism. He supported institutionalism, and yet he saw his work as being continuous with that of his father, John Bates Clark. Allyn Young (1876–1929), who exerted an immense influence in a short career, during which he worked at Chicago, Harvard and LSE, is another such figure whom it is hard to classify as either neoclassical or institutionalist.

Neoclassical economics clearly included mathematical economists such as Fisher. There was, however, a great difference between his approach and the more traditional, non-mathematical and more ethical approach of J. B. Clark. Fisher and Clark had different attitudes towards both the use of mathematics and the meaning of the concept of utility. There were other economists who were closer to Marshall or even to the English classicals, such as Jacob Viner (1892–1970), Frank Taussig (1859–1940) and Frank Knight (1885–1972). If such economists are to be described by a single term, 'traditionalist' is probably better than 'neoclassical'.

What united institutionalists was a commitment to making economics scientific through basing it on strong empirical foundations and abandoning theories that rested simply on axioms about human behaviour for which there was little evidence. Though he was not the originator of this approach, the clearest representative of it is Wesley Clair Mitchell (1874–1948). In his presidential address to the American Economic Association in 1924, he spoke of the need to quantify economic theory. Now that economists were in a position to estimate directly relationships such as that between the demand for a quantity and its price, 'it seems unlikely that the quantitative workers will retain a keen interest in imaginary individuals coming to imaginary markets with ready made scales of bid and offer prices. Their theories will probably be theories about the relationships among the variables that measure objective processes.'[8]

In similar vein Mitchell interpreted Veblen's distinction between business and industry in terms of the relationship between two groups of time series, one group measuring physical quantities of goods, the other sums of money. Quantitative workers would enjoy tackling the relationships between these two groups of data. Such a programme was consistent with Mitchell's role in the National Bureau of Economic Research, founded in 1920. This was an outgrowth of the sense of frustration at the inadequacies of the statistics available during the First World War, and was responsible for a wide range of statistical and empirical investigations into income, wealth and the business cycle.

Inter-War Studies of Competition

These features of US economics during the inter-war period can be illustrated by the work of three economists: Frank Knight, J. M. Clark and Edward Chamberlin. All three tackled the problem that the theory of competition appeared inadequate to explain the behaviour that was observed in most capitalist economies, but they tackled this problem in very different ways.

Knight was a social scientist with wide-ranging interests, spanning ethics and political philosophy, but was a traditionalist in economic theory. In his Ph.D. dissertation, published as *Risk, Uncertainty and Profit* (1921), he described his task as being one of 'refinement, not re-construction',[9] and he argued that the essentials of his arguments differed little from ones to be found in J. S. Mill or Marshall. Critics of the theory of competition had, he argued, never understood it properly. He was also a fervent liberal. In 1927 he moved to the economics department at the University of Chicago. There, with Viner, he was instrumental in consolidating the Chicago school, established by James Laurence Laughlin (1850–1933), on the basis of a commitment to the virtues of free markets and competition. Knight is therefore a major figure in the history of neoclassical economics, even though his own approach was pluralistic and encompassed ideas that hardly fit into conventional views of the neoclassical approach.

Knight's most well-known analytical contribution was his separation of risk and uncertainty, an idea he attributed to nineteenth-century German writers, in particular Thünen and Mangoldt. Risk is measurable and can be expressed in terms of probabilities. Thus games of chance involve risk – it is impossible to predict which card will be drawn from a well-shuffled pack, but the probability of a particular card is precisely 1 in 52. Uncertainty, on the other hand, cannot be measured. For example, it is impossible to calculate in the same way the probability that a particular new product will be successful, because it depends on too many unknown and unpredictable factors. Having drawn this distinction, Knight went on to argue that there was a connection between uncertainty and profits. Given that the main difference between theory and reality that required explanation was the existence of profits in excess of the normal return on capital, Knight could claim that his theory explained the difference between competition as described in theory and competition as experienced in the United States.

However, although he defended traditional theory, Knight was at the same time acutely aware of its limitations. Like Marshall, he contended that man is a complex creature, driven by a range of motives and values. Economic analysis is concerned only with actions directed towards the satisfaction of wants, and hence with only a small part of human activity or even of economic behaviour. This limitation, he argued, is far more sweeping in its scope and import than is easily imagined. It raises the fundamental question of how far human behaviour is inherently subject to scientific treatment. In his views on this point the writer is very much an irrationalist. In his view the whole interpretation of life as activity directed toward securing anything considered as really wanted, is highly artificial and unreal.[10]

Human behaviour is not predictable, and thus economic laws can be no more than approximations. If science were measurement, Knight claimed, then economic science would not be possible.

Knight also denied that it was possible to separate positive and normative economics – to separate questions about what is from questions about what ought to be. His reasons for this lay in his theory of knowledge. 'Reality is not what is logical, but what it suits our *purposes* to treat as real.'[11] Knowledge is simply a way of making sense of the world in order to achieve our objectives. Given that motives are varied, it follows that strict objectivity is impossible. This in turn means that scientific method is of limited usefulness in economics, for it is necessary to take account of human feelings and attitudes even though these cannot be measured or analysed scientifically.

The orthodox theory of perfect competition, defended by Knight, describes a world in which supply equals demand and resources are efficiently allocated, with labour and capital moving freely into those activities where they are most valuable. J. M. Clark, in his first major work, *Studies in the Economics of Overhead Costs* (1923), sought to explain why the actual economic system did not work like that. Why was it that there was instability in many markets and that capital and labour often lay idle? He found the answer in 'overhead costs'. These were costs that the producer incurred whatever the level of output. If overhead costs were sufficiently high, they would cause unit costs to fall as production increased and there would be no such thing as 'normal' costs at which price would settle. Clark argued that the enormous growth in investment in fixed capital had dramatically increased the importance of overhead costs, and that for many businesses full-capacity operation would require a price so low that it would fail to cover them. Theoretical arguments reinforced this conclusion by suggesting that competition would cause price to cover only variable costs such as the costs of labour and materials.

Clark argued that businesses responded to this situation in two ways. They might try to operate price discrimination, charging different prices to different customers. For example, they might establish brands, charge different wholesale and retail prices, or charge different prices in different places. Alternatively, they might engage in cut-throat competition: pushing prices so low as to drive competitors out of the market in order to establish a monopoly and charge higher prices. If this happened, the higher prices might in turn attract new competition.

In *Studies in the Economics of Overhead Costs*, Clark offered a view of competition that was radically different from the world of perfect competition, in which all firms have to accept the going market price, each being too small to have any influence on the market. Clark's world was one in which unrestrained private enterprise offered too many advantages to large-scale production. It was necessary to find ways in which business could be controlled without undermining competition. In *The Social Control of Business* (1926) he explored how this might be done and steps that had been taken to achieve this in the United States since the 1870s. These included anti-trust laws, regulation of public utilities, labour legislation, minimum-wage laws, food standards, urban planning and many other measures. Significantly, he did not see such control as something imposed on business – as an alternative to laissez-faire. Pure laissez-faire, Clark contended, was impossible. Furthermore, social controls were a part of business activity, involving informal agreements and customs, legislation and rules developed by the legal system in the course of settling disputes. This was very close to the perspective of Commons.

Edward Chamberlin (1899–1967), in a dissertation submitted in 1927 and published as *The Theory of Monopolistic Competition* (1933), addressed the same problem of the discrepancy between competition in theory and in practice. His solution, however, was to focus on market structure. He defined monopoly as the ability of a firm to control price through altering supply, and he defined 'pure' competition as competition in which monopoly elements were absent. Pure competition was not necessarily perfect, for knowledge of the future might be limited, or freedom of movement from one activity to another might be limited. He argued that the reason why real-world competition diverged from pure competition was that firms in practice experienced some degree of monopoly power. Markets were both competitive (firms were competing with each other) and monopolistic (firms had control over the price of the goods they sold).

[I]t is monopolistic competition that most people think of in connection with the simple word 'competition'. In fact, it may almost be said that under pure competition the buyers and sellers do not really compete in the sense in which the word is currently used. One never hears of 'competition' in connection with the great markets [such as those for agricultural commodities], and the phrases 'price cutting', 'underselling', 'unfair competition', 'meeting competition', 'securing a market', etc., are unknown. No wonder the principles of such a market seem so unreal when applied to the 'business' world where these terms have meaning.[12]

In order to explain the world of business it was therefore necessary to construct a theory intermediate between those of monopoly (where competition was absent) and the pure competition to be found in organized markets such as those for commodities or financial assets. Clark, Knight and others, Chamberlin claimed, had been led into confusion by being insufficiently clear in their assumptions about market structure. He reached the conclusion that the reason why economic theory appeared remote from reality was not that its method was wrong but that its assumptions were too far from the facts.

Chamberlin analysed market structure in terms of two dimensions: the number of firms in an industry and the degree to which each one produced a differentiated product. Small numbers led to the problem of oligopoly, in which each firm has to take account of how its competitors will react to any changes in its pricing or sales policy. Product differentiation means that each firm has a degree of monopoly power in that it can raise its price without losing all its customers. In such a world, advertising and selling costs are important in a way that they are not under pure competition.

In seeking to find a theory intermediate between pure competition and monopoly, Chamberlin wanted to develop a theory of value that was more general than Marshall's. His thesis was that elements of monopoly and competition interact in the determination of most prices, and that a hybrid of these two theories was needed to analyse firms' pricing behaviour. His book thus dealt with the whole of value theory. He brought Marshall's theory up to date by taking into account phenomena that had become increasingly important, such as advertising and product differentiation.

The Migration of European Academics

The period from 1914 to 1945 was a time of political turmoil in Europe. The First World War led to the Bolshevik Revolution in Russia, and the post-war settlement led to the redrawing of many national boundaries. Many people were uprooted and forced to find new homes. During the 1920s and 1930s this problem was increased dramatically by the rise of the Nazi Party in Germany. Many people were forced to leave Germany and, as Hitler conquered neighbouring countries, to leave the continent of Europe. The result was that, during this period, many economists migrated to the United States. In the 1920s they came mostly from Russia, and in the 1930s and 1940s mostly from German-speaking countries. Not only were they numerically significant, they also included some very prominent individuals who made a significant impact on the profession. They were particularly important in developing mathematical and quantitative economics.

Harvard attracted two of the most prominent such émigrés: Leontief and Schumpeter. Wassily Leontief (1906–99) was Russian. In 1925 he moved to Berlin to complete a Ph.D., and then in 1930 he moved to the United States, taking up an appointment at Harvard in 1931. While in St Petersburg he had written a paper arguing that Walras's general-equilibrium system could be simplified in such a way as to analyse real-world economies. He spent the rest of his career developing this idea into what is known as input–output analysis. The essential idea is that the economy is divided into a number of industries or sectors, and a table is constructed showing how much each industry buys from each of the other sectors. For example, if there are three industries, the table contains three rows and three columns. If one of these industries is mining and another is the steel industry, one of the cells in the table will contain the steel industry's purchases of coal and iron ore and another cell will contain the mining industry's purchases of steel. If it is assumed that the proportions in which each industry buys other industries' outputs do not change, it is possible to use the input–output table to calculate the effects on all industries of various changes in the economy. For example, if exports of steel were reduced, this would have repercussions on all other sectors of the economy: less coal and iron ore would be bought, and these industries would in turn have to reduce their purchases from other industries, and so on. The changes can be calculated using an input–output table. The limitation of this technique is that it does not take account of price changes, which limits the range of problems to which it can provide useful answers.

Whereas Leontief devoted his career to input–output analysis, the activities of the Austrian-trained Joseph Alois Schumpeter were much more wide-ranging. Schumpeter's *The Theory of Economic Development* (1912) placed the entrepreneur at the centre of the process of capitalist development. Entrepreneurs are responsible for the innovations (new products, new sources of supply, new production methods, new forms of organization) that open up opportunities for profit, disturbing the system. Successful entrepreneurs will earn high profits and will attract imitators. Over time, imitation will eliminate the profits earned by the original innovator and the system will settle down to a new equilibrium until it, in its turn, is disturbed by another innovation. Schumpeter's vision of capitalism was thus one of a system in continuous motion, the impetus for change coming from the entrepreneur.

Schumpeter had a brief political career, at one time being Finance Minister in Austria, but emigrated to the United States in 1932. During the 1930s he worked on the problem of business cycles, building on his earlier work by explaining the cycle in terms of swarms of innovations that create profits that are subsequently eroded by imitators. The result was *Business Cycles* (1939), in two volumes. However it received an extremely critical review from Simon Kuznets (see p. 241), and in the face of Keynesian economics (see pp. 228ff.) it failed to attract support. In contrast, *Capitalism, Socialism and Democracy* (1943), which he viewed as a potboiler, was very successful. In this book, Schumpeter argued that Marx was wrong in his diagnosis of why capitalism would break down. The success of capitalism would create rising living standards for all classes. The proletariat would have no reason to rise up and overthrow the system. Nevertheless, capitalism would eventually destroy itself, for it would destroy the values on which its success was based. Entrepreneurs would give way to bureaucracies, self-interested individualism would undermine workers' loyalties, and capitalist values would give way to a desire for security, equality and regulation. By weakening the resistance to change, the Second World War had contributed to this process, as the First World War had done in Europe.

Schumpeter was also the author of one of the classic books on the history of economics – his *History of Economic Analysis* (1954), edited by his wife, Elizabeth Boody Schumpeter (1898–1953), and published posthumously. (Views from this book are discussed on pp. 325–6.)

US Economics in the Mid Twentieth Century

It is hardly an exaggeration to say that the position of US economics had been transformed since the middle of the nineteenth century. Up to 1914 it was still true that the dominant economic ideas came from Europe and that, although it contained some distinguished and original economists, the United States followed Europe. By the 1940s, however, this was no longer true. To take the example discussed earlier in this chapter, new theories of competition were being developed in Cambridge by critics of Marshall, such as Piero Sraffa (1898–1983) and Joan Robinson (1903–83). Theories of oligopoly were also developed in Germany, by Heinrich von Stackelberg (1905–46), Frederik Zeuthen (1888–1959) and others. The American theories, however, were developed independently and had characteristics that set them apart from their European counterparts. American economics exhibited a breadth of approaches to the subject that was absent in the smaller

British profession. With the substantial migration of economists from Germany and other parts of Europe in the 1930s and 1940s, and the effects of the Second World War on the discipline, the strength of American economics was increased still further.

10

Money and the Business Cycle, 1898–1939

Wicksell's Cumulative Process

The central figure in early-twentieth-century work on money and the business cycle was the Swedish economist Knut Wicksell. In *Interest and Prices* (1898) and his *Lectures on Political Economy* (1906) he developed a theory of the relationship between money, credit and prices – his so-called 'cumulative process'. Wicksell's theory was based on the theory of capital developed by the Austrian economist (and student of Menger) Eugen von Böhm-Bawerk (1851–1914), in which the rate of interest is essentially the price of time. There are two sides to this coin. If someone is receiving an income, she has a choice to make. She can spend it on consuming goods and services immediately, or she can save it in order to be able to consume goods at a future date. The way people save is to buy financial assets, thereby lending income to someone else, and in return for this they receive interest. The higher the rate of interest, the more future consumption can be 'bought' by deciding to save rather than to consume now. If the rate of interest rises, people have a greater incentive to postpone their consumption by saving part of their income.

The other side of the coin is investment. Businesses have to choose between investing in production processes that yield revenues very quickly and investing in other processes that are more productive but take longer to yield revenue. For example, the owner of a vineyard can choose whether to sell grapes immediately after the harvest or to ferment them and produce wine. Having produced the wine, there is then a choice of how long to store it. If the wine is allowed to mature, it will become more valuable. Wicksell followed Böhm-Bawerk in assuming that 'long' processes of production (ones which take a long time to yield a revenue) will be more productive than 'short' processes. However, because resources are committed for longer, such processes will require more capital. This means that, if the rate of interest rises, long processes of production will become more expensive relative to shorter ones.

The rate of interest, therefore, influences consumers' decisions about whether to consume goods now (using short processes) or in the future (using long processes), and also influences producers' decisions about whether to invest in processes that will produce goods now or in the future. A rise in the rate of interest will cause a rise in saving, as consumers decide it is worth postponing more consumption, and a fall in investment, as producers move towards shorter production processes. Wicksell argued that there will be some rate of interest at which these two types of decision are balanced. This is his 'natural' rate of interest. At the natural rate of interest, the amount that consumers wish to lend is exactly equal to the amount that producers wish to borrow in order to finance their investment: there is inter-temporal equilibrium.

This part of Wicksell's theory drew on Böhm-Bawerk. The next stage was to introduce a banking system that created credit. The rate at which banks lent money was the 'market' or 'money' rate of interest. The cumulative process arose when the market rate of interest, for some reason, fell below the natural rate. Businesses would increase their investment, borrowing from the banking system the funds that they could not obtain from savers. The increase in investment would cause an increase in demand for resources, with the result that prices would be bid up. At the same time, the increased supply of credit would enable purchasers to pay these higher prices. Wicksell went on to show that, in what he called a pure credit economy, where goods were bought and sold using only bank money, not gold and silver, this process could continue indefinitely. As long as the market rate of interest was lower than the natural rate, prices would continue to rise. (Conversely, if it were higher than the natural rate, prices would fall indefinitely.) This was his cumulative process. If the country concerned were on a gold standard, the process would be brought to an end when the banks began to run out of gold reserves. This would force them to raise interest rates and cut back their lending, bringing the process to a halt.

Wicksell held a 'real' theory of the business cycle, in the sense that he believed that the cycle arose because of changes in the natural rate. For example, inventions that raised productivity would cause the natural rate to rise, as would wars that destroyed resources. But the interest rate would not respond immediately to such changes, the result being that cumulative rises and falls in prices would be initiated. Furthermore, the quantity of currency (gold) played a purely passive role in the process. The active element in the system was the banking system. There was no fixed link between the volume of credit and the supply of currency. Despite this, however, Wicksell did not consider himself as a critic of the quantity theory but as elaborating on it, showing *how* changes in the quantity of money changed prices.

Though the basic theory was simple, there were several serious problems with it. Two of these were particularly important for subsequent developments. The first concerned the use of the Austrian theory of capital to determine the natural rate of interest. Though the notion of a period of production is an appealing one, capturing the insight that capital is associated with taking time to produce goods, it is riddled with technical problems. There may be no clear link between the period of production and the rate of interest. A fall in the rate of interest may cause the period of production to rise or fall, with damaging consequences for the notion of inter-temporal equilibrium. The second major problem can be explained by noting that the natural rate of interest is the rate of interest at which (1) savings equal investment, (2) there is no new credit being created, and (3) prices are constant. In general, however, it is not clear that all three conditions will be satisfied at the same rate of interest. For example, in a growing economy, stable prices will require an increasing quantity of credit to finance the growing volume of transactions. This means that some credit creation, resulting in an inequality of saving and investment, may be compatible with price stability. In addition, if productivity is rising, equality of the money and real rates of interest will lead to falling prices.

Wicksell was aware of these problems, and carefully made assumptions that avoided them. His successors, however, responded to them in very different ways and, as a result, developed very different theories.

To understand these, it is necessary to understand some of the economic events of the inter-war period.

The Changed Economic Environment

The inter-war period was one of unprecedented economic instability. By the end of the First World War the dominant country in the world economy was clearly the United States. Like much of the world, it experienced a brief boom in 1920, followed by a very sharp depression, when prices fell and unemployment rose, in 1921. For the rest of the 1920s, however, the country experienced unparalleled industrial growth and prosperity. Unemployment remained low, electricity spread throughout the country, with profound effects for industry and domestic life, the number of cars registered rose from 8 million to 23 million, and there was an enormous amount of new building. At the end of the decade, Herbert Hoover, as a presidential candidate, claimed that the country was close to triumphing over poverty. The stock market boomed, and investors thought that prosperity would continue indefinitely. Few other countries fared as well as the United States (Japan and Italy were unusual in growing faster), but most countries prospered during the 1920s. Countries that stagnated included many in eastern Europe (including the newly formed Soviet Union), Germany and Britain.

Britain, like the United States, shared in the immediate post-war boom and the depression that followed. Prices rose by 24 per cent in 1920, and then fell by 26 per cent in 1921. Unemployment rose to 15 per cent of the workforce in 1921, and remained around 10 per cent for the rest of the decade. Prices fell, and industry stagnated. In 1925 – by which time US industrial production had risen to 48 per cent above its 1913 level – British industrial production was still 14 per cent below its level in 1913. The British economy had not recovered from the effects of the war.

However, the most spectacular examples of instability in the 1920s were in central Europe. In Germany, prices nearly doubled in 1919, and then more than trebled in 1920. After a brief respite in 1921, they then rose by over 1,600 per cent in 1922. In 1923 the currency completely collapsed. Prices rose by 486 million per cent – true hyperinflation. The value of the mark fell so far that the exchange rate, which had been US\$1 = 4.2 marks in 1913, fell to US\$1 = 4.2 billion marks. At the same time, unemployment rose to almost 10 per cent of the workforce. At the end of the year a new currency was issued, and prices rose gently for the rest of the decade. However, unemployment remained high, averaging over 10 per cent.

The Great Crash came in October 1929. In the United States, the downturn which had begun earlier that summer developed into an enormous slump in which industrial production, agricultural prices and world trade collapsed. Unemployment rose dramatically. In the next few years US industrial production fell to a little over half of its 1929 level, and unemployment rose to over 25 per cent of the labour force. It was not until 1937 that unemployment fell below 15 per cent, and then a further slump pushed it back up to 19 per cent. Similar levels of unemployment were recorded in many other countries. In 1933, unemployment was 26 per cent in Germany, 27 per cent in the Netherlands, 24 per cent in Sweden, 33 per cent in Norway, and 21 per cent in Britain. It was a problem affecting the entire capitalist world, and it persisted throughout the 1930s. In some countries, such as the Netherlands, unemployment remained at similar levels right up to 1939. In others, such as Britain and Sweden, unemployment recovered slowly to just over 10 per cent by the end of the decade. Only in Germany, under the Nazi regime brought to power by the crisis in 1933, was unemployment brought down to low levels (2 per cent by 1938).

Almost inevitably, these events attracted the attention of the world's economists. Though the underlying causes of the period's economic instability remained controversial, it became clear to most economists that the dominant theories of the pre-war period were inadequate to explain what was going on. Most important, it became clear that it was necessary to be able to offer a coherent theory of the level of economic activity. Changes in the level of industrial production and unemployment, on both of which statistics were beginning to be calculated during the 1920s, had become too important to be regarded as a secondary phenomenon. It was also clear that, in some way, changes in the level of economic activity were linked to money and finance. The German case, where hyperinflation completely destroyed the value of the currency and rendered normal economic activity virtually impossible, may have been an extreme example, but it was a very important and salutary one. It was also hard not to look for a connection between the financial activities that caused boom and bust in the US stock market and the unprecedented depth of the following depression.

In addition, behind all this was a world economy that was very different from before the war. In particular, intergovernmental debts, almost unknown before 1914, were a major problem. European governments had borrowed heavily from each other and, in particular, from the United States. They sought to recover these costs from Germany through extracting reparations. There was, and is, scope for disagreement over the role played by reparations in the German hyperinflation, or how far the causes of the Crash and the Depression should be sought in Germany and eastern Europe. There was, however, no doubt that the new situation in international finance was an integral part of the world trading system that, after 1929, proved to be so fragile.

The different experiences of the European countries and the United States meant that, though the economists involved formed a single community in the sense that Europeans drew on American literature, and vice versa, their perspectives were different. In the United States it was natural throughout the 1920s to be optimistic about the prospects for the long-term stability of the economy. When the Great Depression came, it was natural to see it, at least at first, as an unusually bad cyclical downturn. In contrast, by the end of the 1920s British economists had come to see unemployment as a structural problem, not a cyclical one. There was a further difference in that, whereas Britain had not experienced financial panic and bank failures since the 1860s, these were still regular events in the United States. The Federal Reserve System, established in 1913, had yet to establish a reputation as lender of last resort comparable with that of the Bank of England. The result was that Americans were much more interested in finding policy rules that would alleviate the cycle. The situation was different again on the Continent. In Germany, for example, memories of the hyperinflation of 1922–3 remained long after the event.

Austrian and Swedish Theories of the Business Cycle

The main proponents of the Austrian theory of the business cycle were Ludwig von Mises (1881–1973) and Friedrich von Hayek (1899–1992). Both were from Vienna, but Hayek moved to the London School of Economics in 1931. Mises's main ideas were set out in *The Theory of Money and Credit*, first published in 1912, but they came into their own only in the 1920s and early 1930s. They were apparently vindicated by the German hyperinflation and the sudden collapse of the American economy after the greatest boom in its history.

Mises and Hayek started from Wicksell's theory, but developed it into a monetary theory of the cycle. They placed great stress on the Austrian theory of capital underlying Wicksell's natural rate of interest, and argued that monetary policy was liable to interfere in the normal working of credit markets. In a credit economy, not constrained by the gold standard, bankers would be under pressure to keep interest rates low. If they yielded to this pressure, and the market interest rate fell below the natural rate, this not only would cause inflation but would also interfere with the inter-temporal allocation of resources. What would happen was that low interest rates would cause entrepreneurs to invest in production processes that were too long – too capital-intensive – compared with what was appropriate given the level of saving. Because investment in capital goods was too high, capital-goods prices would rise relative to the prices of consumer goods. This would cause a problem because, although producers were shifting resources into processes that would yield returns only in the future, consumers were given no incentive to postpone their consumption. The result would be excessive demand for consumer goods.

As long as credit continued to expand, such a situation might continue for a long time, but eventually the credit expansion would have to end. When the credit expansion ended, interest rates would rise and the result would be a fall in output and a rise in unemployment. The reason would be that the long, capital-intensive production processes that were started when interest rates were low would suddenly become unprofitable and be closed down. The resources put into them (embodied in stocks of unfinished goods, equipment and so on) would typically be unsuitable for the newly profitable shorter processes, and would lie idle.

Mises and Hayek used this theory to condemn the use of expansionary monetary policy as a means of raising the level of economic activity. It might be possible, they argued, to use credit expansion to sustain a boom, but the result would be that, when it came, the eventual collapse would be greater. This fitted the American experience of the 1920s. An exceptionally long boom, sustained by massive credit expansion, had been followed by an equally massive depression. According to Mises and Hayek, this was inevitable. They advocated non-intervention and a policy of 'neutral' money whereby the rate of interest would be set so as to keep the level of money income constant. Even in a depression as severe as that of 1929–32, it would be foolish to lower interest rates and expand the money supply, for it was important that the structure of production be allowed to adjust.

In contrast, the Stockholm school – Erik Lindahl (1891–1960), Erik Lundberg (1907–89), Gunnar Myrdal (1898–1987) and Bertil Ohlin (1899–1979) – developed Wicksell's theory in a completely different way. They argued that technical problems with Austrian theory of capital meant that it was impossible to argue that the natural rate of interest was determined by the productivity of capital. Such a concept was impossible to define. Instead, they took up the idea, previously developed by Irving Fisher, that capital should be understood as the value of an expected stream of income. The demand for loans would depend on expectations about the future. This perspective led them to take issue with the idea of neutral money, claiming that equilibrium between saving and investment was compatible with *any* rate of inflation. The reason was that, so long as it was correctly anticipated, the rate of inflation could be taken into account in all contracts for the future and therefore need not have any effect. It was unexpected changes in prices that would disrupt the relationship between saving and investment.

Members of the Stockholm school were therefore led to abandon two of the ways in which Wicksell defined the natural rate of interest and to focus on the relationship between saving and investment. They

analysed this through investigating dynamic processes, tracing the interaction of incomes, spending, prices and so on from one period to the
next. Among other problems, they analysed how it was that a discrepancy between savers' and investors' plans (termed an *ex ante* imbalance
between saving and investment) could be turned, by the end of the
relevant period (*ex post*), into an equality. For the most part the
processes they analysed started from a situation of full employment,
with the result that they analysed cumulative processes similar to Wicksell's. However, they took very seriously the idea that prices and wages
might be very slow to change, with resulting consequences for output.
They also investigated processes that started with a situation of
unemployment, and were able to show how lowering interest rates
might lead to a prolonged increase in production.

One reason why the Swedish economists did not reach a more definite
view of the cycle was that their theory was very open-ended. They
explored a series of related models, showing that a wide range of
outcomes was possible. This fitted in with their very pragmatic attitude
towards policy. They were open to the idea of using not only monetary
policy but also government spending to reduce unemployment. This
was in marked contrast to the rigid liberalism of the Austrians.

Britain: From Marshall to Keynes

Leaving aside Hayek and his followers at LSE, British thinking on
money and the business cycle had its roots in the work of Alfred
Marshall. His first work on the problem was in *The Economics of
Industry* (1879), written jointly with Mary Paley Marshall and strongly
influenced by J. S. Mill. In a period of rising demand, confidence is
high, the level of borrowing increases, and prices rise. At some point,
however, lenders reassess the situation and start to cut back on their
loans, with the result that interest rates rise. This precipitates a fall in
prices as confidence falls. Businesses are forced to sell their stocks of
goods, causing further falls in prices. The reason why this leads to
fluctuations in output is that prices fluctuate more than costs, in particular wages and fixed costs. In the boom, prices rise faster than costs,

causing firms to increase their production. After the crisis, prices fall more rapidly than costs, causing businesses to reduce output.

The main factor underlying this account of fluctuations in economic activity is confidence. Referring to the depression stage, Marshall and Marshall wrote:

The chief cause of the evil is want of confidence. The greater part of it could be removed almost in an instant if confidence could return, touch all industries with her magic wand, and make them continue their production and their demand for the wares of others . . . [The revival of industry] begins as soon as traders think that prices will not continue to fall: and with a revival of industry prices rise.[1]

Crises occur because businessmen, including those who supply credit, become overconfident, causing expansions to go on too long.

Over the following forty years, Marshall integrated into his account of the cycle a clear statement of the quantity theory of money and the distinction between real and nominal interest rates. However, the essentials of the theory remained unchanged. In particular he continued to argue that fluctuations in demand caused prices to fluctuate. Output changed only when prices and costs moved in such a way as to raise or lower profits. This was the framework underlying the work of his followers. The most important of these were Arthur Cecil Pigou, Marshall's successor as professor at Cambridge, Dennis Robertson (1890–1963), Ralph Hawtrey (1879–1975) and John Maynard Keynes (1883–1946). The theories they developed were all firmly rooted in the Marshallian tradition, emphasizing the role of expectations and errors made by businessmen in explaining the cycle. However, this tradition encompassed a great variety of views.

Hawtrey, whose most influential book was *Currency and Credit* (1919, revised in 1927 and 1950), held a purely monetary theory of the cycle. His theory had several distinctive features, but the most important was his emphasis on what he termed 'effective demand' – the total level of spending, including both consumers' spending and investment. He argued that changes in the money supply would affect the level of effective demand and that, because prices and wages were slow to respond to this, output would change. The existence of time lags in the various processes involved meant that expansions and contractions of credit would go too far, with the result that there would be cycles, not steady growth.

In contrast, Robertson, in his *Theory of Industrial Fluctuations* (1915), explained the cycle in terms of shocks caused by inventions that raised productivity. Following Aftalion, Robertson used the gestation lag (the time that elapses between undertaking an investment and obtaining the output) and other features of investment to explain why such shocks would produce a cycle. A decade later, in *Banking Policy and the Price Level* (1926), his emphasis shifted. Though he did not abandon the idea that inventions caused fluctuations in economic activity, he switched to arguing that, because of monetary factors, cyclical fluctuations were much larger than they needed to be. Suitable banking policy could mitigate this, but, unlike the Austrians, he did not believe that this could completely stabilize the economy.

Pigou's work is revealing because it illustrates the way in which British economists reacted to the persistence of high unemployment during the 1920s. He published a theory of the business cycle, first in *Wealth and Welfare* (1912) and later in *Industrial Fluctuations* (1927). Like several of his contemporaries, he emphasized the importance of entrepreneurs' expectations of profit, and, like Hawtrey, he stressed the role of demand. If demand were sufficiently low, there might be no positive wage rate at which entrepreneurs would wish to employ the whole labour force. However, in discussing the cycle, Pigou was thinking primarily of cycles experienced before 1914. He did not think of himself as explaining the unemployment experience of the 1920s, for which a different approach was required. To explain this, he focused much more on wages and the labour market, publishing *The Theory of Employment* in 1933. This was very Marshallian in discussing the problem in terms of supply and demand for labour.

One of the most orthodox Marshallians in the early 1920s was Keynes. He had achieved celebrity status in 1919 when he resigned from the Treasury team at the Versailles peace conference to write his best-selling pamphlet *The Economic Consequences of the Peace*. This provided a devastating critique of the peace treaty and of the way in which the negotiations were conducted. He argued not only that it was immoral for the allied governments to demand high reparations payments from Germany, but also that Germany would not be able to pay what they were demanding. Then, in 1923, he turned his attention to monetary policy and the cycle in his *Tract on Monetary Reform*. The analytical framework he adopted was Marshall's version of the quantity theory, though, in common with his Cambridge colleagues, he emphasized the role of expectations. Because the demand for cash balances (the key element in Marshall's quantity theory) depended on expectations about the future, it was liable to change at any time. In the absence of suitable changes in the money supply, the result would be fluctuations in the price level. Strict proportionality of the price level to the money supply was true only in the long run. Referring to the notion that doubling the money supply would double the price level, Keynes argued:

Now 'in the long run' this is probably true. But this *long run* is a misleading guide to current affairs. *In the long run* we are all dead. Economists set themselves too easy, too useless a task if in tempestuous seasons they can only tell us that when the storm is long past the ocean is flat again.[2]

There were also disturbances caused by changes in foreign prices, which were linked to British prices via the exchange rate.

This posed a dilemma for the monetary authorities. If they stabilized the domestic price level (increasing the supply of money when demand for it rose, and contracting it when demand fell) the result might be changes in the exchange rate. Alternatively, if they chose to stabilize the exchange rate (as Britain was then doing by trying to return to the gold standard) the result would be instability of domestic prices. Keynes argued two things. The first was that the evils of falling prices were worse than the evils of either rising prices or changing exchange rates. In the context of the early 1920s, when prices were being pushed downward as the government sought to raise the exchange rate to its pre-war value, this led Keynes to oppose returning to the gold standard. The second was that the authorities had to make a decision about the exchange rate: it was necessary for them to recognize that the economy had to be managed and that they could not claim that the price level was determined by forces beyond their control:

In truth, the gold standard is already a barbarous relic. All of us . . . are now primarily interested in preserving the stability of business, prices and employment, and are not likely, when the choice is forced on us, deliberately to sacrifice these to the outworn dogma . . . of £3.17s 10½d per ounce [the pre-war exchange rate in terms of gold]. Advocates of the ancient standard do not observe how remote it now is from the spirit and the requirements of the age. A regulated non-metallic standard has slipped in un-noticed. *It exists*. Whilst the economists dozed, the academic dream of a hundred years, doffing its cap and gown, clad in paper rags, has crept into the world by means of the bad fairies – always so much more potent than the good – the wicked ministers of finance.[3]

He developed this idea, that policy-makers had to take conscious decisions about managing the economy, in *The End of Laissez Faire* (1926).

During the 1920s Keynes worked closely with Robertson and other Cambridge economists on problems of money and the cycle, and in 1930 he published *A Treatise on Money*, intended to be his definitive treatment of the problem. The core of his analysis was thoroughly Wicksellian. He defined saving and investment in such a way that they need not be equal. They would be equal only if 'windfall profits' (profits over and above the normal level of profits necessary to keep firms in business) were zero. He then used the relationship between saving and investment to analyse the impact of monetary policy on the level of activity. For example, a low interest rate would cause a rise in investment and a fall in saving. This would raise prices and windfall profits, causing firms to increase production. Conversely, if the interest rate rose, investment would be less than saving, windfall profits would become negative, the price level would fall, and output would contract. As with his previous work, he emphasized the role of expectations in this process. The link between money and interest rates would depend on the level of 'bearishness' – or the degree to which people were worried about the future. If bearishness were high, for example, people would want to hold more money as a hedge against future uncertainty, with the result that an increase in the money supply would be needed to prevent interest rates from rising.

In 1931 Hayek arrived at LSE, and he and Keynes clashed over the theory of the cycle. Their theories were both in the Wicksellian tradition, but they reached diametrically opposed conclusions about the role of monetary policy. They completely failed to understand each other in what was a heated dispute.

The American Tradition

For reasons mentioned earlier, there arose a distinctive American tradition in monetary economics. The 1920s were a time of immense prosperity, and the Federal Reserve System was only beginning to work out how it should conduct its operations. The result was that, unlike in Europe, American economists paid great attention to the question of designing rules to govern the conduct of monetary policy. However, although there was widespread support for using monetary and fiscal expansion to combat the depression after 1929, without the strong opposition to such policies associated with Mises and Hayek, there was no consensus on any underlying theory. In the words of a recent commentator:

It is difficult to think of any explanation for the event itself [the Great Depression], or any policy position regarding how to cope with it, that did not have its adherents. Moreover, virtually every theme appearing in the European debates . . . found an echo somewhere in American discussions.[4]

The variety of ideas discussed means that it is possible to do no more than outline a few of them.

The most prominent exponent of the quantity theory throughout this period was Irving Fisher. He expressed great scepticism about the existence of anything that deserved to be termed a business cycle. Prices fluctuated, which meant that sometimes they would be high and sometimes low (he used the phrase 'the dance of the dollar'). That was not enough to make a cycle, which implied a regular pattern of cause and effect. What was needed was to stabilize prices, which was why he was active in organizing the Stable Money League in 1921 (which subsequently developed into the National Monetary Association and the Stable Money Association). He was also influential, during the 1920s, in promoting legislation to require the Federal Reserve System to use all its powers to promote a stable price level. Consistent with this, in the early 1930s he argued for a series of schemes to raise the price level, thereby helping to restore stability. He continued to argue that the idea of a cycle was a myth, but he produced several theories that might explain how a recession could be so severe. The most prominent was his debt-deflation theory. According to this, falling prices raised the real value of debts, forcing debtors to cut back on their spending, which forced prices still lower, worsening the situation.

At the other extreme were those who argued that there was no link between monetary policy and the price level, justifying this with a version of the real-bills doctrine. They argued that prices normally changed for non-monetary reasons, and that, if the money supply was not allowed to expand to accommodate this, the velocity of circulation would rise instead. Provided the banking system lent money only for proper commercial transactions, the result would not be inflationary. When the Great Crash came, such economists argued that credit had been overextended (a view not unlike that of the Austrians) and that no useful purpose would be served by monetary expansion. Thus Benjamin Anderson (1886–1949) wrote, 'it is definitely undesirable that we should employ this costly [cheap money] method of buying temporary prosperity again. The world's business is not a moribund invalid that needs galvanizing by an artificial stimulant.'[5]

Austrian views were represented in America, but few economists took them up. Gottfried Haberler (1900–1997), who arrived in 1931, used Hayekian arguments about capital to explain why the Depression was more than a monetary phenomenon and would last a long time. Schumpeter, who went to Harvard in 1932, did not adopt a Hayekian approach. His explanation of the Depression was that it was so severe because it marked the coincidence of a number of cycles, all of different length. There was the Kondratiev long cycle (around forty years long), the Juglar cycle (around ten years long) and the Mitchell–Persons short cycle (around forty months long). These were cycles for which previous economists claimed to have found statistical evidence, and all of them turned down in 1930–31. This perspective was shared by Alvin Hansen (1887–1975). Hansen added the hypothesis that this coincidence of the three cycles came on top of a long-term decline in prices caused by a world shortage of gold and an accumulation of gold stocks in France and the United States. Both Schumpeter and Hansen were sceptical about the possibility of using monetary expansion to get out of the Depression. The Depression might be painful, but it paved the way for improved production methods and higher standards of living.

Another strongly anti-quantity-theory position was that of the underconsumptionists, most prominent of whom were William Truffant Foster (1879–1950) and Waddil Catchings (1879–1967). Foster and Catchings argued that monetary expansion would stimulate activity only if it stimulated consumers' spending. Any other form of monetary expansion, even if linked to rises in government spending, would have no effect. J. A. Hobson (1858–1940), a British economist who had first put forward underconsumptionist theories in 1889, and who had coined the term 'unemployment' in 1896, was widely read.

Other economists adopted a more moderate position. One of the most influential of these was Allyn Young (who had many students while at Harvard), who was in turn strongly influenced by Hawtrey's *Currency and Credit*. Young argued that monetary policy was needed to stabilize business, but that this required the establishing of sound traditions, not the imposition of a simple rule such as Fisher and others were proposing. He also supported the use of government spending to alleviate the cycle. He was able to show, through a detailed statistical analysis, that bank reserve ratios fluctuated greatly with seasonal movements of funds between New York and the rest of the country. Following Hawtrey, he emphasized the instability of credit – something that a strict quantity theorist would not accept. Young died in 1929, but one of his students, Laughlin Currie (1902–93), applied Hawtrey's theory to the Depression, finding evidence that monetary factors were important. He used statistics on the behaviour of a range of measures of the money supply to argue that the Federal Reserve System could have prevented much of the collapse had it chosen to do so. The claim that it was powerless was not borne out by the evidence.

During this period the economist most firmly associated with empirical research on the business cycle was Wesley Clair Mitchell, director of the National Bureau of Economic Research. He popularized the notion of the cycle, and sought to document, statistically, exactly what happened during cycles. He was sceptical about theories that sought to explain the cycle in terms of a single cause, preferring to analyse individual cycles in detail. However, he was convinced that its causes lay in what Veblen had called the 'pecuniary' aspects of economic life. The cycle could not be divorced from its monetary aspects, though these were not all that mattered. When the Depression came in 1929, Mitchell argued that the only puzzle was why it was so severe and so prolonged. His explanation was that several shocks happened to occur on top of each other: depression in agriculture, the after-effects of excessive stock-market speculation, political unrest, increased tariff barriers and so on. The effects of these shocks were exacerbated by changes that reduced the powers of the economic system to stabilize itself. People were buying more semi-durable goods (such as cars and electrical appliances), with the result that if incomes fell they could more easily reduce their spending. There was less self-sufficiency in agriculture, and large firms were increasingly reluctant to cut prices when demand fell. Mitchell's response to this was that laissez-faire was proving inadequate and that greater national planning was required. However, beyond supporting public-works policies and the dissemination of information and forecasts, he did not work out plans in any detail.

In the early 1930s a number of economists, with very different theoretical views, endorsed the idea of requiring the banking system to hold 100 per cent reserves. Supporters of such a rule included Currie, Paul Douglas (1892–1976), Fisher, and Henry Simons (1899–1946), all for different reasons. Currie supported the rule on the grounds that, if the government issued the entire money supply, this would provide the government with the best possible control over it. It would be easy to expand or contract the money supply as much as was required. In contrast, Simons supported it because he regarded 'managed currency without definite, stable, legislative rules [as] one of the most dangerous forms of "planning"'.[6] In the 'Chicago plan' in 1933, Simons argued for 100 per cent reserves combined with a constant growth rate of the money supply and a balanced-budget rule for government spending. This, he believed, would stabilise prices and restrain government spending. However, by 1936 he had come round to the view that this rule would merely lead to variability in the amount of 'near monies' (assets that do not count as money but which can be used instead of money). As a result, he moved towards setting price stability as the goal of policy.

The history of the support for 100 per cent money illustrates the way in which, even though there was enormous diversity within American monetary economics at this time, there were also great overlaps. Simons moved from a money-growth rule towards Fisher's price-stability rule. At the same time, Fisher took up the Chicago position of 100 per cent money. Though the case for 100 per cent money was based on a monetary interpretation of the Great Depression, later associated with Simons and his fellow Chicago economist Milton Friedman (see pp. 295–7), this interpretation originated with Currie. He worked within the theoretical framework laid down by Hawtrey and developed by Young, his teacher at Harvard. Other overlaps include the views on monetary policy shared with Austrian economists and the advocates of the real-bills doctrine.

Keynes's *General Theory*

In his early work, in the 1920s and before, Keynes was a quantity theorist in the Marshallian tradition. In *A Treatise on Money* he moved away from this to a perspective closer to Wicksell's, focusing on the links between money, saving, investment and the level of spending. However, he still considered the price level as central to the whole process. Changes in spending led to changes in prices and profits, thereby inducing businesses to change their production plans. This raised a technical problem at the heart of his analysis. He developed a theory to explain changes in prices and profits on the assumption that output did not change. He then used that theory to explain why output would change. This was unsatisfactory, and soon after the book was published he began to rethink the theory with the help of younger colleagues at Cambridge. The results of this process of rethinking were eventually published in 1936 as *The General Theory of Employment, Interest and Money*.

Perhaps the crucial transition made in the *General Theory* was towards thinking in terms of an economy where the first thing to change in response to a change in demand was not prices but sales. If demand fell, firms would find that their sales had fallen, and that their inventories of unsold goods were higher than they had anticipated. They would then adjust their production plans. One stimulus to this way of thinking came as a result of discussions on employment policy in the 1920s and early 1930s. It was commonly agreed that public-works expenditure could raise employment, but there was no basis for working out by how much employment would rise. This problem was tackled by Richard Kahn (1905–89), who in an article published in 1931 put forward the idea of the multiplier. (This idea was also found in Hawtrey's work in the 1920s, though not named as such.) The question he asked was the following. If an additional worker is employed on a public-works scheme, and that worker buys goods that need to be produced by other workers, how many additional workers will end up being employed? He found that the mathematics of the problem yielded a clear answer, and that it depended on how much of the newly generated income was spent on consumption goods. In a subsequent article a Danish economist, Jens Warming (1873–1939), pointed out that if a quarter of income were saved, a rise in investment of 100 million would lead to a rise in income of 400 million. Saving would rise by 100 million – exactly enough to finance the initial increase in investment. The size of the multiplier (the ratio of the rise in income to the initial investment) was determined by the fraction of income saved.

The multiplier provided Keynes with a link between investment and the level of demand in the economy. He based this link on the notion of what he called the 'fundamental psychological law' that, when someone's income rises, his or her consumption rises, though by less than the full amount. He labelled the ratio of the rise in consumption to the rise in income the 'propensity to consume'. He then needed a theory of investment. He adopted an approach similar to Fisher's, arguing that the level of investment depended on the relationship between the expected return on investment (which he termed the 'marginal efficiency of investment') and the rate of interest. For a given marginal efficiency of investment, a rise in the interest rate would cause a fall in investment and vice versa. However, although he talked of a negative relationship between investment and the interest rate, Keynes placed equal emphasis on the role of expectations and the importance of uncertainty in influencing investment.

He analysed the relationship between uncertainty and investment through arguing that the marginal efficiency of capital depended on what he called 'the state of long-term expectation'. This covered all the factors that were relevant to deciding the profitability of an investment, including the strength of consumer demand, likely change in consumers' tastes, changes in costs, and changes in the types of capital good available. All these had to be evaluated over the entire lifetime of the investment, and were matters about which investors knew little.

The outstanding fact is the extreme precariousness of the basis of knowledge on which our estimates of prospective yield have to be made. Our knowledge of the factors which will govern the yield of an investment some years hence is usually very slight and often negligible. If we speak frankly, we have to admit that our basis of knowledge for estimating the yield ten years hence of a railway, a copper mine, a textile factory, the goodwill of a patent medicine, an Atlantic liner, a building in the City of London amounts to little and sometimes to nothing.[7]

Faced with this uncertainty, investment would depend not on rational calculation of future returns, but on the state of confidence.

In practice, expectations are governed by conventions – in particular the convention that 'the existing state of affairs will continue indefinitely, except in so far as we have specific reasons to expect a change'.[8] The implication of this is that, because expectations are based on conventions, they are liable to change dramatically in response to apparently minor changes in the news. The situation is made worse in a world, such as Keynes saw around him, where investment policy is dominated by professional speculators. Such people are not trying to make the best long-term decisions but are concerned with working out how the stock market will move, which means they are forever trying to guess how other people will react to news. The result is great instability.

The other determinant of investment is the rate of interest. To explain this, Keynes introduced the idea that money is required not only to finance transactions in goods and services but also as a store of value. People may hold money because they are uncertain about the future and wish to be able to postpone their spending decisions, or because they expect holding money to yield a better return than investing in financial assets. (If the price of bonds or shares falls, the return may be negative – less than the return from holding money.) This was the theory of liquidity preference, which led Keynes to argue that the demand for money would depend on the rate of interest. He even claimed that, under some circumstances, the demand for money might be so sensitive to the rate of interest that it would be impossible for the monetary authorities to lower the rate of interest by increasing the money supply – the liquidity trap.

When put together, these three components – the propensity to consume, the marginal efficiency of investment, and liquidity preference – formed a theory of output and employment. For example, given liquidity preference, a rise in the money supply would cause a fall in the rate of interest. Given the state of long-term expectations, this would cause a rise in investment and hence a rise in output and employment. It was a theory in which output was determined by the level of effective demand, independently of the quantity of goods and services that businesses wished to supply.

Keynes's strategy in developing his theory was to take the wage paid to workers as given. Towards the end of the book he considered what would happen if wages were to change, and advanced a variety of arguments about why changes in wage rates would have no effect on employment. Cutting wages would not raise employment unless doing so raised the level of effective demand. He went through all the ways this might happen, concluding that this was very unlikely.

The Keynesian Revolution

Keynes presented his book as an assault on an orthodoxy – the 'classical' theory that, he claimed, had dominated the subject for a hundred years, since the time of Ricardo. According to this orthodoxy, the level of employment was determined by supply and demand for labour, and if there were unemployment it must be because wages were too high. The 'classical' cure was therefore to cut wages. If wages were flexible, the only unemployment would be frictional (associated with turnover in the labour market) or structural (caused, for example, by the decline of certain industries). The classical theory was also characterized by Say's Law, according to which there could be no general shortage of aggregate demand. Keynes went on to argue that the classical theory was a special case, and that his own theory was more general. 'Moreover, the characteristics of the special case assumed by the classical theory happen not to be those of the economic society in which we actually live, with the result that its teaching is misleading and disastrous if we attempt to apply it to the facts of experience.'[9]

This dramatic claim, together with Keynes's celebrity status, was one reason why the *General Theory* made such an enormous impact on its publication. It appealed in particular to young economists who relished the prospect of overthrowing the orthodoxy supported by their elders. Paul Samuelson (see pp. 258–9), perhaps the most prominent Keynesian in the early post-war period, and a student at Harvard when the book came out, compared Keynesian economics to a disease that infected everyone under the age of forty, but to which almost everyone over forty was immune. In so far as the reaction of the older generation was generally critical, Samuelson's point appears justified. Older economists found fault with Keynes's logic and took issue with his claim to be revolutionizing the subject. There was, however, much more to the Keynesian revolution than this.

For economists who read the *General Theory* for the first time in the late 1930s or the early 1940s, it was a difficult book. For some of the older generation, the reason lay in the mathematics – by the standards of the time, it was a mathematical book. There were, however, deeper reasons. The first was that Keynes spoke of a classical orthodoxy, but, as will not be surprising in view of the range of theories surveyed in this chapter, it was not clear just what the classical orthodoxy was. The second difficulty was that the *General Theory* contained many lines of argument, and it was not clear which ones mattered and which could be left to one side. This was a problem not only for non-economist reviewers, many of whom said that they awaited the judgement of Keynes's professional peers, but also for economists who read the book. Economists, therefore, had to make sense of what Keynes was saying.

A number of economists tried to make sense of Keynes's central argument by translating it into a system of equations. The first was David Champernowne (1912–2000), who, in an article published in 1936, within months of the *General Theory*, reduced Keynes's system to three equations. Over the next few months, other economists worked with similar sets of equations, trying to use these to explain what Keynes was saying. The most influential of these was John Hicks (1904–89). Hicks's equations were very similar to those developed by Champernowne and others, but he managed to reduce Keynesian economics to a single, simple diagram showing relationships between output and interest rate. The LM curve showed combinations of output and the rate of interest that gave equilibrium in the money market, and the IS curve showed combinations that made savings equal to investment. Hicks then argued that, if the LM curve were fairly flat, Keynes was right – increases in government spending would shift the IS curve to the right, and output would rise. On the other hand, if the LM curve were vertical, shifts in the IS curve caused by changes in government spending would simply change the rate of interest, leaving output unaffected. Hicks provided a solution to the puzzle about what the differences between Keynes and the classics really were. His diagram also provided a valuable teaching tool, for students could learn how to manipulate the IS and LM curves to show the effects of a wide range of policy changes. The maze of pre-Keynesian business-cycle theory was apparently simplified into a single diagram.

Hicks's diagram was taken up by Hansen, who became the leading exponent of Keynesian ideas in the 1940s. He refined Hicks's diagram into what became known, after the labels attached to its two main

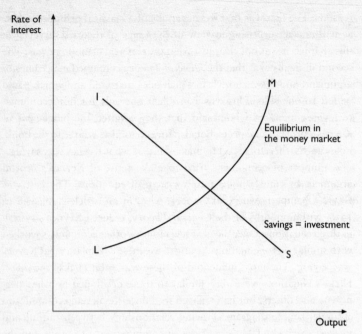

Fig. 4 Hicks's curves showing relationships between output and interest rate

components, as the IS–LM model. At the same time, other economists such as Franco Modigliani (1918–) and Don Patinkin (1922–97) continued the process of making sense of Keynes's theory. They translated it into mathematical models that made microeconomic sense, working out just what had to be assumed in order to get Keynesian results. Keynesian ideas also entered into the elementary textbooks, of which Samuelson's was the most successful. By the end of the 1940s, in a survey of contemporary economics organized by the American Economic Association to help with training returning servicemen, Keynes was far and away the most frequently cited author.

The myth of the Keynesian revolution, which Keynes himself propagated, is that Keynes overthrew something called 'classical economics'. It is that he showed for the first time how changes in government spending and taxation could be used to stabilize the level of employment, thereby laying the foundations of modern macroeconomics. This, however, is a serious distortion of what happened. The literature of the 1920s and 1930s contained a wide range of approaches to macroeconomic questions by economists working in many countries, notably the United States, Britain and Sweden. That literature paid attention to problems of expectations – the relation between saving, investment and effective demand – and much of it supported the idea that both monetary policy and control of government spending might be needed to alleviate unemployment. The *General Theory* arose out of that literature and did not mark a complete break with what went before it. This resolves the puzzle of how, if the *General Theory* was as revolutionary as the myth suggests, Keynesian policies were being employed in several countries long before the book was published. Roosevelt's New Deal, for example, began in 1932.

The Transition from Inter-War to Post-Second World War Macroeconomics

The main reason why post-war macroeconomics was so different from pre-war monetary economics and business-cycle theory is that, from the late 1930s, macroeconomics began to be based, as never before, on working out the properties of clearly defined mathematical models. These include the mathematical models of Keynesian economics associated with Hicks and Champernowne, as well as the dynamic business-cycle models of Samuelson and Ragnar Frisch (see p. 248). This process affected not just macroeconomics, but also other branches of economics. The reason why Keynesian economics dominated the subject so completely is that it provided a framework that could be translated into a mathematical model that proved extremely versatile. In this sense, therefore, the outcome of the Keynesian revolution was the IS–LM model.[10] Having said this, two important qualifications need to be made. The first is that, though it is arguable that the IS–LM model captures the central theoretical core of the *General Theory*, much is left out. This is an inevitable consequence of formalizing a theory. In the case of the *General Theory*, what was left out included Keynes's discussions of dynamics and of expectations. As a result, there are many economists who argue that Keynes's most important insights were lost, and that the IS–LM model represents a 'bastard' Keynesianism, to use Joan Robinson's phrase. If we make the comparison between post-war economics and the entire business-cycle literature of the 1920s and 1930s, the amount that was forgotten appears even greater. One reason for this may be that, by the 1960s, many economists had (mistakenly) come to believe that Keynesian macroeconomic policies had made the business cycle a thing of the past.

The second, and perhaps more important, qualification is that, despite the triumph of Keynesianism (at least in its IS–LM version), the earlier traditions did not die out completely, even though they became marginalized. Hayek, for example, dropped out of mainstream economics, moving into what is usually considered political philosophy. In the 1970s, however, there was a resurgence of interest in his ideas. More significantly, the institutionalist tradition represented by Mitchell left an influential legacy. Hansen, though he presented himself as a Keynesian, was making arguments that can be traced back to what he was doing before the *General Theory* appeared. Even more significantly, the monetary economics of Milton Friedman lies squarely in the tradition established by Mitchell at the National Bureau, emphasizing the importance of detailed statistical work of a type very different from much modern econometrics. Friedman's influential *Monetary History of the United States, 1867–1960* (1963) (see p. 296) is very much in Mitchell's style, and his explanation of the Great Depression is similar to that offered by Currie in the early 1930s. It can also be argued that the 'Chicago' view of monetary policy, with which Friedman has been so strongly associated, goes back via Simons to Currie, and through him to Hawtrey. Behind all this, however, the influence of Fisher, with his analysis of the rate of interest as the price linking the present and the future, is pervasive.

11

Econometrics and Mathematical Economics, 1930 to the Present

The Mathematization of Economics

Between the 1930s and the 1970s economics became mathematized in the sense that it became the normal practice for economists to develop their arguments and to present their results, at least to each other, using mathematics. This usually involved geometry (particularly important in teaching) and algebra (particularly differential calculus and matrix algebra). In the 1930s only a small minority of articles published in the leading academic journals used mathematics, whereas by the 1970s it was unusual to find influential articles that did not. Though the speed of the change varied from one field to another, it affected the whole of the discipline – theoretical as well as applied work.

Mathematics is used in two ways in economics. One is as a tool of theoretical research. Algebra, geometry and even numerical examples enable economists to deduce conclusions that they might otherwise not see, and to do so with greater rigour than if they had used only verbal reasoning. This use of mathematics has a long history. Quesnay and Ricardo had made such extensive use of numerical examples in developing their theories that they were criticized in much the same way that the use of mathematics in present-day economics is criticized – critics argued that mathematics rendered their arguments incomprehensible to outsiders. Marx also made extensive use of numerical examples. The use of algebra goes back at least to the beginning of the nineteenth century, though in retrospect the most significant development was the use of differential calculus by Thünen (1826) and Cournot (1838). With the work of Jevons, Walras and their turn-of-the-century followers – notably Fisher – the use of mathematics, in particular calculus and simultaneous equations, was clearly established as an important method of theoretical inquiry.

The second use of mathematics is as a tool in empirical research – to generalize from observations (induction) and to test economic theories using evidence (usually statistical data) about the real world. Given that calculating averages or ratios is a mathematical technique, this has a very long history. A precondition for the use of such methods is the availability of statistical data. This has meant that the scope for such work increased dramatically with the extensive collection of such data early in the nineteenth century by economists and statisticians such as McCulloch, Tooke and William Newmarch (1820–82), Tooke's collaborator on his *History of Prices* (1838–57). More formal statistical techniques, including correlation and regression analysis, were developed in the late nineteenth century by Francis Galton (1822–1911), Karl Pearson (1857–1936), and Edgeworth. Jevons had speculated that it might one day be possible to calculate demand curves using statistical data, and early in the twentieth century several economists tried to do this, in both Europe and the United States. In the period before the First World War, economists began to address the problem of how to choose between the different curves that might be fitted to the data.

Despite these long histories of the use of mathematics in deductive and inductive arguments, the mathematization of economics since the 1930s represents a major new departure in the subject. The reason is that it has led to a profound change in the way in which the subject has been conceived. Economics has come to be structured not around a set of real-world problems, but around a set of techniques. These include both theoretical and empirical techniques. Theoretical techniques involve not just mathematical techniques such as constrained optimization or matrix algebra but also received assumptions about how one represents the behaviour of individuals or organizations so that it can be analysed using standard methods. Similarly, empirical techniques involve assumptions about how one relates theoretical concepts to empirical data as well as statistical methods.

This development has had profound effects on the structure of the discipline. The subject has come to be considered to comprise a 'core'

of theory (both economic theory and econometric techniques) surrounded by fields in which that theory is applied. Theory has been
separated from applications, and, at the same time, theoretical and
empirical research have become separated. The same individuals frequently engage in both (mathematical skills are highly transferable),
but these are nonetheless separate enterprises. These changes have also
loosened the links (very strong in earlier centuries) between economic
research and economic problems facing society. Much research has
been driven by an agenda internal to the discipline, even where this has
not helped solve any real-world problems.

The theoretical basis for this approach to the subject was provided,
in 1933, by Lionel Robbins (1898–1984) in *The Nature and Significance
of Economic Theory*. In this book, Robbins argued that economics was
not distinguished by its subject matter – it was not about the buying
and selling of goods, or about unemployment and the business cycle.
Instead, economics dealt with a specific aspect of behaviour. It was
about the allocation of scarce resources between alternative uses. In
essence it was about choice. The theory of choice, therefore, provided
the core that needed to be applied to various problems. The message
that economics was centred on a common core that could be applied to
a variety of problems was also encouraged by Paul Samuelson in his
extremely influential *The Foundations of Economic Analysis* (1947),
even though his concerns were in other respects different from those of
Robbins. (Unlike Robbins, he did not denigrate data collection and
analysis as inferior activities.) Samuelson started by presenting the
theory of constrained optimization, and then applied it to problems of
the consumer and the firm. By doing this, he emphasized the mathematical structure common to seemingly different economic problems.

Robbins also encouraged the view that the major propositions of
economics could be derived without knowing much more than the fact
that resources are scarce. This suggested that theory could be pursued
largely independently of empirical work. Furthermore, for many years
economists found a large research agenda in working out the properties
of very general theoretical models; detailed reference to empirical work
was frequently thought not to be necessary. It became more common
for economists to be classified as theorists, econometricians or applied

economists (who were frequently econometricians). Theorists could ignore empirical work, on the grounds that testing theories was a task for econometricians. When economists wrote articles that had both theoretical and empirical content, it became standard practice for these articles to be divided into separate sections, one on theory and another on empirical work.

The Revolution in National-Income Accounting

These changes in the structure of the discipline came about at the same time as another major change was taking place. This was the large-scale, systematic collection of economic statistics and national accounts. In the 1920s, comprehensive national-income accounts did not exist for any country. The pioneering attempts by people such as Petty and King had involved inspired guesses as much as detailed evidence, and were not based on any systematic conceptual framework. Even in the nineteenth and early twentieth centuries, when estimates of national income were made in several countries, including the United States and Britain, gaps in the data were so wide that detailed accounts were impossible. In the United States, the most comprehensive attempt was *The Wealth and Income of the People of the United States* (1915) by Willford I. King (1880–1962), a student of Irving Fisher's. King showed that national income had trebled in sixty years, and that the share of wages and salaries in total income had risen from 36 to 47 per cent. He concluded that, contrary to what socialists were claiming, the existing economic system was working well. In Britain, A. L. Bowley (1869–1957) was producing estimates based on tax data, population censuses, the 1907 census of production, and information on wages and employment. However, this work, like that being undertaken elsewhere, remained very limited in its scope. In complete contrast, by the 1950s, national-income statistics were being constructed by national governments and coordinated through the United Nations. By 1950, estimates existed for nearly a hundred countries.

In the inter-war period, national-income statistics were constructed right across Europe. Interest in them was stimulated by the immense problems of post-war reconstruction, the enormous shifts in the relative economic power of different nations, the Depression of the 1930s, and the need to mobilize resources in anticipation of another war. During the 1930s Germany was producing annual estimates of national income with a delay of only a year. The Soviet Union constructed input–output tables (showing how much each sector of the economy purchased from every other sector) through most of the 1920s and the early 1930s. Italy and Germany had worked out a conceptual basis for national accounting that was as advanced as any in the world. By 1939, ten countries were producing official estimates of national income. However, because of the war, the countries that had most influence in the long term were Britain and the United States. Unlike these two, Germany never used national income for wartime planning, and stopped producing statistics.

In the United States there were three strands to early work on national-income accounting. The first was that associated with the National Bureau of Economic Research, established by Mitchell in 1920. Its first project was a study of year-to-year variations in national income and the distribution of income. Published in 1921, its report provided annual estimates of national income for the period 1909–19. These were extended during the 1920s, and were supplemented in 1926 by estimates made by the Federal Trade Commission. The FTC, however, failed to continue this work. With the onset of the Depression, the federal government became involved. In June 1932 a Senate resolution proposed by Robert La Follette, senator for Wisconsin, committed the Bureau of Foreign and Domestic Commerce to prepare estimates of national income for 1929, 1930 and 1931.

In January 1933, after six months in which little was achieved, the BFDC's work was handed to Simon Kuznets (1901–85), who had been working on national income at the NBER since 1929. At the NBER he had prepared plans for estimating national income, later summed up in a widely read article on the subject in the *Encyclopedia of the Social Sciences* (1933). Within a year, Kuznets and his team produced estimates for 1929–32. (Recognizing the importance of up-to-date statistics, they had included 1932 as well as the years required by La Follette's resolution.) Kuznets moved back to the NBER, where he worked on savings and capital accumulation, and subsequently on problems of long-term growth. The BFDC study of national income became permanent under the direction of Robert Nathan (1908–). The original estimates were revised and extended, and new series were produced (for example, monthly figures were produced in 1938).

At this time, the very definition of national income was controversial. Kuznets and his team published two estimates: 'national income produced', which referred to the net product of the whole economy, and 'national income received', which covered payments made to those who produced the net product. In order to base estimates on reliable data, they had excluded many of the then controversial items. These estimates of national income covered only the market economy (goods that were bought and sold), and goods were valued at market prices. The basic distinction underlying Kuznets's framework was between consumers' outlay and capital formation.

At the same time, Clark Warburton (1896–1979), at the Brookings Institution, produced estimates of gross national product (a term he was the first to use, in 1934). This was defined as the sum of final products (i.e. excluding products that are remanufactured to make other products) that emerge from the production and marketing processes and are passed on to consumers and businesses. This was much larger than Kuznets's figure for national income, because it also included capital goods purchased to replace ones that had been worn out, government services to consumers, and government purchases of capital goods. Warburton argued that GNP minus depreciation was the correct way to measure the resources available to be spent. He produced, for the first time, evidence that spending on capital goods was more erratic than spending on consumers' goods. Economists had long been aware of this, but had previously had only indirect evidence.

The third strand in American work on national income was the work associated with Laughlin Currie. In 1934–5 he began calculating the 'pump-priming deficit'. This was based on the idea that, for the private sector to generate enough demand for goods to cure unemployment, the government had to 'prime the pump' by increasing its own spending. Currie and his colleagues focused on the contribution of each sector to national buying power – the difference between each sector's spending and its income. A positive contribution by the government (i.e. a deficit) was needed to offset net saving by other sectors.

In Britain, the calculation of national-income statistics was the work of a small number of scholars with no government assistance throughout the inter-war period. Of particular importance was Colin Clark (1905–89). In 1932 Clark used the concept of gross national product and estimated the main components of aggregate demand (consumption, investment and government spending). This work increased in importance after the publication of Keynes's *General Theory* (1936), and soon after its publication Clark estimated the value of the multiplier. His main work was *National Income and Outlay* (1937). One of his followers has written of this book that it 'restored the vision of the political arithmeticians [Petty and Davenant] . . . [It] brought together estimates of income, output, consumers' expenditure, government revenue and expenditure, capital formation, saving, foreign trade and the balance of payments. Although he did not set his figures in an accounting framework it is clear that they came fairly close to consistency.'[1]

Clark's work was not supported by the government. (When he had been appointed to the secretariat of the Economic Advisory Council in 1930, the Treasury had even refused to buy him an adding machine.) Questions of income distribution were too sensitive for the government to want to publish figures. Industrialists did not want figures for profits revealed. The government did calculate national-income figures for 1929, but denied their existence because the estimates of wages were lower than those already available. Official involvement in national-income accounting did not begin until the Second World War. Keynes used Clark's figures in *How to Pay for the War* (1940).

In the summer of 1940 Richard Stone (1913–91) joined James Meade (1907–94) in the Central Economic Information Service of the War Cabinet. During the rest of the year, encouraged and supported by Keynes, they constructed a set of national accounts for 1938 and 1940 that was published in a White Paper accompanying the Budget of 1941. The lack of resources available to them is illustrated by a story about their cooperation. They started with Meade (the senior partner) reading numbers which Stone punched into their mechanical calculator, but soon discovered that it was more efficient for their roles to be reversed.

Though the Chancellor of the Exchequer said that the publication of their figures would not set a precedent, estimates were from then on published annually.

During the Second World War, estimates of national income were transformed into systems of national accounts in which a number of accounts were related. Its position in the war effort, together with the work of Kuznets and Nathan at the War Production Board, ensured that the United States was the dominant country in this process. However, the system that was eventually adopted owed much to British work. In 1940 Hicks introduced the equation that has become basic to national-income accounting: GNP = C + I + G (income equals consumption plus investment plus government expenditure on goods and services). He was also responsible for the distinction between market prices and factor cost (market prices minus indirect taxes). Perhaps more important, Meade and Stone provided a firmer conceptual basis for the national accounts by presenting them as a double-entry production account for the entire economy. In one column were factor payments (national income), and in the other column expenditures (national expenditure). As with all double-entry accounts, when calculated correctly the two columns balanced.

From 1941 the United States moved away from national accounts as constructed by Kuznets and Nathan to ones constructed on Keynesian lines, using the Meade–Stone framework. This was the work of Martin Gilbert (1909–79), a former student of Kuznets's, who was chief of the National Income Division of the US Commerce Department from 1941 to 1951. One reason for this move was the rapid spread of Keynesian economics, which provided a theoretical rationale for the new system of accounts. There was no economic theory underlying Kuznets's categories, which derived from purely empirical considerations. The change also appeared desirable for other reasons. In wartime, when the concern was with the short-term availability of resources, it was not necessary to maintain capital, which meant that GNP was the relevant measure of output. In addition, it was important to have a measure of income that included government expenditure. Finally, the Meade–Stone system provided a framework within which a broader range of accounts could be developed. After the war, in 1947, a League of

Nations report, in which Stone played an important role, provided the framework within which several governments began to compile their accounts so that it would be possible to make cross-country comparisons. Subsequently, Stone was also involved in the work of the Organization for European Economic Cooperation and the United Nations, which in 1953 produced a standard system of national accounts.

The Econometric Society and the Origins of Modern Econometrics

The Econometric Society was formed in 1930, in Chicago, at the instigation of Charles Roos (1901–58), Irving Fisher and Ragnar Frisch (1895–1973). Its constitution described its aims in the following terms:

The Econometric Society is an international society for the advancement of economic theory in its relation to statistics and mathematics . . . Its main object shall be to promote studies that aim at a unification of the theoretical-quantitative and the empirical-quantitative approach to economic problems and that are penetrated by constructive and rigorous thinking similar to that which has come to dominate in the natural sciences.[2]

In commenting on this statement, Frisch emphasized that the important aspect of econometrics, as the term was used in the Society, was the *unification* of economic theory, statistics and mathematics. Mathematics, in itself, was not sufficient.

In its early years the Econometric Society was very small. Twenty years before, Fisher had tried to generate interest in establishing such a society but had failed. Thus when Roos and Frisch approached him about the possibility of forming a society he was sceptical about whether there was sufficient interest in the subject. However, he told them that he would support the idea if they could produce a list of 100 potential members. To Fisher's surprise, they found seventy names. With some further ones added by Fisher, this provided the basis for the Society.

Soon after the Society was formed, it was put in touch with Alfred Cowles (1891–1984). Cowles was a businessman who had set up a

forecasting agency but who had become sceptical about whether forecasters were doing any more than guessing what might happen. He
therefore developed an interest in quantitative research. When he wrote
a paper under the title 'Can stock market forecasters forecast?' (1933),
he gave it the three-word abstract 'It is doubtful.' His evidence came
from a comparison of the returns obtained from following the advice
offered by sixteen financial-service providers and the performance of
twenty insurance companies with the returns that would have been
obtained by following random forecasts. Over the period 1928–32 there
was no evidence that professional forecasts were any better than random
ones. With Cowles's support, the Econometric Society was able to
establish a journal, *Econometrica*, in 1933. In addition, Cowles supported the establishment, in 1932, of the Cowles Commission, a centre
for mathematical and statistical research into economics. From 1939 to
1955 it was based at the University of Chicago, distinct from the
economics department, after which it moved to Yale. This institute
proved important in the development of econometrics.

   Econometrics grew out of two distinctive traditions – one American,
represented by Fisher and Roos, and the other European, represented
by Frisch (a Norwegian). The American tradition had two main strands.
One was statistical analysis of money and the business cycle. Fisher and
others had sought to test the quantity theory of money, seeking to find
independent measures of all the four terms in the equation of exchange
(money, velocity of circulation, transactions, and the price level). Mitchell, instead of finding evidence to support a particular theory of the
cycle, had redefined the problem as trying to describe what went on in
business cycles. This inherently quantitative programme, set out in his
Business Cycles and their Causes (1913), was taken up by the National
Bureau of Economic Research, under Mitchell's direction. It resulted in
a method of calculating 'reference cycles' with which fluctuations in
any series could be compared. An alternative approach was the 'business
barometer' developed at Harvard by Warren Persons (1878–1937) as a
method of forecasting the cycle. There was also Henry Ludwell Moore
(1869–1958) at Columbia University, who sought, like Jevons, to establish a link between the business cycle and the weather. A few years
later, in 1923, he switched from the weather to the movement of the

planet Venus as his explanation. Moore's work is notable for the use of a wider range of statistical techniques than were employed by other economists at this time. The other strand in the American tradition was demand analysis. Moore and Henry Schultz (1893–1938) estimated demand curves for agricultural and other goods.

None of this work brought mathematical economic theory together with statistical analysis. Fisher's dissertation had involved a mathematical analysis of consumer and demand theory, but this remained separate from his statistical work, which was on interest rates and money. Mitchell was sceptical about the value of pursuing simplified business-cycle theories that emphasized one particular cause of the cycle. For him, statistical work provided a way to integrate different theories and suggest new lines of inquiry. Mitchell was also, like Moore, sceptical about standard consumer theory. He hoped that empirical studies of consumers' behaviour would render obsolete theoretical models, in which consumers were treated as coming to the market with ready-made scales of bid and offer prices. In other words, statistical work would replace abstract theory rather than complement it. Moore criticized standard demand curves for being static and for their *ceteris paribus* assumptions (assumptions about the variables, such as tastes and incomes, that were held constant). As long as the attitude of statisticians was one of scepticism concerning mathematical theory, this theory was unlikely to be integrated with statistical work. This unlikelihood was reinforced by the scepticism expressed by many economists (including Keynes and Morgenstern – see p. 263) about the accuracy and relevance of much statistical data.

The European tradition, which overlapped with the American at many points, including research on business cycles and demand, had different emphases. Work by a variety of authors in the late 1920s led to an awareness of some of the problems involved in applying statistical techniques, such as correlation, to time-series data. George Udny Yule (1871–1951), a student of Karl Pearson's, explored the problem of 'nonsense correlations' – seemingly strong relationships between time series that should bear no relation to each other, such as rainfall in India and skirt lengths in Paris. He argued that such correlations often did not reflect a cause common to both variables but were purely accidental. He also used experimental methods to explore the relationship between random shocks and periodic fluctuations in time series. The Russian Eugen Slutsky (1880–1948) went even further in showing that adding up random numbers (generated by the state lottery) could produce cycles that looked remarkably like the business cycle: there appeared to be regular, periodic fluctuations. Frisch also tackled the problem of time series, in a manner closer to Mitchell and Persons than to Yule or Slutsky, by trying to break down cycles into their component parts.

Frisch, Tinbergen and the Cowles Commission

The first econometric model of an entire economy was constructed by the Dutch economist Jan Tinbergen (1903–94), who came to economics after taking a doctorate in physics and spent much of his career at the Central Planning Bureau in the Netherlands. However, to understand what Tinbergen was doing with this model, it is worth considering the theory of the business cycle that Frisch published in 1933. He took up the idea (taken from Wicksell) that the problem of the business cycle had to be divided into two parts – the 'impulse' and 'propagation' problems. The impulse problem concerned the source of shocks to the system, which might be changes in technology, wars, or anything outside the system. The propagation problem concerned the mechanism by which the effects of such shocks were propagated through the economy. Frisch produced a model which, if left to itself with no external shocks, would produce damped oscillations – cycles that became progressively smaller, eventually dying out – but which produced regular cycles because it was subject to periodic shocks. Following Wicksell, he described this as a 'rocking-horse model'. If left to itself, the movement of a rocking horse will gradually die away, but if disturbed from time to time the horse will continue to rock. Such a model, Frisch argued, would produce the regularly occurring but uneven cycles that characterize the business cycle.

The distinction between propagation and impulse problems translated easily into the mathematical techniques that Frisch was using.

The propagation mechanism depended on the values of the parameters in the equations and on the structure of the economy. In 1933 Frisch simply made plausible guesses about what these might be, though he expressed confidence that it would soon be possible to obtain such numbers using statistical techniques. The shocks were represented by the initial conditions that had to be assumed when solving the model. Using his guessed coefficients and suitable initial conditions, Frisch employed simulations to show that his model produced cycles that looked realistic.

In 1936 Tinbergen produced his model of the Dutch economy. This went significantly beyond Frisch's model in two respects. The structure of the Dutch economy was described in sixteen equations plus sufficient accounting identities to determine all of its thirty-one variables. The variables it explained included prices, physical quantities, incomes and levels of spending. It was therefore much more detailed than Frisch's model, which contained only three variables (production of consumption goods, new capital goods started, and production of capital goods carried over from previous periods). Most important, whereas Frisch had simply made plausible guesses about the numbers appearing in his equations, Tinbergen had estimated most of his using statistical techniques. He was able to show that, left to itself, his model produced damped oscillations, and that it could explain the cycle.

Three years later Tinbergen published two volumes entitled *Statistical Testing of Business-Cycle Theories*, the second of which presented the first econometric model of the United States (which contained three times as many equations as his earlier model of the Netherlands). This work was sponsored by the League of Nations, which had commissioned him to test the business-cycle theories surveyed in Haberler's *Prosperity and Depression* (1936). However, although Tinbergen managed to build a model that could be used to analyse the business cycle in the United States, the task of providing a statistical test of competing business-cycle theories proved much too ambitious. The available statistical data was limited. Most theories of the cycle were expressed verbally and were not completely precise. More important, most theories discussed only one aspect of the problem, which meant that they had to be combined in order to obtain an adequate model. It was impossible to test them individually. What Tinbergen did manage to do, however, was to clarify the requirements that had to be met if a theory was to form the basis for an econometric model. The model had to be complete (containing enough relationships to explain all the variables), determinate (each relationship must be fully specified) and dynamic (with fully specified time lags).

With the outbreak of the Second World War in 1939, European work on econometric modelling of the cycle ceased and the main work in econometrics was that undertaken in the United States by members of the Cowles Commission. However, many of those working there were European émigrés. A particularly important period began when Jacob Marschak (1898–1977) became the Commission's director of research in 1943. (Marschak illustrates the extent to which many economists' careers were changed by world events. A Ukrainian Jew, born in Kiev, he experienced the turmoil of 1917–18. He studied economics in Germany and started an academic career there, but in 1933 the prospect of Nazi rule made him move to Oxford. In 1938 he visited the United States for a year, and when war broke out he stayed.) Research moved away from seeking concrete results towards developing new methods that took account of the main characteristics of economic theory and economic data, of which there were four. (1) Economic theory is about systems of simultaneous equations. The price of a commodity, for example, depends on supply, demand and the process by which price changes when supply and demand are unequal. (2) Many of these equations include 'random' terms, for behaviour is affected by shocks and by factors that economic theories cannot deal with. (3) Much economic data is in the form of time series, where one period's value depends on values in previous periods. (4) Much published data refers to aggregates, not to single individuals, the obvious examples being national income (or any other item in the national accounts) and the level of employment. None of these four characteristics was new – they were all well known. What was new was the systematic way in which economists associated with the Cowles Commission sought to develop new techniques that took account of all four of them.

Though many members and associates of the Cowles Commission were involved in the development of these new techniques, the key contribution was that of Trygve Haavelmo (1911–). Haavelmo argued that the use of statistical methods to analyse data was meaningless unless they were based on a probability model. Earlier econometricians had rejected probability models, because they believed that these were relevant only to situations such as lotteries (where precise probabilities can be calculated) or to controlled experimental situations (such as the application of fertilizer to different plots of land). Haavelmo disputed this, claiming that 'no tool developed in the theory of statistics has any meaning – except, perhaps, for descriptive purposes – without being referred to some stochastic scheme [some model of the underlying probabilities]'.[3] Equally significant, he argued that uncertainty enters economic models not just because of measurement error but because uncertainty is inherent in most economic relationships:

The necessity of introducing 'error terms' in economic relations is not merely a result of statistical errors of measurement. It is as much a result of the very nature of economic behaviour, its dependence upon an enormous number of factors, as compared with those which we can account for, explicitly, in our theories.[4]

During the 1940s, therefore, Haavelmo and others developed methods for attaching numbers to the coefficients in systems of simultaneous equations. The assumption of an underlying probability model meant that they could evaluate these methods, asking, for example, whether the estimates obtained were unbiased and consistent.

In the late 1940s this programme began to yield results that were potentially relevant for policy-makers. The most important application was by Lawrence Klein (1920–), who used models of the US economy to forecast national income. Klein's models were representative of the approach laid down by Marschak in 1943. They were systems of simultaneous equations, intended to represent the structure of the US economy, and they were devised using the latest statistical techniques being developed by the Cowles Commission. Klein's approach led to the large-scale macroeconometric models, often made up of hundreds of equations, that were widely used for forecasting in the 1960s and 1970s.

The founders of the Econometric Society and the Cowles Commission sought to integrate mathematics, economics and statistics. This programme was only partly successful. Mathematics and statistics became an integral part of economics, but the hoped-for integration of economic theory and empirical work never happened. Doubts about the value of trying to model the structure of an economy using the methods developed at Cowles remained. It was not clear whether structural models, for all their mathematical sophistication, were superior to simpler ones based on more 'naive' methods. The aggregation problem (how to derive the behaviour of an aggregate, such as market demand for a product, from the behaviour of the individuals of which the aggregate is composed) proved very difficult. The outcome was that towards the end of the 1940s the Cowles Commission shifted towards research in economic theory. (Research into econometrics continued apace, mostly outside Cowles, but without the same optimism as had characterized earlier work.) The Commission's motto, 'Science is measurement' (adopted from Lord Kelvin), was changed in 1952 to 'Theory and measurement'. As one historian has expressed it, 'By the 1950s the founding ideal of econometrics, the union of mathematical and statistical economics into a truly synthetic economics, had collapsed.'[5] There are, however, two other strands to this story that need to be considered.

The Second World War

In the 1930s the British Air Ministry started to employ civilian scientists to tackle military problems. Though some of the problems related to physics and engineering, it was increasingly realized that certain questions had an economic aspect, and from 1939 the scientists turned to economists for advice. For example, the question of whether it was worth producing more anti-aircraft shells involved balancing the numbers of enemy bombers shot down (and the damage these might have inflicted) against the resources required to produce the shells. This was an economic question. The US forces followed, employing economists through the Office of Strategic Services (the forerunner of the CIA). These economists became engaged in a wide range of tasks, ranging from estimating enemy capacity and the design of equipment to problems of military strategy and tactics. The last of these included problems such as the selection of bombing targets and the angle at which to fire torpedoes. These were not economic problems, but they involved statistical and optimization problems that economists trained in mathematics and statistics proved well equipped to handle. This was, of course, in addition to the role of the economist in planning civilian production (see pp. 291–2), price control and other tasks more traditionally associated with economics.

Many of these tasks involved optimization and planning how to allocate resources. These required the development of new mathematical techniques in order to obtain precise numerical answers. As many of the problems involved random errors, statisticians were particularly important. The result was intense activity on problems that are best classified as statistical decision theory, operations research and mathematical programming. After the war, the US military, in particular, continued to employ economists and to fund economic research.

These activities by economists had a significant effect on post-war economics. They raised economists' prestige. Many of them were directly related to the war effort and, though less obvious than the achievements of natural scientists, who had produced new technologies such as nuclear weapons, they were widely recognized to have been important. In addition, the economists involved in these activities worked in close proximity with physicists and engineers. The boundaries between statisticians and economists were blurred. Much of these professionals' work was closer to engineering than to what had been traditionally thought of as economics.

Some of the research undertaken to solve problems of specific interest to the military proved to have wider applications. The most important example was linear programming. This is most easily explained using some examples. If goods have to be transported from a series of factories to a set of retail stores, how should transport be arranged in order to minimize total transport costs? If a person needs certain nutrients to survive, and different foods contain these in different proportions, what diet supplies the required nutrients at minimum cost? To solve these problems and others like them, it was assumed that all the relationships involved (such as between cost and distance travelled, or health and nutrient intake) were straight lines.

Linear programming was developed independently by two statisticians, George Dantzig (1914–), working for the US Air Force, and Tjalling Koopmans (1910–85), a statistician with an interest in transportation problems who also made significant contributions to econometrics at the Cowles Commission. During the war, Koopmans was involved with planning Allied freight shipping, and Dantzig was trying to improve the efficiency with which logistical planning and the deployment of military forces could be undertaken. After the war, linear programming and the related set of techniques that went under the heading of 'activity analysis' proved to be of wide application.

The development of such techniques depended on developments before the war. Dantzig's starting point was the input–output model developed by Wassily Leontief. By assuming that each industry obtained inputs from other industries in fixed proportions, this had reduced technology to a linear structure. Koopmans's interest in transport dated from before the war. Unknown to either of them, Leonid Kantorovich (1912–86), at Leningrad, where input–output techniques had a comparatively long history, had arrived at linear programming as a way to plan production processes. Other techniques developed during the war arose even more directly out of pre-war civilian problems. Statistical methods of quality control, for example, had been used in industry before the war, but were taken up and developed by the military.

General-Equilibrium Theory

In the 1940s and 1950s general-equilibrium theory (also termed competitive-equilibrium theory) became seen as the central theoretical framework around which economics was based. It remained a minority activity, requiring greater mathematical expertise than most economists possessed, but one with great prestige. Its roots went back to Walras and Pareto, but during the 1920s, when Marshall's influence was dominant, it had been neglected. Interest in general-equilibrium theory remained low until the 1930s, when several different groups of economists began to investigate the subject.

One of these groups was based on the seminar organized in Vienna in the 1920s and early 1930s by the mathematician Karl Menger (1902–85) – not to be confused with his father, Carl Menger. The so-called Vienna Circle's manifesto, *The Scientific View of The World*, was published in 1929, and Vienna was attracting mathematicians and philosophers from all over Europe. One of these was Abraham Wald (1902–50), a Romanian with an interest in geometry. He was put in touch with Karl Schlesinger (1889–1938), whose *Theorie der Geld- und Kreditwirtschaft* (*Theory of the Economics of Money and Credit*, 1914) had developed Walras's theory of money. They discussed the simplified version of Walras's set of equations for general equilibrium found in *The Theory of Social Economy* (1918), written by the Swedish economist Gustav Cassel (see p. 276). Cassel had simplified the set of equations by removing any reference to utility. Schlesinger noted that, if a good was not scarce, its price would be zero, which led him to reformulate the equations as a mixed system of equations and inequalities. For those goods with positive prices, supply was equal to demand, but where goods had a zero price, supply was greater than demand. In a series of papers discussed at Menger's seminar, Wald proved that, if the demand functions had certain properties, this system of equations would have a solution. Using advanced mathematical techniques (in particular a fixed-point theorem, a mathematical technique developed in the 1920s), and using Schlesinger's reformulation of the equations, Wald had been able to achieve what Walras had tried to do by counting equations and unknowns. He proved that the equations for general equilibrium were sufficient to determine all the prices and quantities of goods in the system. In 1937 Wald (like Menger) was forced to leave Austria and he moved to the Cowles Commission, where he worked on mathematical statistics.

Another mathematician to take an interest in general equilibrium was John von Neumann (1903–57), a Hungarian who, after several years in Berlin, joined Princeton in 1931, having spent the previous year there as a visitor. In 1932 he wrote a paper in which he proved the existence of equilibrium in a set of equations that described a growing economy. He discussed this work at Menger's seminar in 1936, after which it was published in *Ergebnisse eines mathematischen Kolloquiums* (*Results of a Mathematical Colloquium*, 1937) in an issue edited with Wald. Von Neumann focused on the choice of production methods, and he developed a novel way of treating capital goods. This was in contrast to Wald's focus on the problem of allocating given resources. However, they had used similar mathematical techniques to solve the problem of existence of equilibrium.

It was, however, not mathematicians such as Wald and von Neumann who revived interest in general-equilibrium theory. At the London School of Economics, Lionel Robbins, who had a greater knowledge of Continental economics than most British economists of his day, introduced John Hicks to Walras and Pareto. In the early 1930s Hicks, with R. G. D. Allen (1906–83), reformulated the theory of demand so as to dispense with the concept of utility, believed to be a metaphysical concept that was not measurable. Individuals' preferences were described instead in terms of 'indifference curves'. These were like contours on a map: each point on the indifference-curve diagram represented a different combination of goods, and each indifference curve joined together all the points that were equally preferred (that yielded the same level of welfare). In the same way that moving from one contour on a map to another means a change in altitude, moving from one indifference curve to another denotes a change in the consumer's level of welfare – the consumer is moving to combinations of goods that are either better or worse than the original one. The significance of indifference curves was that, in order to describe choices, it was not necessary to measure utility (how well off people were – the equivalent of altitude). So long as one knew the shape of the contour lines and could rank them from lowest to highest, it was possible to find the highest point among those that were available to the consumer. Hicks and Allen argued that this was sufficient to describe behaviour.

This was followed by Hicks's *Value and Capital* (1939). This book contained an English-language exposition of general-equilibrium theory. It restated the theory in modern terms (albeit using mathematics

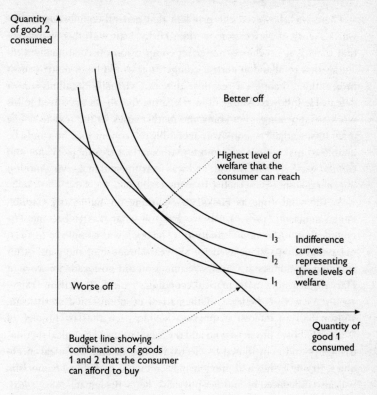

Fig. 5 Indifference curves

that was much simpler than that used by Wald, von Neumann or peven Samuelson), basing it on the Hicks–Allen theory of consumer behaviour. It also integrated it with a theory of capital and provided a framework in which dynamic problems could be discussed. Though Hicks did not refer to the IS–LM model in *Value and Capital*, most readers, at least by the end of the 1940s, understood him to have shown how macroeconomics could be viewed as dealing with miniature general-equilibrium systems. In short, the book showed that general equilibrium could provide a unifying framework for economics as a whole.

There was, however, the problem that general-equilibrium theory was a theory of perfect competition. Hicks dealt with this by arguing that there was no choice: imperfect competition raised so many difficulties that to abandon perfect competition would be to destroy most of economic theory – a response that was virtually an admission of defeat. He followed Marshall in relegating the algebra involved in his work to appendices, confining the mathematics in the text to a few diagrams, so that the book was accessible to economists who would be unable to make sense of a more mathematical treatment. *Value and Capital* was very widely read, and was instrumental in reviving interest in general-equilibrium theory in many countries.

At the same time as Hicks was working on *Value and Capital*, Paul Samuelson (1915–) was working on what was to become *The Foundations of Economic Analysis*. (The book was completed in 1941, but publication was delayed for six years because of the war.) After studying economics at Chicago, Samuelson did postgraduate work at Harvard, learning mathematical economics from E. B. Wilson (1879–1964). As well as being a mathematical economist and statistician, Wilson had an interest in physics, having been the last protégé of Willard Gibbs, a physicist who laid the foundations of chemical thermodynamics and contributed to electromagnetism and statistical mechanics. (Irving Fisher had previously been taught by Gibbs.) Samuelson was also influenced by another physicist, Percy Bridgman (1882–1961), who proposed the idea of 'operationalism', according to which any meaningful concept could be reduced to a set of operations – concepts were defined by operations. Although Bridgman was responding to what he saw as ambiguities in electrodynamics, Samuelson applied operationalism to economics. In the *Foundations*, he interpreted this idea as meaning that economists should search for 'operationally meaningful theorems', by which he meant 'hypotheses about empirical data which could conceivably be refuted, if only under ideal conditions'.[6] Much of the book was therefore concerned to derive testable conclusions about relationships between observable variables.

Samuelson's starting point was two assumptions. The first was that there was an equivalence between equilibrium and the maximization of some magnitude. Thus the firm's equilibrium (chosen position) could be formulated as profit maximization, and the consumer's equilibrium could be formulated as maximization of utility. The second assumption was that systems were stable: that, if they were disturbed, they would return to their equilibrium positions. From these, Samuelson claimed, it was possible to derive many meaningful theorems. The book therefore opened with chapters on mathematical techniques – one on equilibrium and methods for analysing disturbances to equilibrium, and another on the theory of optimization – and these techniques were then applied to the firm, the consumer and a range of standard problems.

Unlike *Value and Capital*, *Foundations* placed great emphasis on mathematics. Like his teacher, Wilson, Samuelson believed that the methods of theoretical physics could be applied to economics, and he sought to show what could be achieved by tackling economic problems in this way. However, there were important similarities between the two books. Hicks and Samuelson both emphasized that all interesting results in the theory of the consumer could be derived without assuming that utility could be measured. They both discussed dynamics and the stability of general equilibrium. Samuelson's assessment of the relationship between the two books was that '*Value and Capital* (1939) was an expository tour de force of great originality, which built up a readership for the problems *Foundations* grappled with and for the expansion of mathematical economics that soon came.'[7]

One of the most significant features of the revival of general-equilibrium theory in the 1930s and 1940s was that those involved came to it from very different backgrounds. Hicks approached it as an economist, bringing ideas influenced by Robbins and Continental economists into the British context, then dominated by Marshall. Samuelson's background was mathematical physics as developed by Gibbs and Wilson, whose techniques he sought to apply to economics. He emphasized dynamics and predictions concerning observable variables. In contrast, the way in which Wald and von Neumann approached general equilibrium arose directly from their involvement in mathematics.

In the first three decades of the twentieth century, enormous changes in mathematical thinking had taken place. Acceptance of non-Euclidean geometry (discovered early in the nineteenth century but not fully axiomatized until 1899) raised questions concerning the foundations of mathematics. It became impossible to defend the idea that geometry simply formalized intuitive notions about space. Non-Euclidean geometries violated everyday experience, but were quite acceptable from a mathematical point of view. Euclidean geometry became only one of many possible geometries, and after the theory of relativity it was not even possible to argue that it was the only geometry consistent with the physical world. Another blow to earlier conceptions of how mathematics related to the real world came with quantum mechanics. It was possible to integrate quantum mechanics and alternative theories, but only in the sense that it was possible to provide a more abstract mathematical theory from which both could be derived. Mathematics was, in this process, becoming increasingly remote from everyday experience.

David Hilbert (1862–1943) responded to this situation by seeking to reduce mathematics to an axiomatic foundation. In his programme, in which he hoped to resolve several paradoxes in set theory, mathematics involved working out the implications of axiomatic systems. Such systems included definitions of basic symbols and the rules governing the operations that could be performed on them. An important consequence of this approach is that axiomatic systems are independent of the interpretations that may be placed on them. This means that when general-equilibrium theory is viewed as an axiomatic system it loses touch with the world. The symbols used in the theory can be interpreted to represent things like prices, outputs and so on, but they do not have to be interpreted in this way. The validity of any theorems derived does not depend on how symbols are interpreted. Thus when Wald and von Neumann (whose earlier work included axiomatizing quantum mechanics) provided an axiomatic interpretation of general-equilibrium theory, the way in which the theory was understood changed radically.

From the point of view of economists, Wald and von Neumann were on the periphery of the profession. In the late 1940s, however, the Cowles Commission, having moved away from econometric theory, encouraged work on general-equilibrium theory. Two economists working there, Kenneth Arrow (1921–) and Gérard Debreu (1921–), published, in 1954, an improved proof of the existence of general equilibrium. The Arrow–Debreu model has since come to be regarded as the canonical model of general equilibrium. Its definitive statement came in Debreu's *Theory of Value* (1959). In the preface, Debreu wrote:

The theory of value is treated here with the standards of rigor of the contemporary formalist school of mathematics ... Allegiance to rigor dictates the axiomatic form of the analysis where the theory, in the strict sense, is logically entirely disconnected from its interpretations.[8]

It is no coincidence that Debreu came to economics from mathematics, and that as a mathematician he was involved with the so-called Bourbaki group, a group of French mathematicians concerned with working out mathematics with complete rigour, who published their work under the pseudonym 'Nicolas Bourbaki'. *Theory of Value* could be seen as the Bourbaki programme applied to economics.

Debreu's *Theory of Value* provided an axiomatic formulation of general-equilibrium theory in which the existence of equilibrium was proved under more general assumptions than had been used by Wald and von Neumann. The price of this generality and rigour was that the theory ceased to describe any conceivable real-world economy. For example, the problem of time was handled by assuming that futures markets existed for all commodities, and that all agents bought and sold on these markets. Similarly, uncertainty was brought into the model by assuming that there was a complete set of insurance markets in which prices could be attached to goods under every possible eventuality. Clearly, these assumptions could not conceivably be true of any real-world economy.

In the early 1960s, confidence in general-equilibrium theory, and with it economics as a whole, was at its height, with Debreu's *Theory of Value* being widely seen as providing a rigorous, axiomatic framework at the centre of the discipline. The theory was abstract, not describing any real-world economy, and the mathematics involved was understood only by a minority of economists, but it was believed to provide foundations on which applied models could be built. Interpretations of the Arrow–Debreu model could be applied to many, if not all, branches of economics. There were major problems with the model, notably the failure to prove stability, but there was great confidence that these would be solved and that the theory would be generalized to apply to new situations. The model provided an agenda for research. However, this optimism was short-lived. There turned out to be very few results that could be obtained from such a general framework. Most important, it was proved, first with a counter-example and later with a general proof, that it was impossible to prove stability in the way that had been hoped. The method was fundamentally flawed.

In addition, there were problems that could not be tackled within the Arrow–Debreu framework. These included money (attempts were made to develop a general-equilibrium theory of money, but they failed), information, and imperfect competition. In order to tackle such problems, economists were forced to use less general models, often dealing only with a specific part of the economy or with a particular problem. The search for ever more general models of general competitive equilibrium, that culminated in *Theory of Value*, was over.

Game Theory

Though economists have moved away from general-equilibrium theory, they have continued to search for a unifying framework on which economics can be based. They have found it in game theory. Though this has a longer history, modern game theory goes back to work by von Neumann in the late 1920s, in which he developed a theory to explain the outcomes of parlour games. The simplest such game involves two players who cannot cooperate with each other, each of whom has a choice of two strategies. In such a game, there are four possible outcomes. Von Neumann was able to prove that there will always be an equilibrium, defined as an outcome in which neither player wishes to change his or her strategy. To ensure this, however, he had to assume that players can choose strategies randomly (for example by tossing a coin to decide which strategy to play). There was thus a parallel between social interaction and the need for probabilistic theories in physics. Such work was an attempt to show that mathematics could be used to explain the social world as well as the natural.

From 1940 to 1943 von Neumann cooperated with Oskar Morgen-stern (1902–77) on what became *The Theory of Games and Economic Behavior* (1944). Morgenstern was an economist who succeeded Hayek as director of the Institute for Business Cycle Research in Vienna from 1931, until he moved to Princeton in 1938. In the course of his work on forecasting and uncertainty, he introduced the Holmes–Moriarty problem, in which Sherlock Holmes and Professor Moriarty try to outguess each other. If Holmes believes that Moriarty will follow him to Dover, he gets off the train at Ashford in order to evade him. However, Moriarty can work out that Holmes will do this, so he will get off there too, in which case Holmes will go to Dover. Moriarty in turn knows this . . . It is a problem with no solution. Though expressed in different language from the problems that von Neumann was analys-ing, it is a two-person game with two strategies.

In Vienna, Morgenstern became involved with Karl Menger and came to accept that economic problems needed to be handled formally if precise answers were to be obtained. Unlike many Austrian econo-mists, he believed that mathematics could play an important role in economics (he had received tuition in the subject from Wald), and he had an eye for seeing points where mathematics would be able to contribute. However, unlike von Neumann, he was critical of general-equilibrium theory and did not believe that it could provide a suitable framework for the discipline. Game theory provided an alternative. In the course of his cooperation with von Neumann, during which he continually put pressure on him to get their book out, he asked provoca-tive questions and offered ideas on equilibrium and interdependence between individuals that von Neumann was able to develop. In developing their theory, von Neumann and Morgenstern were responding to the same intellectual environment – formalist math-ematics – that lay behind the developments in general-equilibrium theory during the same period. Indeed, some of the key mathematical theorems involved were the same.

The Theory of Games and Economic Behavior was a path-breaking work. It analysed games in which players were able to cooperate with each other, forming coalitions with other players, and ones in which they were not able to do this. It suggested a way in which utility might be measured. Most significant of all, it offered a general concept of equilibrium that did not depend on markets, competition or any specific assumptions about the strategies available to agents. This concept of equilibrium was based on the concept of dominance. One outcome (call it x) dominates another (call it y) 'when there exists a group of participants each one of whom prefers his individual situation in x to that in y, and who are convinced that they are able as a group – i.e. as an alliance – to enforce their preferences'.[9] Equilibrium, or the solution to a game, comprises the set of outcomes that are not dominated by any other outcome. In other words, it is an outcome such that no group of players believes it can obtain an alternative outcome that all members of the group prefer. Given that the notion of dominance could be interpreted in many different ways, this offered an extremely general concept of equilibrium.

The Theory of Games and Economic Behavior was received enthusiastically, but by only a small group of mathematically trained economists. One of the main reasons was that, even as late as 1950, many economists were antagonistic towards the use of mathematics in economics. Another was the dismissive attitude of von Neumann and Morgenstern to existing work in economics. (Morgenstern had published a savage review of *Value and Capital*, and von Neumann was privately dismissive of Samuelson's mathematical ability.) The result was that for many years game theory was taken up by mathematicians, particularly at Princeton, and by strategists at the RAND Corporation and the US Office of Naval Research, but was ignored by economists. The main source of mathematically trained economists was the Cowles Commission, several of whom wrote substantial reviews of *The Theory of Games*, but even they did not take up game theory.

One of the Princeton mathematicians to take up game theory was John Nash (1928–). In a series of papers and a Ph.D. dissertation in 1950–51, Nash made several significant contributions. Starting from von Neumann and Morgenstern's theory, he too distinguished between cooperative games (in which players can communicate with each other, form coalitions and coordinate their activities) and non-cooperative games (in which such coordination of actions is not possible). He proved the existence of equilibrium for non-cooperative games with an arbitrary number of players (von Neumann had proved this only for the two-player case), and in doing this he formulated the concept that has since come to be known as a Nash equilibrium: the situation where each player is content with his or her strategy, given the strategies that have been chosen by the other players. He also formulated a solution concept (now called the Nash bargain) for cooperative games.

During the 1950s there were many applications of game theory to economic problems ranging from business cycles and bank credit expansion to trade policy and labour economics. However, these remained isolated applications that did not stimulate further research. The main exception was due to Martin Shubik (1926–), an economist at Princeton, in touch with the mathematicians working on game theory. His work during the 1950s culminated in *Strategy and Market Structure* (1959), in which he applied game theory to problems of industrial organization. It was not until industrial economists became disillusioned with their existing models (notably what was termed the structure–conduct–performance paradigm, which assumed a hierarchical relationship between these three aspects of markets) that game theory became widespread in the subject. During the 1970s, industrial economics came to rely more and more on game theory, which displaced the earlier, empirically driven approach which contained relatively little formal theory. By the 1980s game theory had become the organizing principle for underlying theories of industrial organization. From there it spread to other fields, such as international trade, where economists wanted to model the effects of imperfect competition and strategic interaction between economic agents.

The Mathematization of Economics (Again)

In the 1960s and 1970s, economics was transformed. The mathematization of the subject, which had gained momentum in the 1930s, became almost universal. Though there were exceptions, training in advanced mathematics came to be considered essential for serious academic work – not least because without it it was impossible to keep up with the latest research. It became the norm for articles in academic journals to use mathematics. The foundations for this change, which was so profound that it can legitimately be described as a revolution, were laid in the preceding three decades and encompassed econometrics, linear models, general-equilibrium theory and game theory. Ideas and techniques from these four areas spread into all branches of economics.

The use of mathematical models enabled economists to resolve many issues that were confusing for those who used only literary methods and simple mathematics. Topics on which economists had previously been able to say little (notably strategic interaction) were opened up. However, the cost was that economic theories became narrower, in the sense that issues that would not fit into the available mathematical frameworks were ignored, or at least marginalized. Theories became simpler as well as logically more rigorous and more numerous. There were equally dramatic changes in the way in which economic theories were related to empirical data. Though older, more informal, methods never died out, statistical testing of a mathematical model became the standard procedure.

The variety of economists involved is evidence against any very simple explanation of this process. The motives and aims of Tinbergen, Frisch, Hicks, Samuelson, von Neumann and Morgenstern were all very different. However, some generalizations are possible. The subject saw an enormous influx of people who were well trained in mathematics and physics. They brought with them techniques and methods that they applied to economics. More than this, their experience in mathematics and physics affected their conception of economics. This extended much more widely than the obvious example of von Neumann. The mathematization of economics was also associated with the forced migration of economists in the inter-war period. In the 1920s the main movement was from Russia and eastern Europe, and in the 1930s from German-speaking countries, with some economists being involved in both these upheavals. By the 1950s there had been an enormous movement of economists from central and eastern Europe to the United States. The mathematicians involved in Menger's seminar in Vienna (including Menger himself) were merely the tip of an iceberg. In 1945 around 40 per cent of contributors to the *American Economic Review*, most of whom lived in the United States, had been born in central and eastern Europe, and a large number of these were highly trained in mathematics.

The aim of the Econometric Society, which fostered much of the early work involving mathematics and economics, was to integrate mathematics, statistics and economics. In a sense, its goals were realized, perhaps more conclusively than its founders had hoped. It became increasingly difficult to study economics without knowledge of advanced mathematics and statistics. However, less progress was made in integrating economic theory with empirical work. From the late 1940s econometrics and mathematical theory developed as largely separate activities within economics. There have been times when they have come together, and there has been considerable cross-fertilization; however, the goal that econometric techniques would make it possible for economic theory to be founded securely on empirical data, instead of on abstract assumptions, has not been achieved. In part this reflects the influence of formalist mathematics. In part it reflects the overconfidence of the early econometricians and their failure to appreciate the difficulty of the task they had set themselves. The main justification for the key assumptions used in economic theory remains, as for Marshall and his contemporaries, that they are intuitively reasonable.

Economists have responded to this situation in different ways. The one most complimentary to economic theory is to argue that theory is 'ahead of' measurement. This implies that the challenge facing economists is to develop new ways of measuring the economy so as to bring theories into a closer relationship with evidence about real economic activity. An alternative way to view the same phenomenon is to argue that economic theory has lost contact with empirical data – that the theoretical superstructure rests on flimsy foundations. From this perspective the onus is on theorists to develop theories that are more closely related to evidence as much as on empirical workers to develop new evidence.

Doubts about the mathematization of economics have gone in cycles. In the long post-war boom, confidence in economics grew and reached its peak in the 1960s. General-equilibrium theory was the unifying framework, affecting many fields, and, as the cost of computing power fell, econometric studies were becoming much more common. As inflation increased and unemployment rose towards the end of the decade, however, doubts were increasingly expressed. With the emergence of stagflation (unemployment and inflation rising simultaneously) in the mid-1970s, and the failure of large-scale econometric models to forecast accurately, confidence in economics was shaken even further. In the 1980s confidence returned as game theory provided a new unifying framework for economic theory and the advent of powerful personal computers revolutionized econometrics. However, this increased confidence in the subject has been accompanied by persistent dissent. Outsiders and some extremely influential insiders have argued that the assumptions needed to fit economics into the mathematical mould adopted since the 1930s have blinded economists to important issues that do not fit. These include problems as diverse as the transition of the Soviet Union from a planned to a free-market economy or the environmental catastrophe that will result from population growth and policies of laissez-faire.

12

Welfare Economics and Socialism, 1870 to the Present

Socialism and Marginalism

The closing decades of the nineteenth century saw the rise of socialism as a large-scale movement. Socialist parties were formed across Europe, and in many countries their support grew rapidly. Extension of the franchise to include the working class led to an expansion of socialist representation in European parliaments. There was great pressure for social reform, both from socialist parties themselves and from conservatives (such as Bismarck, the German Chancellor, and Disraeli, the British Prime Minister) who sought to lessen the pressure for more radical change. Government activity was extended into many new fields, new organizations emerged, and the role of the state increased. Labour unions were expanding to include unskilled as well as craft workers, and were beginning to exact improved working conditions. Though there were clear exceptions, the rise of trade unions and the rise of socialism were strongly linked.

The socialist movements that arose across Europe and in the United States took many forms. They covered a spectrum ranging from mild reformism to revolutionary Marxism. For economists, the rise of socialism presented two types of challenge. The first was to develop principles for working out the appropriate role of the state. When, where and how should the state intervene in economic life? The second was to evaluate socialist and communist schemes for reorganizing society. Could an economy organized on socialist principles operate successfully? Though these questions clearly overlapped, they provide a useful way to think about some of the main lines of economic thought during this period.

The challenges posed by socialism came at the time when economists were increasingly taking up marginalist theories. These theories provided a framework within which problems such as the regulation of industry, the provision of welfare benefits, the establishment of government enterprises and tax policy could be tackled that was very different from that available to previous generations of economists. Smith and J. S. Mill had discussed the problem of state intervention, but their analysis had centred on long-run growth. They offered general principles by which state activities could be judged, and their observations on specific cases contained many perceptive insights, but their ability to tackle specific questions about how resources should be allocated was severely limited. Marginalism, with its mathematical apparatus of utility and profit maximization, appeared to be able to fill this gap.

Some of the early marginalists – notably the Austrians – acquired a reputation for being hostile to socialism. Some undoubtedly were. For the rest, however, although they may generally have been biased in favour of laissez-faire and individualism, this was in practice outweighed by more pragmatic considerations. Most marginalists were on the side of reform, even if their approach was sometimes paternalistic or if they were hostile to radical change. For example, although Jevons started his career a supporter of laissez-faire, by his last book, published in 1882, he had arrived at a position where he saw 'hardly any limits to the interference of the legislator'.[1] What had happened was that, during the 1870s, he found more and more contexts where state intervention was justified, to be financed mostly by continual increases in local taxation: public health, working conditions, education, transport, and many others. Marshall, the dominant economist of the following generation, saw a smaller role for state intervention than did Jevons. However, he still assigned a significant role to the state, going along with the wider movement towards support for progressive taxation (where the rich are subject to higher tax rates than the poor). Though his socialism was somewhat limited, Walras even described himself as a socialist. If there was a causal link between socialism and marginalism, therefore, it did not involve marginalism being adopted as a way of defending laissez-faire against socialist criticism. Marginalism was used to argue in favour of social reform.

The State and Social Welfare

In the English-speaking world, the dominant approach to problems of social welfare and reform was, for several decades, the Cambridge tradition, which originated with Henry Sidgwick (1838–1900). The fundamental part of Sidgwick's argument was a distinction between two senses in which the term 'wealth' was used. The first was as the sum of goods produced, valued at market prices. The second was as the sum of individuals' utilities – what we would now term welfare. He offered reasons why these might be different. The clearest example is free goods: goods for which no price is paid. Such goods raise individuals' utilities – people value them – but they do not enter into the first concept of wealth at all, for their price is zero. More generally, the market value of a good to a consumer will measure the value of the last unit consumed. If the value of an additional unit falls as consumption rises, this will be less than the average value of the good to that consumer. If the ratio of price to average utility were the same for all goods, this would not matter at all. However, the ratio of price to average utility will depend on how fast marginal utility falls, and there is no reason to suppose that this will be the same for all goods. Some goods have an average utility that is high relative to their price and will be undervalued in calculations of wealth at market prices. Free goods, which have positive value but a zero price, are enough to make this point.

In developing these arguments, Sidgwick made use of Jevons's utilitarianism, according to which individuals' utilities could be measured and compared. This meant that if the marginal utility of a particular good were higher for one person than for another, total utility could be raised by redistributing goods to those who valued them most. This would leave wealth at market prices unchanged. For example, the value of an additional loaf of bread to a poor person may be higher than its value to a rich person; it may therefore be possible to increase welfare by taking a loaf from the rich person and giving it to the poor person. In other words, a community's welfare depends on how goods are distributed, not simply on the value of goods being consumed.

Having provided reasons why wealth and welfare might differ, Sidgwick argued that, for practical reasons, wealth had to be measured using market prices, except in specific cases where 'the standards of the market fail us'.[2] This provided the justification for an approach to welfare economics similar to that of the classical economists such as Smith and Mill, tackling problems of welfare by analysing first the production and then the distribution of wealth. Sidgwick also followed Mill in his analysis of the role of government. The general principle was laissez-faire, but this was subject to numerous exceptions that he explored in detail. These included cases where individuals could not obtain adequate reward for the services they provided to society (lighthouses, afforestation and scientific discovery) and also those where the gains to individuals exceeded those to society (duplicating an existing railway line). There were also cases, such as the control of disease, where cooperation was required. However, even though Sidgwick defended the classical perspective, his separation of two concepts of wealth made it possible, arguably for the first time, to conceive of welfare economics as something distinct from economics in general.

Marshall followed in the same tradition, but made Sidgwick's analysis more precise. He defined wealth very clearly as a sum of money values – national income, or national dividend as he called it – that was distinct from utility or welfare. His main contribution, however, was to develop a way to measure utility in terms of money. This was the theory of consumers' surplus. An individual consumer's surplus is the difference between what the consumer is willing to pay for a commodity and what he or she actually pays. Marshall showed that such surpluses could be added together and used to measure changes in social welfare only under certain circumstances: in particular, the value of an additional unit of income had to be the same for all individuals. In general, this would not be true. His response was to confine his use of consumers' surplus to situations where it could plausibly be argued that it was approximately true.

On the whole, however, it happens that by far the greatest number of events with which economics deals, affect in about equal proportions all the different classes of society; so that if the money measures of the happiness caused by two events are equal, there is not in general any very great difference between the amounts of happiness in the two cases.[3]

Marshall confined his use of consumers' surplus to goods that accounted for only a small proportion of consumers' spending. This meant that a change in price would have a negligible effect on real income and would have only a minor effect on the value to the consumer of an additional unit of income.

The practical, utilitarian approach to welfare economics reached its culmination in the work of Pigou (who gave the subject its name), in his two books *Wealth and Welfare* (1912) and *The Economics of Welfare* (1920). Pigou's welfare economics was utilitarian, in that he regarded the elements of welfare as 'states of consciousness' that could be compared with each other.[4] Like Sidgwick and Marshall, he focused on national income and the way in which it was distributed. National income was linked to what he called 'economic welfare' – 'that part of welfare that can be brought, directly or indirectly, into relation with the measuring rod of money'.[5] In other words, he recognized that there were aspects of welfare about which economists could say little.

Pigou's main innovation was to replace Marshall's concept of consumers' surplus with an analysis of marginal private and social products. If the marginal private product of an activity (the benefits obtained by the person undertaking the activity) were different from its marginal social product (the benefits to society), welfare was unlikely to be maximized. There were, Pigou argued, many situations where private and social products would be different from each other. One was where one person owned an asset (for example, land or a building) that was managed by a tenant. If the benefits accrued to the landlord, the tenant might have no incentive to improve or even to maintain the asset. The marginal social product of improving land, therefore, would be higher than the marginal private product to the tenant. Another situation was where one person's activities directly affected someone else's welfare. The obvious examples of this are pollution and traffic congestion. Monopoly would also cause private and social products to differ: instead of simply looking at the value of the additional output, the monopolist will also take account of the effect of increased sales on the price of goods that are already being produced. Economic policy therefore involved eliminating differences between marginal private and social products. Using this approach, Pigou offered a detailed programme for economic policy, virtually providing a blueprint for the welfare state.

The Lausanne School

Unlike the Cambridge economists, Walras and Pareto at Lausanne did not assume that the welfare of different individuals could be measured and added together. Instead, Walras started from the notion of justice in exchange – 'commutative justice'. He argued that this type of justice required that every trader faced the same price for a given product and that prices did not change. He then showed that, given justice in exchange, free competition would produce maximum welfare. The significance of this result was that it offered a way in which questions of welfare could be analysed without either adding up or comparing the well-being of different individuals. This approach was developed by Pareto, who defined a social optimum as a situation in which any change would be agreeable to some individuals and disagreeable to others – in other words, a position where it was impossible to make anyone better off without making someone else worse off.

Though Walras, like his English counterparts, proposed detailed policies of social reform, centred on getting rid of monopolies, he also considered the question of socialism at a more abstract level. Central to this was a proposal for land nationalization that would, he contended, provide a way to reconcile individualism and socialism. Pareto took the discussion of socialism a stage further, paying attention to the question of how a socialist state might be organized. He observed that, even if the state owned the entire stock of capital and prohibited all buying and selling, prices and rates of interest would have to remain, at least as accounting entities:

The use of prices is the simplest and easiest means for solving the equations of equilibrium; if one insisted on not using them, he would probably end up by using them under another name, and there would then be only a change of language, and not of things.[6]

Without prices and interest rates, 'the ministry of production would proceed blindly and would not know how to plan production'.[7] Individuals' desires and the obstacles to satisfying them would be the same under a collectivist organization of society as under capitalism, with the result that both societies would have to solve similar problems. The main difference between socialism and capitalism was the principles by which the distribution of income was determined. Under capitalism, incomes were linked to ownership of means of production (and hence by the way in which society has evolved), whereas under socialism they were determined according to ethical and social considerations.

Pareto's argument was in turn taken a stage further by one of his students, Enrico Barone (1859–1924). Barone pointed out that the same conditions had to be fulfilled in a collectivist economy seeking to maximize the welfare of its members as in a perfectly competitive equilibrium. The ministry of production in a socialist state could start with the prices and wages inherited from the previous regime. It could then raise or lower them, in a process of trial and error, until two conditions were fulfilled: prices were equal to costs of production and costs of production were minimized. These arguments led him to claim that such a ministry would face an immense task, though not an impossible one.

The Socialist-Calculation Debate

The period of 'war communism' in Soviet Russia in 1918–21 was a brief attempt to dispense completely with markets and prices – the basis of capitalist economies – replacing them with centralized planning. This resulted in chaos, and was followed in the early 1920s by the New Economic Policy, which reintroduced markets for many goods, though maintaining extensive state control over the economy. The time was thus right for a more detailed examination of socialism. Had the Soviet experiment in instituting a non-market economy collapsed because of the intense pressures created by wartime, or because it was theoretically flawed? Several economists took up the challenge of showing that it was the latter.

One such economist was Gustav Cassel (1866–1945), who used the example of a socialist economy to make certain points that applied to any exchange economy. The socialist economy had the advantage that it was the simplest possible economy, with the result that it offered a benchmark against which more complex economies could be assessed. Comparison with socialism would reveal which institutions were essential and which could be dispensed with. This led him to elaborate on Barone's point that, even if a socialist state tried to dispense with prices and wages, these would inevitably re-emerge, for they reflected fundamental economic realities. However, he went further than Barone in arguing that, in the absence of private property and a fully developed system of exchange, a socialist state would be unable to direct production in the best way. The necessary prices would not be available.

The economist who provided the most radical critique of socialism was Mises, in his article 'Economic calculation in the socialist common-wealth' (1920). This provoked what has come to be known as the socialist-calculation debate, in which many of the period's leading economists participated. In his article, Mises argued, in uncompromising terms, that socialism was impossible – it could never work. His reasoning was that, in any economy, rational calculation required the existence of freely established money prices for both consumers' and producers' goods. Without such prices it would be impossible for anyone to work out how resources should best be used. This was, Mises emphasized, not a purely technical problem, as some socialists seemed to assume. The main difficulty arose not with consumer goods (one might not need prices to say, for example, that 1,000 litres of wine was more valuable than 500 litres of oil) but with producers' goods. A railway, for example, is valuable because it reduces costs for other industries, enabling them to produce more of the goods that consumers require. Without money prices, it would be impossible to calculate whether or not it should be built.

In a static economy, where nothing changed, rational calculation might be possible. A socialist state could continue the pattern of production that prevailed under a previous competitive system. However, the world is not static. Tastes and technology are forever changing, with the result that new ways of producing goods have continually to be worked out. In a socialist state, there would be no one with the responsibility and initiative to change the way in which activities were organized in response to these changes. Managers of capitalist enterprises, Mises argued, have an interest in the businesses they administer that is quite different from anything that could be found in public concerns. 'Commercial-mindedness' will not exist when people are moved from business into public organizations. Even if human nature could be changed so that people all exerted themselves as much as if they were subject to the pressure of free competition, there would still be a problem. In the absence of prices, people would not know what it meant to economize – to balance the costs and benefits of alternative activities.

The main response to Mises came from a group of economists who have come to be known as 'market socialists', including Fred M. Taylor (1855–1932), H. D. Dickinson (1899–1969) and Oskar Lange (1904–65). The reason for this label is that they argued that it was possible to design an economy that was socialist in the sense that the state owned the means of production but in which there were markets for consumer goods and labour. Households would thus be free to sell labour and to buy consumption goods in response to market wages and prices. Production would be organized by plant managers, who would be given the task of producing at minimum average cost and setting prices equal to marginal cost (the cost of an additional unit of output). Behind these plant managers would be industry managers, who would make investment decisions, including when to open new plants and close old ones. A central planning board would monitor the whole process, setting the prices on which the decisions of industry managers would be based.

The reasoning behind these rules was that, if they were followed, it would be possible for a socialist economy to mimic the behaviour of a perfectly competitive one. If the market-socialist system were correctly administered, both systems would give the same outcome. There might be practical problems with socialism (no one disputed this), but it was argued that socialism was theoretically possible.

The most forceful response to this came from Hayek, in a series of articles the first of which appeared in 1935. Hayek argued that the market socialists had not shown that rational calculation was possible under socialism. They had just shown that if one had complete knowledge of all the relevant data (including knowledge of consumers' tastes and of all the technical possibilities for producing goods) it would be possible to solve a set of equations to determine what goods should be produced. However, this did not solve the problem of how efficiency could be achieved under socialism – it showed that it had not been understood. In a real-world economy, full information on technical conditions of production does not exist. What does exist is engineers with techniques of thought that enable them to discover new solutions when confronted with new problems. In other words, the knowledge required by socialist planners does not exist – it needs to be created. This means that the initiative in adopting new methods, developing new products and so on has to come not from planners, but from managers who are aware of new developments and are able to respond to them. The problem with socialism is not merely a computational problem: it is one of generating the information required for the system to operate. The market socialists, by taking technical conditions as given, simply assumed the problem away.

Hayek also raised further problems with the market-socialist arguments. In equilibrium, prices can be calculated by solving a set of simultaneous equations. But the economy never is in equilibrium. It is not clear how the planners should operate out of equilibrium. It might not even be appropriate to start with existing prices, for there was no reason to believe that the transition to socialism would not produce large changes in equilibrium prices. Such problems would be compounded by the problem of new goods: planners would have no idea about which new goods should be produced and in what quantities. Comparisons with state enterprises in a capitalist economy would provide no guidance, for it would no longer be possible to make comparisons with the private sector.

This critique of the so-called 'competitive solution' to the problem of socialist planning was developed by Hayek into a theory of competition that differed radically from the one that had, by the 1930s, come to dominate the profession. Where the theory of perfect competition focused on an equilibrium in which no firm was able to affect the prices it faced, Hayek focused on rivalry. The essence of competition was that businesses competed with each other, discovering new technologies and new ways in which production could be organized. The importance of the market was that it provided a means whereby decentralized decision-making by individual firms could be coordinated. Prices conveyed information that would not otherwise be available to decision-makers. Competition was not only a means of moving the economy towards equilibrium, but also a procedure for discovering new ways of doing things.

Welfare Economics, 1930–1960

The socialist-calculation debate overlapped with another controversy that arose in the 1930s. This was about the foundations of welfare economics. Lionel Robbins argued that there was no scientific basis on which interpersonal comparisons of welfare could be made. Though people made such judgements all the time, they should not form part of the science of economics. This undermined the foundations of the Cambridge tradition in welfare economics. There was therefore a need to rebuild the subject. The outcome was what came to be called the 'new welfare economics', developed by Lange and a group of Robbins's younger colleagues at LSE, notably Hicks, Abba Lerner (1903–82) and Nicholas Kaldor (1908–86). There was a close link with the calculation debates, for it was impossible to ask whether a socialist economy could operate efficiently without examining what an efficient allocation of resources might look like. Lange, one of the architects of market socialism, was also a major contributor to the new welfare economics.

The main contribution of the new welfare economics was the development of the concept that came to be known, using the term coined by Ian Little (1918–) in 1950, as 'Pareto optimality' or 'Pareto efficiency' (the two terms are used interchangeably). This is the situation, described by Pareto, where it is impossible to make one person better off without making someone else worse off. The contribution made by Hicks, Lange, Lerner and their contemporaries in the 1930s was to work out the conditions that had to be met if this condition were to be satisfied. There was, however, a problem with the criterion of Pareto optimality and the associated concept of a Pareto improvement (a change that would make at least one person better off without making anyone worse off): they failed to provide any guidance on real-world policy changes, which virtually always benefited some people and harmed others. A stronger criterion was required.

Hicks and Kaldor, again taking up an idea found in Pareto, tried to strengthen the Pareto criterion by introducing the idea of a 'compensation test'. A change would be beneficial if the gainers could compensate the losers and still remain better off. If this criterion were met, the result would be a *potential* Pareto improvement. It would not be an actual Pareto improvement, of course, unless compensation was actually paid; however, the concept of a compensation test was thought to provide a way in which the question of whether resources were being used efficiently could be separated from questions of income distribution. But the idea turned out to be flawed. Tibor Scitovsky (1910–) showed in 1940 that it was easy to find examples where the compensation test would be satisfied in both directions: it gave contradictory results.

In the course of these discussions, economists approached the problem of social welfare in many different ways, often deriving different versions of the conditions for a social optimum. One of the main problems was that, though economists wrote of 'optimality' and 'ideal output', it was never made clear exactly what it was that was optimized in a social optimum. An answer was provided by Abram Bergson (1914–), who proposed the idea of a social-welfare function. This was a relationship between social welfare and all the variables on which social welfare might depend. In itself, this was entirely devoid of content: it simply stated that social welfare depended on whatever variables it depended on. However, it provided a framework within which different approaches to the problem could be analysed. It was possible to use the social-welfare function to analyse the implications of different value judgements or ethical criteria. For example, individualism implies that the only variables entering the social-welfare function are variables affecting individuals' levels of well-being. The Pareto criterion implies that if an individual's welfare increases (without anyone else's changing) social welfare must increase. Using such arguments, it was possible to clarify the meaning of the concept of Pareto optimality and to resolve the paradoxes surrounding compensation tests.

During the 1950s economists worked extensively on welfare economics. Kenneth Arrow's *Social Choice and Individual Values* (1951) completely reoriented welfare economics by proposing a social-welfare function that was very different from Bergson's. Arrow thought of a social-welfare function (or social-choice function) as being similar to a voting mechanism. Every voter has a preference for a particular political party, and a voting mechanism is a rule that translates such individual preferences into a social choice (a government is elected). Possible mechanisms include simple majority voting as well as much more complicated procedures. Arrow viewed the problem of social choice in exactly the same way – as the problem of getting from individuals' views about how society should be organized to a social decision.

The way in which Arrow managed to say anything about such an abstract problem was by specifying a list of conditions that any voting procedure, or social-choice function, should satisfy. These included conditions such as 'If everyone prefers A to B, then A should be chosen' (this is known as the Pareto principle); 'No individual should be a dictator'; and so on. He then proved that, although every condition looked extremely reasonable, there was no social-welfare function that would satisfy all of them. This was his so-called 'impossibility' theorem. It stimulated the emergence of an entirely new field of economics – social-choice theory – which had strong links with the analysis of voting rules by political scientists.

At around the same time, Arrow, together with Gérard Debreu, formulated what have become known as the two 'fundamental theorems of welfare economics'. These results formalized what had been discovered in the 1930s with the new welfare economics. The first theorem is that every competitive equilibrium is Pareto efficient. In other words, that in a competitive equilibrium it is impossible to make anyone better off without making someone else worse off. The second theorem approaches the problem the other way round. It is that any Pareto-efficient allocation of resources can be made into a competitive equilibrium, provided that income is distributed in an appropriate manner.

The Arrow–Debreu theorems mark the culmination of a particular approach to welfare economics, as their inventors' existence proof did for the theory of general competitive equilibrium. They establish all that can be said about the merits of perfect competition as a way in which to allocate resources. Their limitations, however, are that Pareto optimality is an extremely weak optimality criterion and that they tell us nothing about what happens when some of the criteria for optimality are not satisfied. For example, if there are monopolies in several other industries, will it be socially beneficial to remove a tax that distorts incentives in a particular industry? In 1956 Richard Lipsey (1928–) and Kelvin Lancaster (1924–), worked out their theory of the 'second best', which showed that this would generally not be the case. If there were distortions in other parts of the economy (such as monopolies or taxes) then removing a distortion was as likely to make the overall situation worse as to improve it.

The result of these developments was that by the end of the 1950s the outlook for welfare economics looked very bleak. The new welfare economics had failed to provide any welfare criterion stronger than Pareto optimality. Arrow's impossibility theorem had shown that there was no acceptable way to get from individual preferences to a social preference. Lipsey and Lancaster had undermined the idea that piecemeal reforms could be shown to be beneficial. Arrow and Debreu had established the precise relationship between perfect competition and Pareto efficiency, but nothing could, in general, be said about whether actual policy changes would raise or lower social welfare.

Market Failure and Government Failure

The displacement of the 'old' welfare economics of Sidgwick, Marshall and Pigou by the 'new' welfare economics did not mean that the old problems were neglected. In 1951 Samuelson worked out the theory of pure public goods. Public goods are goods (like the services of a light-house, a healthy environment, or a public fireworks display) that, if they are provided at all, are provided for everyone. People cannot be excluded from benefiting from them, and one person can benefit from them without reducing the benefits available to anyone else. (The qualification 'pure' is used to acknowledge that these conditions describe an ideal – problems of congestion, for example, mean that after some point many goods cease to exhibit these characteristics.) The significance of public goods is that, as Samuelson showed, the amount supplied will typically be less than the amount that is socially desirable. Everyone benefits, but no one has an incentive to pay. Similar problems arise with externalities (of which pollution is the main example), where one person's action causes harm (or possibly benefit) to a third party.

Public goods and externalities are both examples of market failure – where competitive markets fail to allocate resources in a Pareto-efficient way. If allocations are not Pareto-efficient, it means that there can be unanimous agreement that a better allocation of resources is possible (at least one person can be made better off without anyone being harmed). These concepts have been widely used to justify government intervention. The government has the responsibility to provide goods that the market will not supply in sufficient quantities, and to use its power to tax in order to correct defects in the market mechanism. In the 1960s such beliefs fitted in well with the belief that the government also had to intervene at the macroeconomic level to ensure full employment. Since then, however, this rationale for government intervention has been challenged.

The first challenge arose with what has come to be called the 'Coase theorem', proposed by Ronald Coase (1910–) in 1960. Coase made the point that most discussions of externalities, like Pigou's, failed to take account of the legal framework within which economic activities were undertaken. The failure of markets to allocate resources efficiently should, Coase argued, be attributed not to a failure of competition but to the absence of clearly defined property rights. If property rights were clearly defined, markets could develop that would ensure efficient use of resources. For example, if the rights over the use of a river were clearly established, a factory owner wishing to pollute the river and fishermen with an interest in clean water could negotiate over the amount of pollution that would be allowed. If the factory owner held rights over the river, fishermen could pay him or her to limit pollution; if fishermen held the rights, the factory owner could buy the right to pollute. The result of this perspective was that Coase saw a much greater scope for the market and a more limited role for the state than did Pigou.

The second challenge to the conventional view of the role of government, also around 1960, came with the development of theories of how voters, governments and bureaucracies behaved. These theories, developed by economists such as James Buchanan (1919–), Gordon Tullock (1922–), Mancur Olson (1932–98) and Anthony Downs (1930–), abandoned the notion that governments are disinterested organizations that act in the public interest (see p. 312). They replaced it with a view of governments as made up of individuals who are seeking to achieve their own ends. Politicians offer policies that will maximize support in elections. Managers run their organizations in ways that increase their own status and income. Taxes and government spending came to be seen as the outcome of political processes in which competing interests were expressed. The result was that the concept of government failure came to be placed alongside that of market failure.

Conclusions

Since at least the eighteenth century economists have been concerned with the question of whether the market mechanism is an effective way to organize economic activity. In this sense they have always been concerned with welfare economics. The major theme in Adam Smith's *Wealth of Nations* was that a system of natural liberty, or free competition as it came to be called, would promote economic growth and hence increase welfare. Producers would be led, as if by an invisible hand, to serve the public good even though they were concerned only with furthering their own interests. This was a theorem about competition and economic welfare.

During the period covered by this chapter, the way in which welfare economics was conceived changed dramatically. Theories of marginal utility provided a new way to analyse markets. Economists began to focus on whether the resources available at any moment were allocated efficiently. Concern with the growth of resources faded into the background. At the same time, economists began to think of competition in a different way. Instead of Smith's vision of natural liberty, in which competition meant actively competing with other people, competition came to mean a situation in which market power – the ability to influence prices – was absent. This change was clearly illustrated in the socialist-calculation debate, in which the market socialists – for many years perceived as the clear victors – defended socialism on the grounds that it was possible to design a socialist system in which resources would be allocated efficiently. They failed to recognize that Mises and Hayek, like Smith and the classical economists, had a different vision of what competition involved and of how the efficiency of an economic system should be judged.

Economists were, as so often in the history of the subject, also trying to make economics more 'scientific'. In the 1930s many of them interpreted this to mean that value judgements should be eliminated from the core of the discipline. In this they were possibly influenced by the arguments made in philosophy by the Viennese logical positivists (and brilliantly conveyed to the English-speaking world by A. J. Ayer). The 'old' welfare economics of Sidgwick, Marshall and Pigou was strongly criticized and replaced by the 'new' welfare economics based on the principle of Pareto-optimality. It turned out, however, that few clear results could be obtained. The Pareto criterion was too weak a foundation on which to base welfare economics. However, the Arrow–Debreu theorems about the efficiency of a competitive equilibrium made it possible to claim that Smith's problem of the invisible hand had now been rigorously proved. What was less often noted, however, was that the interpretation of the invisible-hand theorem had changed dramatically. It was no longer (as it was for Smith) a proposition about the dynamic effects of competitive rivalry in the real world; instead it had become a theorem about optimal resource allocation in an abstract world where market power was absent.

From around the 1970s the situation began to change. The work of

Buchanan, Tullock and others has already been mentioned. In addition, social-choice theory developed as an abstract discipline that sat somewhere between economics, ethics and political science, strongly influenced by Arrow's impossibility theorem. Social-choice theorists such as John Harsanyi (1920–) and Amartya Sen (1933–) explored issues such as whether it might be possible to measure individuals' utility, the nature of individual rights, and the ethical criteria on which social decisions might be based. More widely, economists began to use models not to provide a value-free science but to explore the consequences of different possible value judgements.

There were also important changes in the way in which markets were conceived. In the mid-1970s 'Austrian' economics experienced a revival. It was actively promoted as an alternative to conventional economics, based on radically different conceptions of knowledge and the market process. However, although support for this approach grew, and Hayek once again became a widely known figure within the profession, it remained very much a minority tradition. Within the mainstream of the subject, economists began to construct models in which there was uncertainty about the future and information was scarce. Joseph Stiglitz (1943–) showed that, once information was introduced, markets could not be completely efficient. If someone tried to use information he or she possessed (say by trading on the stock exchange), the very act of trading would reveal information to others, reducing its value. Differences in the information available to different agents were shown to produce results that were far removed from the perfectly competitive ideal. For example, if banks were unable properly to monitor the performance of businesses to whom they had made loans, it might be rational for them to maintain a low rate of interest and ration borrowers. There were also attempts to construct more dynamic models of competition in which firms actively competed against other firms, trying to be the first to patent a new technology.

The economics of socialism versus capitalism received a sharp stimulus from the break-up of the Soviet Empire around 1990. It is too soon to see this in proper perspective. To many economists it seemed to offer the final vindication of the claim made by Mises and Hayek that socialism could not work, although it was only one type of socialism, implemented in very peculiar circumstances, that had failed. However, it is tempting to argue that the developments described in this chapter proved of little help in designing a rational transition from socialism to capitalism. One might claim that the most important lesson the reformers needed was to be found in Adam Smith, who emphasized the importance to any capitalist system of a secure framework of law, morality and property rights. The socialist-calculation debate, along with most welfare economics, missed this point entirely.

13

Economists and Policy, 1939 to the Present

The Expanding Role of the Economics Profession

Since the Second World War the economics profession has grown enormously. There have been rises both in the number of economics graduates and in the number obtaining postgraduate degrees. In part this has reflected a rise in the number of people entering higher education, and in part a general expansion in the social sciences. Demand for the rising supply of graduates, at both first-degree and Ph.D. levels, has come not just from academia but increasingly from business, government and international organizations. Economists have been employed as technical experts on a scale unknown before the war. With this have come changes in the way the subject has been conceived.

One reason why the Second World War was, in many countries, a watershed in the growth of the profession was that this was when economists first became firmly established in government. In the United States, in 1940 Laughlin Currie became economic adviser to the President – the first economist to be employed full-time at such a high level. The role of economists at the heart of the US government was institutionalized with the establishment, in 1946, of the Council of Economic Advisers. The exact scope and the effectiveness of this varied according to the economic climate and the attitudes of the Council's chairman, but its existence indicated that economists had acquired a new role. The list of economists serving on the Council or associated with it includes some of those whose academic work shaped the post-war discipline: Robert Solow (1924–), James Tobin (1918–) and Joseph

Stiglitz. Similar developments occurred in Britain with the establishment, in 1941, of the Economic Section in the War Cabinet Secretariat. After the war, however, the Economic Section and its successor, the Government Economic Service, remained small (around twenty members) until 1964, but by 1970 the numbers employed had risen tenfold. In both countries there was also a large increase in the number of statisticians as governments became increasingly involved in the production of national accounts and economic statistics.

Economists were also employed in international organizations. There was a precedent for this in that the League of Nations and the International Labour Organization (ILO) had both employed economists. The League of Nations had sponsored economic research by Haberler and Tinbergen on the business cycle. After 1945, however, the number of such organizations increased dramatically, and with it the employment of economists. In addition to the ILO (established before the war) there were the United Nations, which had regional commissions, the International Monetary Fund (IMF), the World Bank (originally the International Bank for Reconstruction and Development) and the General Agreement on Tariffs and Trade (GATT). These were later followed by the Organization for Economic Cooperation and Development (OECD), originally the Organization for European Economic Cooperation (OEEC), and the United Nations Conference on Trade and Development (UNCTAD).

These organizations were largely concerned with practical policy questions, and economists were not always influential. However, despite the fact that the organizations' primary goals were technical, economists based in them undertook important economic research, including theoretical research, and could make an impact on economic thinking. One example was Jacques Polak (1914–), who at the IMF in the 1950s was engaged in influential work on exchange rates and the role of money in determining a country's balance of payments. Another was Raúl Prebisch (see pp. 302–3), who at the UN's Economic Commission for Latin America developed a theory about the relationships between industrial and developing countries.

In its early years the World Bank was concerned more to establish its credibility as a sound banking institution than with applying economic analysis, with the result that, as in most other international organizations, economists were marginalized. This situation did not change until the 1960s, under Robert McNamara (1916–), when between 1965 and 1969 the number of economists employed rose from 20 to 120. McNamara also encouraged the idea that, because the World Bank's loans would always be small relative to any country's total investment, the dissemination of ideas was important. As a result the importance attached to economic research increased, and by the early 1990s the World Bank employed around 800 economists, many doing research comparable with that done in universities. Nowhere else was there such a large concentration of economists. Given that these were all working on issues related in some way to development, they had a noticeable influence.

Keynesian Economics and Macroeconomic Planning

These changes in the economics profession were closely linked to the spread of Keynesian ideas. The relationship is, however, not a simple one. Keynes's *General Theory* provided an enormous stimulus to the idea that governments could, and should, take responsibility for controlling the level of economic activity. It was also of great importance to the development of national-income statistics. Interest-rate policy and changes in government spending and taxation could be used to keep unemployment low. In the 1940s the United States and Britain both introduced clear commitments to full employment. However, it is important not to exaggerate the influence of Keynesian ideas on these developments. Roosevelt's New Deal, which began four years before Keynes's book was published, owed much to Rexford Tugwell (1891–1979), an advocate of economic planning. The concept of 'American planning' was widely discussed in policy-making circles during the 1930s as something different from the socialist planning found in the Soviet Union or Nazi Germany. Equally important, in both the United States and Britain the Second World War showed that economic planning could be used to achieve national goals. Economists played an important role in the war effort, and arguably made a significant contribution to the Allied victory. In addition, a significant number of economists (or people who subsequently entered economics) spent the war working as statisticians. Although they worked on technical problems, such as quality control in munitions production, making the best use of limited shipping resources, or even the design of gunsights, many of the techniques they developed and the attitudes they acquired influenced the discipline when the war was over.

A further factor was that, although Keynesian economics swept through the universities, governments were more resistant. Britain introduced a Budget organized along Keynesian lines in 1940, and the concept of the inflationary gap – described by Keynes in *How to Pay for the War* (1940) – was used to calculate how much could be spent without causing inflation, and hence how much needed to be taken out of the economy by taxation or compulsory saving in order to avoid inflation. However, it is arguable that Keynesian ideas were not fully accepted in the Treasury until 1947. In the United States it was only in the 1960s, under the Kennedy administration, that Keynesian full-employment policies were systematically applied. In much of continental Europe (notably France and Germany) Keynesian ideas never dominated the policy agenda.

Macroeconomic planning of the type that governments tried to use during the post-war decades was made possible by the revolution that took place in national accounting and the provision of statistics during the inter-war period and the Second World War (see pp. 240–45). The use that could be made of national-income analysis was clearly demonstrated by wartime experiences in Britain and the United States. In Britain, the estimates of national income produced by Meade and Stone were used to calculate the inflationary gap. In the United States, Kuznets and Nathan used national income to show that Roosevelt's 'Victory Program', in which he promised vast increases in military production in 1942–3, was achievable. (It was achieved.) After the attack on Pearl Harbor, when the military dramatically increased its demand for hardware, Kuznets and Nathan (at the War Planning Board) continued to apply these methods. This time, however, goals had to be revised down, not up. Gilbert, in charge of national-income accounts, focused on providing rapidly available information on the state of the war economy.

The work of Kuznets and Nathan has been described as 'one of the great technical triumphs in the history of the economics discipline'.[1] They set targets that turned out to be feasible at a time when military procurement rose from 4 per cent to 48 per cent of US national income in four years. Not only was this an invaluable contribution to the war effort, it also provided a clear indication of what could be achieved using national accounting as a tool for economic planning. It amounted to turning military procurement into a science: if too little were demanded, war would be prolonged unnecessarily; if too much were demanded, costs would rise without any more being produced.

Keynesian economics and national-income accounting came together in econometric models. During the 1960s, as electronic (mainframe) computers became more widely available, these models grew in both size and sophistication compared with the earlier models of Tinbergen (see p. 249) and Klein (see p. 251). For example, in 1964 Klein produced a model of the United States based on quarterly data, comprising thirty-seven equations and estimated using more advanced statistical techniques than had been employed in his earlier work. The larger size of the model was the result of a much more detailed modelling of variables such as consumption (broken down into durable goods, non-durables and services) and investment (where Klein took account of inventories and new orders). The key development, however, was the Brookings model, first published in 1965. This started with around 200 variables, which later increased to over 400, and provided a much more detailed analysis of the economy than smaller models could provide. For example, it had separate equations for automobile sales and for spending on food and drink. Housing was distinguished from non-residential construction, and several industries were analysed. Equally important, it was the result of a collaborative research effort, involving economists from different universities and other institutions. This was followed by a series of other models on a similar scale during the 1960s and 1970s. Unlike the earlier models, several of the new models were produced by commercial organizations. As this happened, the emphasis shifted away from exploring new techniques and developing new concepts towards keeping the models up to date so that they could provide business with the forecasts that were being demanded. The hope was that, by using an increasingly detailed model, estimated by ever more sophisticated statistical techniques, more accurate forecasts would be produced. Though there were national differences, similar developments occurred in other countries.

Though there were exceptions, these models were generally Keynesian in their broad structure: aggregate demand for goods and services was modelled in great detail, being broken down into various categories following the national accounts. These accounts adopted the Keynesian categories of consumption, investment, government spending on goods and services, exports, and imports. Each of these was then subdivided into a more detailed classification. This core, in which national income was determined by the level of aggregate demand, was supplemented by other equations to determine variables such as productive capacity, prices, wages and interest rates.

A particularly important equation was the Phillips curve. Its author, A. W. Phillips (1914–75), was an engineer who turned to economics at LSE and was responsible for the 'Phillips machine', in which coloured water was pumped through a system of transparent tanks in such a way that flows of water represented flows of income in the Keynesian system. This was 'hydraulic Keynesianism' in the most literal sense of the term: the metaphor of a circular flow of income was translated into real flows of water. Phillips's curve, published in 1958, showed a negative relationship between inflation and the unemployment rate – high unemployment was associated with low inflation, and vice versa. Because unemployment could not fall below zero, however high inflation might be, and because wages fell by little, even when unemployment rose to 20 per cent during the Great Depression, the result was a curve rather than a straight line.

Phillips's curve was an empirical relationship that he found in British data. It was, however, soon given a theoretical interpretation by Lipsey, who in 1960 also provided an interpretation of the curve's distinctive shape. His explanation of the curve was based on the idea that if supply of any good (including labour) exceeds demand the price will fall, and if demand is greater than supply the price will rise. This means that there will be a negative relationship between wage inflation and the gap between supply and demand for labour. Unemployment, when adjusted for so-called 'frictional unemployment' (unemployment that arises because workers are different from each other and have to be matched with the right job before they can be employed), was a measure of the difference between demand for and supply of labour.

In the same year, Samuelson and Solow found a similar relationship for the United States. They also argued that the Phillips curve could provide a framework within which to think about economic policy. Governments faced a trade-off between inflation and unemployment, but could use monetary policy and changes in government spending and taxation to achieve the point on the curve that they preferred. Some governments might choose to have low unemployment at the cost of a high inflation rate, whereas others might prefer lower inflation at the cost of higher unemployment.

Its relevance for policy-making was one reason why economists took up the idea of the Phillips curve with such enthusiasm. There were, however, two further reasons. The first was that it provided a satisfactory way to 'close' the macroeconomic models that were in use at the time. The IS–LM model (see pp. 233–4) had become the standard model of how the levels of output and employment were determined, but it did not explain the price level. The Phillips curve provided the missing link, completing the model. In so far as they were constructed along Keynesian lines, the same was true of the large econometric forecasting models: when augmented with a Phillips curve, they could be used to forecast prices – something that clearly needed to be forecast. The second reason was that during the 1960s, as more and more economists had access to mainframe computers, estimating the Phillips curve provided an ideal agenda for econometric research. It was soon found that the original formulation of the Phillips curve did not fit the data very well, and numerous attempts were made to improve it by adding new variables and modifying the form of the equation.

Inflation and Monetarism

The 1960s saw the high tide of Keynesian economics. In the United States, under President Kennedy, Keynesian policies were used to move the economy towards full employment by the end of the decade. However, this coincided with the escalation of the war in Vietnam and an enormous rise in military expenditure. In the rest of the world, too, the late 1960s and early 1970s were a period of rapid expansion, and inflation began to rise rapidly. The collapse of the Bretton Woods system, dating from 1944, which had fixed exchange rates for the previous quarter-century, meant that countries could expand without worrying about the effect it would have on their balance of payments. An important feature of this boom was a rise in commodity prices. In 1973 the Organization of Petroleum Exporting Countries contributed to this rise by successfully reaching an agreement to cut supplies of crude oil in order to raise its price. The Yom Kippur War, between Israel and the Arab states, disrupted oil supplies. The outcome was that oil prices rose by 66 per cent in October 1973 before doubling again in January 1974, and there was an acute shortage of oil. Furthermore, because oil revenues rose more rapidly than oil exporters could spend them, there was a sudden shortage of demand in oil-importing countries, which found themselves with unprecedented balance-of-payments deficits. The world was plunged into recession.

The novel feature of this depression was that inflation and unemployment rose simultaneously. The Phillips curve 'broke down' (the negative relationship between inflation and unemployment disappeared), and Keynesian theory no longer provided an adequate framework on which policy-making could be based. Rising unemployment implied that spending should be increased, but high inflation required that it be reduced. A further consequence was that, as the decade went on, it became clear that the large-scale econometric models that were used for forecasting were not performing well. Something had gone seriously wrong with the way in which economists were analysing current problems. It was under these circumstances that the profession took a more serious interest in monetarism as expounded by Milton Friedman (1912–).

Starting with a widely read article in 1956, Friedman had been trying to revive interest in the quantity theory of money. This theory argued that the main factor explaining inflation was increases in the quantity of money (the stock of currency in circulation plus the stock of bank deposits). This ran counter to the Keynesian consensus of the time, which emphasized fiscal rather than monetary policy. Friedman sought to prove his case through extensive empirical work on the relationship between money, prices and interest rates, culminating in his *Monetary History of the United States, 1867–1960* (1963), written jointly with Anna J. Schwartz (1915–). He argued, in particular, that the money supply did not respond passively to other developments in the economy, and that changes in the money supply exerted a powerful effect on the economy. In the short run a rise in the money supply would raise output, but eventually output would return to its original level and the only effect would be on the price level. However, it was not possible to use this relationship as the basis for controlling the business cycle, because the effects of monetary changes were felt only after a long and unpredictable lag. If a central bank were to raise the money supply, the effects might be felt a year, or perhaps two years, later. The conclusion Friedman drew was that the aim of policy should be to prevent money from being a source of disturbance, and the way to do this was to ensure that the stock of money grew at a constant, known rate.

Against the background of 1968–73, when many governments had allowed the money supply to increase, Friedman's analysis of inflation was persuasive. Rapid monetary expansion around 1971 had been followed, about two years later, by an equally rapid rise in inflation. (Inflation in 1973 was clearly linked to the oil price rises of that year, though monetarists could argue that, were it not for monetary expansion, prices would not have risen so much.) During the 1970s, therefore, government after government broke with Keynesianism and implemented targets for the growth of the money supply. In some countries, such as Britain, this process was assisted by pressure from the IMF, which had for some years been working on the links between money and the balance of payments.

Overturning the Keynesian consensus, however, required much more than this. Three developments were particularly important: Friedman's expectations-augmented Phillips curve; the failure of Keynesian fore-casting models; and rational expectations. The first of these – Fried-man's alternative to the conventional theory of inflation – was proposed in his presidential address to the American Economic Association in 1967. His argument was that the conventional Phillips curve was incor-rectly specified. What mattered to people negotiating over wages was not the money wage rate but the real wage rate – the wage adjusted for the purchasing power of money. This meant that, when bargaining over wages, people would take account of expected inflation. If people expected inflation to be 5 per cent, they would require wages to rise by 5 per cent more than if they expected the inflation rate to be zero. The result was that, if the inflation rate increased, the Phillips curve would shift upward by the same amount. This implied that there would be no stable trade-off between inflation and unemployment.

Friedman claimed that there was a single unemployment rate – the natural rate of unemployment – that was consistent with a constant inflation rate. He argued that if a government tried to peg unemploy-ment at a level other than the natural rate, the inflation rate would rise or fall indefinitely. Low unemployment could not be bought at the price of a high inflation rate – only at the price of an ever-accelerating inflation rate, which must, at some point, become unsustainable. Governments had to accept that, though they might be able to influence unemployment for a short period (before people realized what was happening to inflation), they could not do this for long. Eventually unemployment would have to return to the natural rate. This completely undermined the basis for Keynesian demand-management policy.

It is interesting to note that the authors of the original Phillips-curve theory – Phillips, Lipsey, Samuelson and Solow – had all been well aware that wage increases would depend on expected inflation. Their economic theory told them this very clearly. However, in the late 1960s there was no such relationship in the data. Inflation was low and had changed little, with the result that there was no detectable relationship between expectations and wage increases. They thus dropped price inflation from their equations. By the early 1970s, however, after inflation rates had risen for a sustained period, econometric studies began to reveal a significant effect of expected inflation on wages, and by the mid 1970s the relationship was the very strong one that Friedman had predicted. This provided empirical support for Friedman's position. From the late 1970s, therefore, economists began to accept that in the long run the Phillips curve must be vertical – that there was no trade-off between inflation and unemployment.

The theory of the expectations-augmented Phillips curve reinforced Friedman's earlier arguments over the quantity theory. If governments could not control unemployment and faced the danger of accelerating inflation, there was a strong case for using monetary policy to control the one variable they could control, namely the rate of inflation. This doctrine came to be known by a term coined by Karl Brunner (1916–89), one of its supporters, as 'monetarism'. Though this is simply a doctrine about the relationship between money and inflation, many of its supporters, such as Friedman, combined it with more general support for free markets and non-intervention. 'Monetarism' therefore came to be associated, especially in the minds of non-economists, with measures such as privatization, deregulation, income-tax cuts and reductions in social-welfare provision. The meaning of the term became even looser where, as under Margaret Thatcher's government in Britain in the 1980s, attempts were made to implement so-called 'monetarist' policies using methods (namely cuts in government spending) that were far removed from those advocated by Friedman. By this stage the term had become almost meaningless.

The New Classical Macroeconomics

In the 1970s, in the wake of the first oil crisis, macroeconometric forecasting models began to forecast very badly. Attempts were made to repair them, introducing new equations and redesigning existing ones. However, such attempts were not very successful. It became clear that, despite the enormous resources that had been put into them, these models did not perform significantly better than much simpler ones. An explanation of why this was so was provided by Robert E. Lucas Jr (1937–) in 1976. The essential argument in what has come to be called the 'Lucas critique' is that the behaviour of the private sector depends on people's expectations of what the government is going to do. For example, consumption patterns will depend on the tax and social-security policies that consumers expect to face. This means that a consumption function estimated under one tax regime will no longer work when tax policy changes. Thus, even if forecasting models offered accurate accounts of the way the economy operated when they were built in the 1960s, they were bound to break down when policy changed during the 1970s. Lucas concluded that a different type of model was required.

In a series of papers starting in 1972, Lucas argued that macroeconomic models ought to be based on the assumption that individuals were completely rational and that they took advantage of all opportunities open to them. He interpreted this to imply that all markets must be modelled as being in equilibrium, with supply equal to demand. If supply were greater than demand, for example, some suppliers would be unable to sell all the goods they wanted to sell. They would thus have an incentive to undercut their competitors, causing prices to fall, so bringing the market into equilibrium. To assume that markets were not in equilibrium, therefore, was to assume that people were not being fully rational. Similarly, he argued that if people were fully rational, their expectations would take account of all the information that was available to them. Here Lucas added the novel twist that modellers should assume that agents in their model know the true structure of the model. There are several ways in which this assumption can be justified, the most convincing of which is the argument that, if they do not do this, agents will make mistakes and change their behaviour. The only possible equilibrium, therefore, is one where people know the true model of the economy.

These two assumptions – known as 'continuous market clearing' and 'rational expectations' – have dramatic implications. They undermine the idea, basic to Keynesian economics, that people are unemployed because they cannot find work. Instead it is assumed that, if people would accept a lower wage rate, they would find work – that they have 'chosen' to be unemployed, in that they have decided that the wage they would obtain from working is not enough to compensate them for the leisure they would lose. Fluctuations in output and employment arise because unanticipated shocks cause people to make mistakes in their estimates of inflation. It follows from this that systematic changes to government policy (such as following a rule that says expand the economy when unemployment is high and contract when unemployment gets low) will have no effect. The effects of such a rule will be predictable and hence will not affect output. The private sector will discount the policy changes in advance.

The business cycle presents a major challenge to such a theory. Though precise changes in output cannot be predicted, the economy generally follows a rough cyclical pattern of boom and slump, with the cycle lasting several years. In the 1970s Lucas tried to explain this as the result of monetary shocks. These would raise or lower demand, causing people to make mistakes that would cause output to fluctuate around its long-term trend. Much effort was put into measuring these shocks and explaining how they might produce fluctuations similar to those observed in the real world. Eventually, however, Lucas's explanation was abandoned in favour of one which explained the cycle in terms of 'real' shocks – primarily shocks to technology (new inventions and so on). The result was the 'real business cycle' theory first proposed by Fynn Kydland (1943–) and Edward Prescott (1940–). This was based on the same assumptions as Lucas's theory – notably continuous market clearing and rational expectations – but differed in its assumptions about the source of shocks to the system and used a new set of econometric techniques (so-called 'calibration' methods).

Though many economists remained sceptical about the extreme policy conclusions reached by what came to be called the 'new classical macroeconomics', the main thrust of the new classical argument – that economic models should assume fully rational behaviour – came to be widely accepted. Keynesians, who in the 1970s had been exploring models where markets were generally out of equilibrium and traders faced rationing, changed their research strategy. They started to search for explanations of unemployment that did not violate the assumption of rationality. They built models using assumptions such as asymmetric information (where firms cannot tell how productive a worker will be until after he or she has been hired) or imperfect competition (where firms or unions have power to influence the prices at which they buy or sell). These models were based on the main new-classical assumptions, but produced Keynesian conclusions.

The main reason why the new classical macroeconomics had such a big impact was that it was in many ways a natural development from what had been happening in microeconomics since the 1930s. There were two elements to this. The first was ever greater mathematical rigour in the analysis of problems. Enough simplifying assumptions were made to permit rigorous mathematical techniques to be applied to whatever problem was being analysed. The second was the modelling of individual behaviour in terms of optimization – assuming that firms maximized profits and individuals maximized utility. In such a world, everything rested, in the last resort, on technology and individual tastes. One result of this was that the distinction between microeconomics, dealing with the behaviour of individual firms and households, and macroeconomics, dealing with the economy as a whole, was broken down.

Development Economics

A field that exhibits certain parallels with macroeconomics is development economics. This emerged in its modern form after the Second World War. The United States – then clearly the dominant Western power – was anti-colonialist, and from the 1940s many colonies began to achieve independence, receiving a political voice through the United Nations. As a result the 'colonial economics' of the inter-war period, with its stress on the development of resources by colonial powers, was clearly out of date. Attention had also been focused on the economics of underdeveloped countries during the war. Paul Rosenstein-Rodan (1902–85) had tackled the theory of underdevelopment, focusing on south-eastern Europe. The statistical work of Colin Clark and Simon Kuznets revealed, for the first time, the extent of income differences between rich and poor countries. Finally, governments in North America and western Europe were taking an active interest in measures that might be taken to promote growth (and capitalism) in the rest of the world, partly in response to competition with the Soviet Union.

Various agencies associated with the United Nations had a commitment to economic development from the start, and later the World Bank's remit extended from 'reconstruction' to include 'development'. The Organization for European Economic Cooperation (OEEC) became the Organization for Economic Cooperation and Development (OECD).

There were strong links between Keynesian economics and early theorizing on problems of development. Keynesian economics was based on the presumption that economies could get stuck in situations of mass unemployment or underemployment (where workers have jobs but are not fully employed) from which they could not escape unaided. Underdeveloped countries were similarly thought to have become stuck in situations from which they needed assistance to escape. (The term 'underdeveloped countries' is used here as it was the one used at the time. Since then, a series of euphemisms for poor countries has been used: 'underdeveloped countries', 'less developed countries', 'developing countries', 'emergent nations', 'the Third World' and, most recently, 'the South'.)

There were several theories about why this was the case. One of the most common focused on the difference between economy-wide growth and growth in a single sector of the economy. If a single industry (or a single business) were to expand, it would soon come up against barriers such as a lack of demand for its products and shortages of skilled labour. In contrast, if it were possible to engineer an expansion of the whole economy, each industry would create demand for other industries' products and would contribute to the growth of a pool of skilled labour on which all industries could draw. Such thinking underlay the theories of Rosenstein-Rodan, economic adviser to the World Bank in its early years, and Ragnar Nurkse (1907–59), an economist at the League of Nations who, after the war, became an advocate of the need for balanced growth.

Not all explanations of underdevelopment were of this type. At the UN Economic Commission for Latin America, Raúl Prebisch (1901–86) explained the contrast between rich and poor countries as being the outcome of unequal interaction between a 'core' of industrial countries, exporting mainly industrial goods, and a 'periphery' of poor countries, whose main exports were primary commodities. Because workers in industrial countries had great bargaining power, productivity gains led to rising real wages. In contrast, workers in underdeveloped countries did not have such bargaining power and so were unable to translate productivity gains into wage rises. Instead, wages stayed the same and prices fell. This difference led to primary commodities becoming ever cheaper in relation to industrial goods. The terms on which trade took place thus became more and more favourable to industrial countries, and it became more difficult for countries in the periphery to escape from poverty. Prebisch drew the conclusion that development required state intervention to develop industries (protected by tariff barriers) that would compete with goods currently being imported – a strategy of 'import substitution'.

Other economists produced theories of 'dualistic' development. Arthur Lewis (1915–91), for example, distinguished between a modern sector in which firms maximized profits and used mechanized production methods and a 'traditional' sector in which family relationships ensured that everyone was employed on the land, even if their presence did not raise output. Economies that were split between sectors in this way were characterized by surplus labour in the traditional sector. Economic development involved the growth of the modern sector. Labour moved out of a sector in which its productivity was zero into one where it was productive.

Few of these theories went unchallenged. 'Big-push' balanced-growth theories, for example, were vigorously challenged by Albert Hirschman (1915–), who argued that development required disequilibrium – unbalanced growth. Expansion of a single industry would create opportunities for other industries and would promote the development of new activities. Prebisch's theories were also challenged. There was a vigorous debate over whether statistical evidence supported the claim of a falling trend in commodity prices. Dualistic theories were vulnerable to the charge that it was in practice very difficult to identify sectors that were as different as the theories required.

The common feature of these theories is that they were 'structural' theories. They attributed the problem of underdevelopment either to the structure of the economies themselves or to the structure of the world economy. These structural features meant that the market mechanism would, on its own, be insufficient to ensure development. Planning and state intervention of some kind were a necessity. This fitted in with the Keynesian perspective in two ways. The first was that different types of theory were seen as being needed for different problems. Just as macroeconomics was needed as a subject distinct from microeconomics in order to tackle problems of unemployment, so development economics was needed to deal with problems specific to underdeveloped countries. The second was that it was believed that markets could not be left alone – that government intervention was necessary if market economies were to operate in a beneficial way.

In the 1970s, however, this way of thinking about development fell out of favour. Attempts to plan development – whether they involved import substitution, export promotion, balanced or unbalanced growth, or the creation of disequilibria – were not particularly successful. It also became increasingly clear that 'developing' countries were far from homogeneous – sub-Saharan Africa had problems that bore little if any relationship to those faced by South-East Asia or Latin America. It had become apparent that economic growth did not automatically reduce poverty. The result might simply be the emergence of an affluent modern sector amid poverty that was as great as before, or even greater. There was also an ideological shift against planning and in favour of solutions that placed greater emphasis on markets. The success stories of economic development were seen as arising from free-market economies such as those of Singapore, Taiwan and Korea (even though these had strong and authoritarian governments that intervened actively in industry). The assumption, central to many structural theories of development, that people in developing countries behaved in some way differently from people in developed countries became harder to sustain. The result was an increasing tendency to apply to problems of developing countries the same analytical techniques as were being used to analyse problems of developed countries. Everyone, whether rich or poor, was assumed to behave according to the precepts of rational behaviour.

There was therefore a significant change in the way in which development was tackled in the 1970s. Grand theories, often based on Keynesian macroeconomics, increasingly gave way to microeconomic theories in which prices played a much greater role. In 1969 Ian Little and James Mirrlees (1936–) produced for the OECD a manual on project evaluation that presented techniques that were widely used. It was argued that projects should be evaluated not on the basis of market prices, which might be seriously distorted, but on so-called 'shadow prices' that reflected the constraints facing developing countries. In a similar vein, the concept of effective protection, first developed in the 1960s, came into more widespread use. Economists also focused more on the concept of poverty, seeking better ways to measure it. 'Basic needs' indices, taking account of factors such as nutrition levels, mortality and literacy rates, became more prominent. Economic growth, though still important, was no longer the sole criterion by which development was measured. The theoretical tools used were, as in macroeconomics, increasingly those of contemporary microeconomics. For example, in the 1970s development economists took up models of risk and incomplete information. In the 1980s, again following macroeconomics, these were extended to include imperfect competition and the latest developments in growth and trade theory. Parallel changes took place both in academia and in international organizations, though there was no uniformity, even among the latter. For example, in the 1970s the OECD and UNIDO (the UN Industrial Development Organization) took up Little–Mirrlees methods of project appraisal and cost-benefit analysis, but the World Bank did not.

One of the main developments during the 1980s was the increasing prominence of the World Bank in setting the agenda for development. In 1980 it abandoned its earlier policy of lending only to finance specific projects and introduced 'structural-adjustment lending'. This was lending designed to help countries get over medium-term balance-of-payments problems without impeding growth. Loans were made on condition that the borrowing countries implemented a programme of reform, including measures such as allowing exchange rates and interest rates to be determined by world markets, reducing the size of the public sector, deregulating markets, and removing controls on investment. This was based on the so-called 'Washington consensus' – the idea that development required free markets and a trade-oriented development strategy. The debt crisis of the early 1980s worsened the situation for many developing countries, and the World Bank's insistence that lending be accompanied by measures to liberalize trade and capital flows and open up domestic markets became a major issue. Critics of the World Bank argued that structural-adjustment policies served to place the burden of adjustment on the poor in developing countries, for the result would frequently be unemployment and cuts in public services. Supporters focused on the need for such reforms if developing countries' problems were to be solved.

The context of development economics changed even more dramatically with the fall of the Soviet Empire in 1989–91. Economists – including both academics and those in international organizations – turned on a large scale to problems of 'transition' and 'emerging markets'. The establishment of market economies in eastern Europe and the former Soviet Union had clear parallels with the situation of 'traditional' developing countries facing structural adjustment. It was believed that, in the long run, the establishment of a market economy would raise living standards, but the short-term effects were high unemployment and extreme poverty alongside extreme affluence.

Conclusions

After the Second World War, economics became a much more technical subject, and mathematical techniques were systematically applied to all its branches. This was not a neutral development, but was accompanied by a transformation of the subject's content as theories were refined in such a way that they could be treated using the available mathematical tools. The meaning attached even to such basic terms as 'competition', 'markets' and 'unemployment' changed. These developments were something that could happen only in an academic environment, for many theories were developed that had only tenuous links, if any, with real-world problems. Comparisons with 'basic' or 'blue-sky' research (not aimed at any specific use) in science and medicine were used to justify such inquiries.

At the same time as economics became more technical, it also became more international. (Cause and effect are hard to tie down, but there were many causes of internationalization other than the spread of mathematical techniques.) While there are still many economists who can be identified with a single country, there are many who cannot. It became common for an economist to be born in one country, to study in another country (or in two other countries), and to spend his or her career moving between institutions in a variety of other countries. Communication networks have also become international. The result is that the nationality of economic ideas has become harder than ever to pin down – there is a real sense in which it has become a meaningless concept. Economic ideas have become essentially international. Even where schools have retained national labels (such as 'Austrian' economics) they have become international.

The country at the centre of this process was the United States. Universities, even in countries with long-established academic institutions, such as Germany and Britain, have increasingly modelled their graduate teaching on the US model. American textbooks have been widely used in all countries. American criteria for academic advancement, emphasizing the publication of articles in learned journals, have become widespread. In addition, because of the sheer size of the US academic system, American economics has increasingly dominated the pages even of European academic journals. Americans clearly dominate the list of Nobel Prize winners, and have been responsible for the most influential new ideas in the subject. The process therefore seems to be one of Americanization rather than internationalization. However, against this has to be set the fact that the ideas on which the current consensus is based have significant European roots: mathematical economics in German mathematics of the 1920s; econometrics in Tinbergen's work in the Netherlands; and macroeconomics, through Keynes, in Cambridge, England. In addition, one of the reasons for the apparent American dominance has been the migration of economists from Europe and elsewhere in the first half of the twentieth century (see p. 207). Many of the key players in the transformation of the subject came from German-speaking countries or eastern Europe. If economics has been Americanized, there is a sense in which this is because the American academic system has been so large, so wealthy and so open to international influences.

This, however, is only one side of the story of economics becoming more technical. The other is the increased involvement of economists in government, international organizations and business. Economists have come to be seen as technical experts whose advice is essential to decision-making – a process greatly stimulated by the Second World War. This has gone beyond simply forecasting, though that remains important. Especially in the United States, where the process has perhaps gone further than elsewhere, economists are regularly used in tasks such as designing the rules by which industries are to be regulated or the procedures by which franchises are to be sold. During the 1990s they were heavily involved in designing measures to protect the environment. In some fields, ideas were developed in academia and then applied by economists working in government or business, as one might expect. However, this simple relationship is not always found. Macroeconomics and development are two fields where it is hard to draw a clear line between research done in academia and research done in government, central banks and international organizations. Research in these fields has been dominated by policy problems, and there has been continual interaction between economists in universities and in other organizations, with many staff moving back and forth between different types of institution. There has therefore been a convergence between, for example, the ways in which central banks and academic economists think about monetary policy, and in ways of tackling economic development.

The academic environment, dominated by the United States, in which economic ideas were developed in the second half of the twentieth century is very important. The way in which economic thought developed during this period cannot be understood apart from it. However, the role of economists as policy advisers should not be neglected, especially in particular fields.

14

Expanding the Discipline, 1960 to the Present

Applied Economics

As economics has become more technical and economic theory more abstract and mathematical, applied fields have proliferated. Writing in the 1940s, Schumpeter distinguished between five types of applied field. The first type comprised fields such as money and banking that were widely considered part of general economics but were taught separately so that they could be treated in more detail. A second type included fields such as actuarial science and insurance that were separate from economics for purely historical reasons. The third included fields based on public policy, such as agriculture, labour, transport and public finance. The last two comprised a mixture of fields such as socialism and comparative economic systems and area studies. Reflecting on this, he commented:

There is evidently no permanence or logical order to this jumble of applied fields. Nor are there definite frontier lines to any of them. They appear or vanish, they increase or decrease in relative importance, and they overlap with one another as changing interests and methods dictate. And ... this is as it should be.[1]

It would be possible to make very similar remarks about the situation at the end of the twentieth century. However, in the second half of the century the situation had changed in several ways. One was that the division of the subject into applied fields became institutionalized. Applied fields ceased to be simply convenient labels attached to courses offered to students, but began to be reflected in the way in which the profession was organized. Much more than in the 1940s, they acquired their own societies, conferences and journals. The most obvious sign was the proliferation of specialist journals. Economists working within applied fields began to talk much more to each other rather than to economists in general.

However, a second development was that economics came increasingly to be viewed as having a theoretical 'core' that is applied to different problems. The core comprises micro- and macroeconomics, which are then applied – along with econometrics (seen primarily as a body of statistical techniques) – to problems such as labour, development, money, the public sector and so on. This hierarchy is reflected in the fact that most degree programmes will require training in core subjects, but will allow students to choose which applied fields to study. This development has had two effects. It provides a much clearer basis for applied fields than was available in the 1940s, when the distinction between the core and applications was much less clearly defined. At the same time it unifies the subject in a specific sense. Because applied fields have increasingly been based on a common core – especially since the 1970s, when the distinction between 'micro' and 'macro' was significantly reduced – there is a level at which all economists can speak to each other, whatever field they specialize in. It could be said that economists speak different dialects of a shared language.

The histories of these applied fields are varied. Some fields are clearly linked to outside, political developments. In the era of the Cold War, 'comparative economic systems' had a clear role. It owed much to the earlier 'economics of socialism', a field whose history went back to the nineteenth century, but it was far from identical with it. With the collapse of the Soviet Empire around 1990 and the extension of market activities in China, the capitalist system appeared, at least to most economists, to have won. Comparative economic systems, focusing on the choice between capitalism and socialism, had lost its *raison d'être*, even if there remained more subtle differences between different types of socialist and capitalist systems that remained to be understood. It gave way to the economics of transition and emerging markets. In contrast, the history of labour economics probably exhibits greater continuity, with problems such as wage determination and the organization of labour markets being of perennial concern. A technical field such as econometrics has no doubt emerged as a separate field because of the specialized range of mathematical techniques employed: a large investment is necessary to learn them. Though external political or ideological changes have had an impact, for example in changing the type of questions that econometricians have been expected to answer, these are probably less important in econometrics than in less technical fields of economics. Developments in information technology have probably been the main external factor influencing the recent history of econometrics, for modern computing has opened up possibilities about which early econometricians could only dream.

Economic Imperialism

A significant development, especially in the 1960s and beyond, was the development of applied fields that extended the boundaries of economics. Economic analysis was applied to problems previously considered to lie in the realm of other social sciences, notably sociology and political science. Gary Becker (1930–) has applied standard price theory to, among other sociological topics, crime and the family. Criminal activity is modelled as an optimization problem in which potential criminals weigh up the gains to be obtained from successful crimes against the potential losses they would incur in the event of being caught and convicted. Given that, even if they are guilty, they are not certain to be caught and convicted, this can be formulated as a standard problem of choice under uncertainty. It is possible to use such models to decide, for example, how effective increased sentences are likely to be in deterring crime. Similar models can be used to analyse decisions within the family, such as the circumstances under which husbands or wives are more likely to go out to work, and even whether changes in economic factors will raise or lower the chances of couples deciding to marry or to divorce. These developments have led to economists becoming the butt of many jokes, such as in an article on the economics of brushing teeth which parodied Becker's method of analysis.[2]

Another applied field that has extended the boundaries of economics is public-choice theory. Although this field has origins that go further back, in particular to the theory of voting and Arrow's impossibility theorem, it originates with the work of Buchanan, Tullock, Downs and Olson around 1960. This applied standard economic techniques to decisions by governments and bureaucracies. Voters, politicians and bureaucrats were all assumed to be rational agents who maximized their own utility. Inability to monitor their actions perfectly and the impossibility of designing contracts that covered every eventuality gave rise to the possibility of government failure. These ideas, however, did more than add a new topic to existing courses in microeconomic theory. 'Public choice' developed as an identifiable applied field, and in the 1970s it acquired its own scholarly society and journal. It went off in new directions. There were several reasons for this. The fact that the two most influential public-choice theorists, Buchanan and Tullock, were to the right of the political spectrum may have helped them obtain funding more easily than might otherwise have been the case. Probably more important, however, was the fact that they preferred verbal arguments to mathematical models. This set them apart from the bulk of the profession and may, at least in part, explain why they found it difficult to get their work published in the major journals. Once regular conferences, graduate programmes and specialist journals were established, it became possible for public choice to develop in ways that would not otherwise have been possible.

This type of imperialism raises difficult questions about where the boundaries of economics should be drawn. Should rational-choice sociology, which has affinities with Becker's work, be regarded as economics? Should public-choice theory be regarded as political science? In themselves, these questions are not interesting. The boundaries of academic disciplines are artificial constructions. However, the fluidity of the boundaries of modern economics echoes similar changes that have taken place over the history of the subject. For most of the period covered by this book, economics did not exist as a distinct discipline. Early chapters trace ideas about questions that we now define as 'economic' in writings on law, philosophy and theology. Even after the subject emerged, in England, as a distinct body of ideas around the beginning of the nineteenth century, its boundaries remained very fluid. They could hardly be otherwise when the identities of 'neighbouring' disciplines (such as psychology, sociology, geography and political science) were also not clear.

The process of differentiation continued throughout the twentieth century as new disciplines and new fields in economics emerged. The development of management science raised a fresh set of boundary questions. For example, personnel management – now clearly located in management – was at one time considered part of economics. Another example is economic history, settled uneasily on the boundaries of economics and history, with its place influenced by institutional factors as well as by intellectual developments. In the field of development, economics, politics and sociology continually confronted each other. (Hirschman described his career as involving 'crossing boundaries' and 'trespassing'.)[3] Demography, associated with economics since Petty and Graunt, has almost dropped out of the discipline, even though it thrives. New developments such as public-choice theory and rational-choice sociology continually challenge conventional assumptions about where boundaries should be drawn.

Many of these are developments of which many other social scientists have been critical. Economists have spoken of economics as the 'hardest' of the social sciences (on account of its use of rigorous mathematical theory, comparable with that used in physics) or as the 'queen of the social sciences'. The response to this has been to regard economists as arrogant and imperialistic.

Heterodox Economics

The last quarter of the twentieth century saw enormous homogenization within the mainstream of economic thought. When economics became professionalized towards the end of the nineteenth century, there was still great variety within the discipline. It encompassed historical economics (especially in Germany), a wide variety of interpretations of marginalism (from the mathematical approach of Walras and Fisher to the less mathematical and very different approaches of J. B. Clark and the Austrians), Veblen's evolutionary economics, and Commons's law-based institutional economics. The historian may look back and say that these were all 'economics' in some sense, but it is hard to claim that this plethora of approaches rested on a single foundation. The differences between, for example, Fisher, Commons and Veblen were simply too great.

In the second half of the twentieth century, however, this began to change. On the basis of developments that took place during the 1930s – notably new ways of modelling individual behaviour and Keynesian macroeconomics – the range of approaches began to narrow significantly. Most noticeably, historical economics was either assimilated (it became applications of standard economics) or pushed aside into other fields, and institutionalism withered away as a significant force in the discipline. However, there was still no uniform approach to the subject. It was accepted that general-equilibrium theory – the dominant paradigm in microeconomics – could not explain everything. As a result, Keynesian macroeconomics and development economics were regarded as distinct, each being appropriate to its distinctive subject matter. Even industrial economics, centred on the structure–conduct–performance paradigm, developed as a partly autonomous, empirically driven discipline.

From the 1970s, however, with the waning of Keynesianism, this too began to change. There was a narrowing of the subject as field after field came to be based on rigorous rational-choice foundations. The mathematical level of the discipline moved up a step. For most of the profession, increasingly dominated by those trained after 1950, who took for granted the need for mathematics in economics, these changes constituted progress. Even when economists disagreed with the assumptions being made (for example, those underlying the new classical macroeconomics), most of them could accept the principle that more rigorous theorizing was essential. There were, however, minorities whose dissent remained more radical.

Some dissenting groups have a long history. Marxist economics, sustained by its political dimension, goes back to the nineteenth century. American institutionalism never completely died out. John Kenneth Galbraith (1908–), whose *The Affluent Society* (1958) offered a withering critique of consumerism and the role of large corporations in American society, fits into the institutionalist tradition. However, though he became president of the American Economic Association, and though his books were best-sellers, his ideas were never taken seriously by the majority of the profession. (In 1950, on the eve of what became known as the German economic miracle, he told the American Economic Association that removing price controls would wreck the German economy.) In the 1970s, however, the coalescing of economics around a central core stimulated the rise of new 'heterodox' groupings that brought together economists who felt that their ideas were being systematically excluded from the profession's main journals. In 1973 Alfred Eichner (1937–88) and Jan Kregel (1944–) argued the case for a 'post-Keynesian' alternative to orthodox economics. This was to integrate Eichner's theory of oligopoly pricing with Keynesian economics as interpreted in particular by Joan Robinson. She had never accepted the IS–LM interpretation of the *General Theory*, and in her later career she repudiated her earlier work on imperfect competition, along with neoclassical economics, as paying insufficient attention to problems of time and uncertainty. Using terminology from the historian of science Thomas Kuhn (1922–96), Eichner and Kregel argued that post-Keynesian economics offered a new paradigm for the subject: a radically new conceptual framework within which to think about economic problems.

Another dissenting movement that emerged at this time was 'radical economics', established after the 1968 meeting of the American Economic Association. This grew out of disillusion with the American Establishment and opposition to the Vietnam War. Radical economics had much in common with Marxist economics, in that it emphasized exploitation, discrimination and the inequalities produced by American society, and was critical of the role of the military in the American economy. However, it did not commit itself to the Marxist theoretical framework, and sought new ways to analyse these issues. Like post-Keynesian economics, it became established as an identifiable group (the Union of Radical Political Economy) within the profession.

At around the same time, 'Austrian' economics began to coalesce into an organized, heterodox school of economics. A conference in 1974 brought together a wide-ranging group of economists, united in finding inspiration in the work of Carl Menger and his followers, in particular Mises and Hayek, who had been marginalized by post-war developments. Politically, the Austrians were conservative (in contrast with the radicals and post-Keynesians, who identified clearly with the Left), and they had considerable success in raising private funds. They emphasized methodological individualism (the doctrine that economic theories should be based on theories about individual behaviour), and they viewed individuals as economizing (making choices in response to the prices and opportunities they faced). However, like Menger, they refused to model this using mathematics, preferring to rely on verbal logic. They took up Hayek's view, which had dropped out of orthodox economics, of competition as a dynamic process – a discovery procedure – viewing the market as a means for disseminating information in a changing, uncertain world.

One of the main reasons why heterodox groups began to organize was the perceived trend towards greater homogeneity of the mainstream. In an environment where academic economists were under continual pressure to publish, economists with unorthodox views felt threatened, and organization was important for their survival. That they were able to organize was a result of the profession having become sufficiently large that it could accommodate dissenting groups. Dissenters were not spread uniformly across universities, but relied on particular institutions for support. Chicago (with Friedman, George Stigler (1911–91), Becker and Lucas) was the centre of orthodox free-market economics, and Yale, Harvard and MIT (Massachusetts Institute of Technology) were the centres of orthodox Keynesianism. Public-choice theory (close to being heterodox, though not quite deserving of the label) was centred in Virginia, and Austrian economics in the New York and Auburn universities. The variety of the American university system was vital.

New Concepts and New Techniques

At the same time as self-styled heterodox economists were trying to break loose from what they saw as the stranglehold of an increasingly entrenched orthodoxy, that orthodoxy began to change. New concepts and new techniques were developed, and these enabled economists to tackle problems that had previously been considered beyond formal economic analysis. Many of these developments are too recent for it to be possible to assess their long-term significance in any detail, but it is nonetheless important to consider them. They illustrate the great variety of ways in which the boundaries of economics are being extended. More important, they show how strands in what is considered mainstream or orthodox economics have abandoned what were previously considered to be central elements in orthodox theory. For example, at one time it would have been said that orthodox 'neoclassical' economics assumed perfect information. However, from the 1960s even Chicago economists – notably Stigler – began to work with theories in which agents had only imperfect or limited information about their environment. These developments explain why it is that many economists fail to recognize the picture painted by 'heterodox' economists of a discipline dominated by a monolithic orthodoxy.

The first example is the set of developments centred on the concept of transaction costs. Transaction costs are the costs of transferring ownership from one person to another. They arise for many reasons:

The parties to a contract have to find each other, they have to communicate and to exchange information. The goods must be described, inspected, weighed and measured. Contracts must be drawn up, lawyers may be consulted, title is transferred and records have to be kept. In some cases, compliance needs to be enforced through legal action and breach of contract may lead to litigation.[4]

The term 'transaction cost' was first used by Marschak in 1950, but the idea has a long history. Economists frequently referred to 'frictions', and used the metaphor of money being the oil that reduces such frictions. In the 1920s Commons argued that transactions (which he defined very broadly, to include much more than the exchange of goods and services) should form the focus of economists' attention. In 1937 Coase argued that transaction costs could explain the existence and size of firms. Coase pointed out that activities could be organized in two ways. One is through the market. The other is by management within a firm. Both methods involve transaction costs, but the costs are different. He then argued that the boundary of the firm – the dividing line between activities organized managerially and those that are organized through the market – should be the one that minimizes transaction costs. In other words, transaction costs explain why firms should exist (why some transactions are undertaken outside the market) and why the economy is not organized as one giant firm (a centrally planned economy). It was not until around 1970 that economists began to see the significance of Coase's idea. Oliver Williamson (1932–) and others began to find ways to make the idea of transaction costs operational. They used it to answer questions such as why certain industries are vertically integrated (the same firms control the supply of materials, production and distribution) whereas others are not.

The significance of this idea was that it offered an alternative to the conventional theory of the firm. The traditional view saw the firm as a technical unit for transforming inputs into outputs. Its size was determined by technology – steel firms are large because production costs are lower for larger firms than for smaller ones, whereas greengrocers can be small because small shops can be as efficient as large ones. Coase, instead, saw the firm as an organization or, as Williamson put it, as a governance structure. This is, of course, obvious. However, it was not until Coase introduced the idea of transaction costs that economists had any way in which to analyse this. Many economists had studied the organization of industry (a classic example is Marshall's *Industry and Trade*, 1919), but such work was largely descriptive. Economists had not found a theoretical framework that could explain why industries were organized as they were. 'Industrial organization' existed as a field within economics, and courses were taught, but they focused on problems such as monopoly, regulation and anti-trust laws. They took the way industry was organized as a datum.

As reinterpreted by Coase, Williamson and others, the theory of the firm becomes a theory about the efficiency of different types of contract. This is an example of a much broader problem – the economic analysis of the law. This field – usually known as 'law and economics' – began to develop in its modern form in the mid-1960s. A 1960 article by Coase on social cost[5] argued that the establishing of property rights (a legal question) was crucial to any efficient solution of externality problems. He analysed how the courts in Britain and the United States had tackled the problem, claiming that the way in which judges had interpreted phrases such as 'reasonable' and 'common or ordinary use' frequently reflected economic considerations. Property rights were also analysed by Armen Alchian (1914–) and Harold Demsetz (1930–). Another dimension was provided by work on torts, such as that by Guido Calabresi (1932–). Though it remained distinct, this work fitted well with the emerging field of public-choice theory.

Although it provoked much empirical research, the concept of trans-action cost was a theoretical innovation – a new way of thinking about economic phenomena. In contrast, experimental economics involved the creation of a new empirical procedure whereby economic theories could be tested. Like the concept of transaction costs, it has a long history. Psychologists have always used experiments to establish and test theories about behaviour, and economists followed suit. The modern literature on the subject dates from the 1930s and 1940s, and the early work addressed several types of problem. The earliest was the use of experiments to determine consumers' preference. In 1931 L. L. Thurstone (1887–1955) did this by asking subjects, repeatedly, to choose between alternative bundles of goods. This was strongly criticized (subjects were not making real choices), but in the early 1950s other economists continued this type of study. A second type of work was the use of experiments to find out how markets operated. In 1948 Chamberlin constructed an experiment to find out whether a group of subjects would hit on the competitive-equilibrium price at which supply equalled demand.

Interest in both types of experiment increased significantly after the publication of von Neumann and Morgenstern's 1944 book on game theory (see p. 263). During the 1950s and 1960s, however – even though some influential results were discovered, and systematic attention began to be paid to questions of how experiments should be conducted – experimental economics remained small-scale. In the 1970s the subject attracted more funding, including support from the National Science Foundation in the USA, and it grew rapidly. By the end of the 1980s it had become a generally recognized (if still controversial) way to do research in economics, and by the end of the 1990s it had entered the mainstream, in that it was discussed in introductory textbooks. It had ceased to be an activity undertaken only by specialists.

The significance of experimental economics is twofold. It provides a way to test economic theories in a manner that had previously been thought impossible. Unfortunately, as far as many economists are concerned, it suggests that some of the fundamental assumptions made by economists, such as utility maximization, are probably false. Experimental evidence suggests that people do not behave as they would if they were maximizing utility. Some economists have responded by developing theories of decision-making that reconcile experimental results with utility maximization. Others simply ignore such results, sometimes expressing scepticism about whether the artificial conditions of the laboratory (often involving students playing abstract games of chance to earn small sums of money) reflect real-world situations.

Experimental economics has also provided a way to try out alternative ideas about how institutions should be designed. For example, much work has been undertaken on auctions. When it was suggested that the winners of competitive tenders for oilfields systematically earned low returns, experiments were able to confirm the phenomenon of the 'winner's curse'. The idea behind this is that, if firms are bidding for oil rights or some other asset whose value is unknown, the winner will typically be someone who has overestimated the asset's value. This provides bidders with an incentive to be cautious in their bids. This is the rationale for awarding contracts to the second-highest bidder: knowing that a bid will be successful only if one other bidder is willing to pay more makes it safer to put in a high bid. Auction design has been an area where experiments have proved useful in testing ideas that economic theorists have produced.

Experimental economics requires organization and resources. (It is now generally considered that real money has to change hands if experimental subjects are to behave as they would in real life.) The establishing of the field in the 1980s and 1990s is therefore to be explained in terms of the sociology of the profession. However, there is in principle no reason why it could not have emerged much earlier had economists been less suspicious of such work.

In contrast, modern econometric methods would have been impossible without recent technological developments. The availability of cheap, powerful computers has been crucial to the transformation of the statistical techniques available to economists. Many of the estimation methods and statistical tests that have proliferated in the past twenty years would have been inconceivable without modern computers.

The use of computers has also produced data that would have been impossible to imagine even ten years ago. For example, the computerization of trading in financial markets means that it is possible to monitor stock prices and individual transactions minute by minute. The result is data sets that contain enough information to study the detailed operation of these markets, such as the way in which news affects prices. The use of new econometric techniques and the availability of large data sets have transformed empirical research in this area. Similarly, computers have made it possible for labour economists to study samples of thousands of individuals. Using such large data sets, economists can calculate things such as the effect on employment of a change in unemployment benefits while controlling for the effects of differences in personal characteristics (gender, education, health and employment history, and so on).

Economics in the Twentieth Century

In 1912, Schumpeter summarized contemporary developments in economics in the following words:

The more we approach modern times the less possible it becomes to characterize briefly the wealth of currents and cross-currents and the more untrue, forced and misleading appears any systematic arrangement and grouping . . . We must add that hand in hand with the progressing specialization resulting from the increase of the subject-matter and from the advances in analysis, which turned many of the best workers into laymen in all branches except their own special ones, a tendency established itself in most recent times to break down the barriers between the various specialized branches.[6]

Though written nearly a century ago, these words sum up many of the themes discussed in the last five or six chapters of this book. Economics, especially since the middle of the twentieth century, has become much larger. The number of economists has increased, as have the range of fields covered by the discipline and the amount to be learned about each. In this book, order was imposed by picking out certain very broad themes, from the rise of mathematical economics and econometrics to the expanded role played by economists in advising governments. However, although a sometimes-bewildering variety of ideas is discussed, even more has been left out. Schumpeter's judgement that as we approach modern times it becomes less possible to offer a brief characterization of the subject remains well justified.

When we turn to Schumpeter's vision of the structure of the discipline, the picture is much more complicated. He wrote at a time when the institution of the academic school, based in a particular institution and often dominated by a single individual (Schmoller and Marshall being the best examples in economics), was at its zenith. Such groupings were, he argued, becoming less important:

The slogans used to designate certain outstanding groups are much simpler than is warranted by the actual conditions. These slogans, moreover, are partly coloured by non-scientific factors ... [T]hey appear with a claim to universal validity, while in fact in every branch of the social sciences, and often with different problems in the same branch, conditions are different.[7]

In other words, the slogans about historical and theoretical methods were oversimplified. People had to use different methods alongside each other, with the result that barriers between different specializations were breaking down.

However, although the academic school as Schumpeter had known it was coming to an end, the division of the subject into schools of thought continued. During the inter-war period, American economics exhibited a variety of approaches, loosely covered by the extremely oversimplified labels of 'institutionalism' (notably Commons, Mitchell and Veblen) and 'neoclassical economics' (of which J. B. Clark and Fisher were the most eminent representatives). In Britain there was the divide between the Cambridge school (continued by Pigou and Keynes) and LSE (where Robbins and Hayek had displaced the historical approach of the Webbs).

In the post-war period, schools continued, their character changing yet again. The neoclassical synthesis of Keynesian economics and general-equilibrium theory developed into the dominant orthodoxy. Self-consciously heterodox schools (such as Austrians and post-Keynesians) formed in rebellion against this. These, however, remained numerically small and marginal to the discipline. More important was the emergence of new approaches to the subject from within the mainstream. These approaches shared much with the prevailing view, but pursued different, controversial, lines of inquiry, with the result that labels such as 'orthodox' or 'heterodox' were hard to apply. Examples include Friedman's 'monetarism' and the Chicago school – resolutely 'neoclassical' and yet challenging the consensus – public-choice theory, transaction-cost economics and so on.

In the late nineteenth century, schools were associated with hierarchical university systems and a lack of international communication and publication opportunities. In contrast, a century later, schools were made possible by easy communications and the burgeoning variety of outlets for economic research. Present-day schools may be dominated by the work of certain individuals, but this is usually because those individuals' ideas have stimulated others to emulate them. Schools are more diffuse and more fluid than a century earlier, for they comprise networks of like-minded economists who do not necessarily share any institutional ties other than choosing to publish in certain places and to join certain societies. The boundaries and significance of schools change as some ideas become common currency and others become unfashionable.

Similar remarks can be made about applied fields. On one hand, the growth of the discipline has increased the barriers between fields (as

Schumpeter perceived). For example, it is difficult for a single economist to be familiar, in detail, with the latest developments in more than one or two fields. This effect has been reinforced by the emergence of specialized journals and conferences, which make it much easier to be unaware of what is happening in other fields. On the other hand, there are forces operating to reduce these barriers. The emergence of a common core of economic theory has served to unify fields. It is possible to be an expert in a particular set of techniques and to apply these in a variety of fields. This means that a theorist who works on models of imperfect competition may write articles on industrial organization, macroeconomics and international trade. Whereas, for previous generations, 'macro' and 'micro' were very separate disciplines, the barrier between them became much lower during the 1980s and 1990s.

Schumpeter had hoped that the 'non-scientific factors' behind the slogans of various groups would diminish, that economists would stop making excessive claims for their ideas. It seems safe to say that this has not happened. General-equilibrium theory and then game theory have both held out hopes of providing the organizing framework within which disputes might be clarified and resolved. However, while some disputes have been resolved, new ones have emerged and old ones have re-emerged. Econometrics has made enormous advances, but its power to settle theoretical disputes arguably remains extremely controversial. Schumpeter's hope of developing scientific economic techniques that would render economics uncontroversial remains a chimera. On top of this, the increased competitiveness of the academic system provides people with an incentive to oversell their ideas – to claim excessive originality. To achieve tenure in an American university typically requires publication of half a dozen articles, and few economists can expect to have this many genuinely original ideas by their late twenties. Once past this barrier, promotion and salary depend on regular publication, and reputations are made by claiming much, not by being modest. The founder of a controversial school will be rewarded by frequent citations of his or her work, and high citation counts are taken as a measure of prestige. Ending a controversy does not produce many citations. On top of this, politics and ideology intrude as much as ever.

Epilogue: Economists and Their History

There have been times in the history of economics in which there has been a strong tendency towards integration. Schumpeter identified two such 'classical situations' in the subject. The first emerged after 1890, based on Smith's *Wealth of Nations*. The second emerged from the innovations made by Jevons, Walras and Carl Menger after the controversy with the historical school had settled down: 'the leading works exhibited a large expanse of common ground and suggest a feeling of repose, both of which created, in the superficial observer, an impression of finality – the finality of a Greek temple that spreads its perfect lines against a cloudless sky'.[1] In such situations it was natural for economists to adopt attitudes such as 'It's all in Marshall.'

It can be argued that the period around 1960 – the age of the 'neoclassical synthesis' – also constituted such a classical situation. Keynes had provided a framework on which macroeconomics could be based, and Hicks, Samuelson, Arrow and Debreu had shown how microeconomics could be built around general-equilibrium theory. Patinkin had synthesized micro- and macroeconomics, and the Cowles Commission had shown how theoretical models could be tested against the rapidly growing quantity of statistical data.

In a time of integration, it becomes easy to view the past from the point of view of the present. McCulloch and many nineteenth-century economists were able to take the view that Adam Smith had established the basic framework of the subject and that all that remained was to fill in the details. In similar vein, Schumpeter was confident that there was one general-equilibrium system and that Walras had discovered it. This enabled him to make remarks such as:

as far as pure theory is concerned, Walras is in my opinion the greatest of all economists. His system of economic equilibrium . . . is the only work by an economist that will stand comparison with the achievements of theoretical physics. Compared with it, most of the theoretical writings of that period – and beyond – . . . look like boats beside a liner, like inadequate attempts to catch some particular aspect of Walrasian truth.[2]

For Schumpeter, Walrasian general-equilibrium theory provided the integrating framework within which all economics could be understood. The history of economic theory was the history of attempts to perceive what Walras was the first to see clearly. For the economists of the neoclassical synthesis, influenced so strongly by Walras, the classic history was *Economic Theory in Retrospect* (1962) by Mark Blaug (1927–). This resolutely sought to appraise past ideas from the perspective provided by contemporary economics. Past economists' ideas were recast using modern theoretical tools.

However, this period of integrative tendencies during which one might have said 'It's all in Samuelson [or Keynes, or Hicks, or Arrow, or Patinkin]' did not last. It has been followed by a proliferation of schools. In macroeconomics there are Keynesians, post-Keynesians, New Keynesians, traditional monetarists, real-business-cycle theorists, and others. In addition, there are econometricians whose approach is inductive, and applied economists who spurn both abstract theories and technical econometrics. In microeconomics there are game theorists general-equilibrium theorists, transaction-cost theorists, experimental economists sceptical about rational-choice theory, Paretian welfare economics, social-choice theory, and various non-Paretian approaches to welfare. 'New' fields (including new growth theory, new economic geography and new trade theory) proliferate. The emphasis is on the originality, or at least partial originality, of ideas.

In such a world, appraising the past from the perspective of the present becomes much more difficult. There are too many modern theories to choose from, each of which may give a different perspective on the past. History starts to matter much more, because it is the only way to get a sense of where the subject is going amid the welter of competing claims. It becomes important for the professional historian of the discipline to expand and correct the partial and often biased histories that economists create in order to justify and explain what they and their colleagues are doing.

In a classical situation, when economic theories are being integrated into a generally accepted framework, it is common to write the history of economics as one of progress. The story can be told by tracing the history of central economic ideas from their inchoate origins in the ancient, medieval or early-modern worlds through to their present-day incarnations. For example, the history of supply and demand in competitive markets can be traced from the ancients, through the scholastics and early-modern writers, to Adam Smith. After Smith, the story becomes one of increasing precision and mathematical rigour, culminating in the work of Arrow and Debreu. Although it may exhibit numerous detours and false trails on the way, the story is one of progress: economic theories become more refined, more rigorous, and more clearly focused on specifically economic problems. Alongside this runs a story of improvements in the data and statistical techniques available to economists.

Such histories, however, conceal as much as they reveal. Behind the façade of increased mathematical rigour and precision lie fundamental changes in the meanings that have been attached to central concepts and in the ways in which economists have understood what they were doing. For Adam Smith and his contemporaries, competition was a process: people competed with each other in the same way that horses competed on the racecourse. Smith spoke of the system of 'natural liberty' or of 'free competition', in which one man could bring his capital into competition with that of any other person. As the concept of competition became formalized and mathematized, however, this concept of competition became lost. Following the lead of Cournot, the profession moved towards a theory of 'perfect' competition. Perfect competition was a situation in which buyers and sellers were so numerous that no buyer or seller had any influence on price and in which no producer was able to earn more than normal profits. Competition had ceased to be a process and had become an end-state – a situation under which no firm had any incentive to engage in competitive activities. As late as the 1930s, economists were still aware of this distinction. Chamberlin, for example, wrote:

One never hears of 'competition' in connection with the great markets [i.e. commodity markets], and the phrases 'price cutting', 'underselling', 'unfair competition', 'meeting competition', 'securing a market', etc. are unknown. No wonder the principles of such a [perfectly competitive] market seem so unreal when applied to the 'business' world where these terms have meaning.[3]

However, by the 1960s the earlier, dynamic, concept was virtually lost. The economics profession failed to understand Hayek because it failed to realize that he was working with the older, process, version of competition.

This example raises doubts about whether the concept of progress itself may be misleading. What constitutes a 'detour' is crucially dependent on what one takes to be the true story against which progress and regress are to be judged. In a period of proliferating schools, it is easier for economists to understand these problems. Different schools will construct their own histories, picking out those ideas that provide a route into their own, while being aware that other stories can be told. The role of the historian is to bring these stories together, correcting and amplifying them where appropriate, showing where they fit into a larger story. The history that is written ceases to be either conservative (celebrating the achievements of modern economics) or revolutionary (revealing its fatal errors in order to overthrow contemporary orthodoxy). It serves to provide economists with a vision of where their own work fits into a wider story.

A Note on the Literature

In one sense, the best suggestion for further reading is to read the original sources cited in the text. Many of these are as accessible as modern commentaries. Smith and J. S. Mill, for example, wrote for a wide audience, and it is tempting to say that no one's economic education is complete without having read them. The suggestions offered here, however, are almost entirely secondary sources. Listing them also serves as a way of acknowledging some of the works on which I drew in writing this book. Nevertheless, I should point out that this list does not indicate everything I read while writing this book. There are many books that I found helpful but which are reflected in only a single sentence or even a short phrase. To list all these would stretch the patience of publisher and readers. In particular, I have cited only references that discuss economic ideas directly. General histories on which I relied for background information are not mentioned here.

Readers should be warned that the dual function of this bibliography means that the technical level of the material listed varies considerably.

General Reading

There exist many histories of economic thought, most written by economists. Perhaps the classic is

J. A. Schumpeter, *History of Economic Analysis*, London: Allen & Unwin, 1954; Routledge, 1986.

Although some of Schumpeter's judgements have not stood up to more recent scholarship, this remains an outstanding book. Also useful is

J. A. Schumpeter, *Ten Great Economists: From Marx to Keynes*, New York: Oxford University Press, 1951; London: Routledge, 1997.

For a more recent attempt to provide a history of economics on the same scale as Schumpeter's *magnum opus*, see

M. Perlman and C. R. McCann, *The Pillars of Economic Understanding*: Vol. 1, *Ideas and Traditions*; Vol. 2, *Factors and Markets*, Ann Arbor, Mich.: University of Michigan Press, 1998, 2000.

Among many textbooks, two stand out:

M. Blaug, *Economic Theory in Retrospect*, 5th edn, Cambridge: Cambridge University Press, 1997;

H. W. Spiegel, *The Growth of Economic Thought*, 3rd edn, Durham, N.C.: Duke University Press, 1991.

Blaug reviews economic ideas from the late eighteenth century to the present day from the point of view of modern economic theory in a manner likely to be accessible only to those trained in economics. Spiegel is wide-ranging and provides a particularly thorough coverage of early material. It is also worth mentioning two sets of lectures, both transcribed from tape recordings and students' notes:

W. C. Mitchell, *Types of Economic Theory: from Mercantilism to Institutionalism*, ed. J. Dorfman, 2 vols., New York: A. M. Kelley, 1967;

L. C. Robbins, *A History of Economic Thought: The LSE Lectures*, Princeton: Princeton University Press, 1998.

The above books are all very substantial works. Readers wanting something shorter and less comprehensive should try the following:

R. L. Heilbroner, *The Worldly Philosophers*, Harmondsworth: Penguin Books, 1973.

The same author has compiled a volume of short extracts from original sources together with brief commentaries:

R. L. Heilbroner, *Teachings from the Worldly Philosophy*, New York: W. W. Norton, 1996.

For readable essays on a selection of important twentieth-century economists, see

W. Breit and R. L. Ransom, *The Academic Scribblers*, 3rd edn, Princeton: Princeton University Press, 1998.

Finally I mention two of my own books. The first attempts to place a selection of economic ideas in the context of the corresponding periods'

economic history. The second focuses on the twentieth century and provided the starting point for some of the later chapters in this book:

R. E. Backhouse, *Economists and the Economy: The Evolution of
  Economic Ideas*, 2nd edn, New Brunswick, N.J.: Transaction Press,
  1994;
R. E. Backhouse, *A History of Modern Economic Analysis*, Oxford:
  Basil Blackwell, 1985.
  Useful reference books include
M. Blaug, *Great Economists before Keynes* and *Great Economists since
  Keynes*, Cheltenham: Edward Elgar, 1997, 1998;
M. Blaug, *Who's Who in Economics*, 3rd edn, Cheltenham: Edward
  Elgar, 1999;
S. Pressman, *Fifty Major Economists*, London: Routledge, 1999.
The most valuable reference work, however, is
J. Eatwell, M. Milgate and P. Newman (eds.), *The New Palgrave: A
  Dictionary of Economics*, 4 vols., London: Macmillan, 1987.
This contains numerous biographical entries as well as entries on
important topics. It can be daunting finding the information required,
but there is a lot of material there.

The Internet

Much material on this subject is available over the Internet. One of
the main sources of out-of-copyright texts, mostly from the sixteenth
to the nineteenth centuries, is the site maintained by Rod Hay at
McMaster University: http://socserv2.socsci.mcmaster.ca/~econ/ugcm/
3113/index. html, with a UK mirror at http://www.ecn.bris.ac.uk/het/
index.htm. The History of Economics Society's site at http://www.
eh.net/HE contains links to further sites.

Ancient and Medieval Economics

Of the textbooks mentioned above, Spiegel is particularly good on this
period. A general survey is provided in

B. Gordon, *Economic Analysis before Adam Smith: Hesiod to Lessius*, London: Macmillan, 1975.

The work of writers from ancient Greece to sixteenth-century scholastics is discussed in

S. T. Lowry and B. Gordon (eds.), *Ancient and Medieval Economic Ideas and Concepts of Social Justice*, Leiden: E. J. Brill, 1998;

B. B. Price (ed.), *Ancient Economic Thought*, London: Routledge, 1997.

The most comprehensive account of ancient Greek ideas, focusing on the idea of an administrative order, is

S. T. Lowry, *The Archaeology of Economic Ideas: The Classical Greek Tradition*, Durham, N.C.: Duke University Press, 1987.

The outstanding writer on scholastic economics is Odd Langholm, who has written a series of books on the subject. The best starting points in his work are his article in the Lowry and Gordon collection cited above and

O. Langholm, *The Legacy of Scholasticism in Economic Thought: Antecedents of Choice and Power*, Cambridge: Cambridge University Press, 1998.

Focusing on the link between justice and compulsion, this book also offers valuable insights into ancient and particularly Roman thought, as well as some links to seventeenth-century and more recent economic thought. The period is also covered by

L. Baeck, *The Mediterranean Tradition in Economic Thought*, London: Routledge, 1994.

Early Modern Economics

A useful collection of primary texts (including translations from languages other than English) is

A. E. Monroe, *Early Economic Thought: Selections from Economic Literature Prior to Adam Smith*, Cambridge, Mass.: Harvard University Press, 1965.

Spanish writings are translated, with commentary, in

M. Grice Hutchison, *The School of Salamanca: Readings in Spanish Monetary Theory, 1544–1605*, Oxford: Clarendon Press, 1952.

For further essays on Spanish thought, see

M. Grice Hutchison, *Economic Thought in Spain*, ed. L. S. Moss and C. K. Ryan, Cheltenham: Edward Elgar, 1993.

The literature on mercantilism goes beyond economic thought to economic policy and economic history. It is, however, worth mentioning what is probably the classic work and some volumes containing reprints of many articles on the subject:

M. Blaug (ed.), *Pioneers in Economics*: Vol. 4, *The Early Mercantilists*; Vol. 5, *The Later Mercantilists*, Cheltenham: Edward Elgar, 1991;

D. C. Coleman (ed.), *Revisions in Mercantilism*, London: Methuen, 1969;

E. Heckscher, *Mercantilism* (1935), 2 vols., London: Routledge, 1994.

Almost compulsory reading on the economic and political thought of this period is

A. O. Hirschman, *The Passions and the Interests: Political Arguments for Capitalism before its Triumph*, Princeton: Princeton University Press, 1977.

English writings are discussed in

J. O. Appleby, *Economic Thought and Ideology in Seventeenth-Century England*, Princeton: Princeton University Press, 1978;

W. Letwin, *The Origins of Scientific Economics: English Economic Thought, 1660–1776*, London: Methuen, 1963;

B. E. Supple, *Commercial Crisis and Change in England, 1600–1642*, Cambridge: Cambridge University Press, 1959.

The only comprehensive survey of the eighteenth century prior to Smith is

T. W. Hutchison, *Before Adam Smith: The Emergence of Political Economy, 1662–1776*, Oxford: Basil Blackwell, 1988.

Biographies of two of the period's most important writers are

A. Murphy, *John Law: Economic Theorist and Policy-Maker*, Oxford: Clarendon Press, 1997;

A. Murphy, *Richard Cantillon: Entrepreneur and Economist*, Oxford: Clarendon Press, 1986.

For a discussion of Cantillon's ideas, see

A. A. Brewer, *Richard Cantillon: Pioneer of Economic Theory*, London: Routledge, 1992.

The Enlightenment and Classical Economics

Once we reach the Physiocrats, Adam Smith and classical economics, the volume of literature, both primary and secondary, expands dramatically. The following represents an even tinier proportion of what is available than is the case with previous periods. A useful short introduction is provided in

D. Winch, 'The emergence of economics as a science, 1750–1870', in C. M. Cipolla (ed.), *The Fontana Economic History of Europe*, Vol. 3, *The Industrial Revolution*, London: Fontana, 1973, Chapter 9.

A useful collection of eighteenth-century readings is contained in

R. L. Meek (ed.), *Precursors of Adam Smith, 1750–1775*, London: Dent, 1973.

On the Physiocrats and Turgot, see

W. A. Eltis, *The Classical Theory of Economic Growth*, London: Macmillan, 1984;

P. D. Groenewegen, *The Economics of A. R. J. Turgot*, The Hague: Martinus Nijhoff, 1977.

As its title implies, the former also discusses classical economics. For an outstanding and concise survey of this subject see

D. P. O'Brien, *The Classical Economists*, Oxford: Clarendon Press, 1975.

Because of his status (whether deserved or not) as a free-market icon and as the major figure in classical economics, one of the most intensively researched areas in the history of economic thought, the literature on Adam Smith is vast. Recent literature is surveyed in

V. Brown, ' "Mere Inventions of the Imagination": a survey of recent literature on Adam Smith', *Economics and Philosophy*, 13 (2), 1997, pp. 281–312.

Mention has to be made of the work of Andrew Skinner, one of the editors of the 'Glasgow' edition of Smith's books (reprinted by Liberty Classics):

A. S. Skinner, *A System of Social Science: Papers Relating to Adam Smith*, Oxford: Clarendon Press, 1979.

See also

D. D. Raphael, *Adam Smith*, Oxford: Clarendon Press, 1985.

The transition to classical economics has been placed in its political context in

E. Rothschild, *Economic Sentiments: Adam Smith, Condorcet and the Enlightenment*, Cambridge, Mass., and London: Harvard University Press, 2001;

D. Winch, *Riches and Poverty: An Intellectual History of Political Economy in Britain, 1750–1834*, Cambridge: Cambridge University Press, 1996.

(The former appeared too late to be used in writing this book.) See also

D. Winch, *Malthus*, Oxford: Oxford University Press, 1987.

From the mass of literature on Ricardo, one of the best accounts is

T. Peach, *Interpreting Ricardo*, Cambridge: Cambridge University Press, 1993.

Accessible editions of major works, with useful introductions, include

T. R. Malthus, *Essay on the Principle of Population*, ed. A. Flew, Harmondsworth: Penguin Books, 1970;

J. S. Mill, *Principles of Political Economy*, ed. D. Winch, Harmondsworth: Penguin Books, 1970;

D. Ricardo, *Principles of Political Economy and Taxation*, ed. R. M. Hartwell, Harmondsworth: Penguin Books, 1971;

A. Smith, *The Wealth of Nations*, ed. A. S. Skinner, Harmondsworth: Penguin Books, 1970.

The French engineering school is discussed in detail in

R. B. Ekelund and R. F. Hebert, *The Secret Origins of Modern Microeconomics: Dupuit and the Engineers*, Chicago: Chicago University Press, 1999.

The literature on Marx is voluminous. A small selection of the most accessible items includes

A. A. Brewer, *A Guide to Marx's Capital*, Cambridge: Cambridge University Press, 1984;

D. McLennan, *The Thought of Karl Marx*, London: Macmillan, 1971.

For a discussion of German economics in relation to Menger's marginalism, see

E. Streissler, 'The influence of German economics on the work of Menger and Marshall', in B. Caldwell (ed.), *Carl Menger and his Legacy in Economics*, Durham, N.C.: Duke University Press, 1990.

The Late Nineteenth and Early Twentieth Centuries

An old, though still extremely valuable, coverage of this period is provided by

T. W. Hutchison, *A Review of Economic Doctrines, 1870–1929*, Oxford: Oxford University Press, 1953.

A useful collection of essays on the so-called 'marginal revolution' is

R. D. C. Black, A. W. Coats and C. D. W. Goodwin (eds.), *The Marginal Revolution in Economics*, Durham, N.C.: Duke University Press, 1972.

Several essays on this period's economics in Britain and the United States are contained in Coats's two volumes of collected papers:

A. W. Coats, *British and American Essays*: Vol. 1, *On the History of Economic Thought*; Vol. 2, *The Sociology and Professionalization of Economics*, London: Routledge, 1992, 1993.

For more detailed discussion of Marshall and English historical economics see

P. D. Groenewegen, *A Soaring Eagle: Alfred Marshall, 1842–1924*, Cheltenham: Edward Elgar, 1995;

A. Kadish, *Historians, Economists and Economic History*, London: Routledge, 1989;

G. M. Koot, *English Historical Economics, 1870–1926*, Cambridge: Cambridge University Press, 1987;

J. Maloney, *The Professionalization of Economics: Alfred Marshall and the Dominance of Orthodoxy*, New Brunswick, N.J.: Transaction Publishers, 1991.

American economics is comprehensively surveyed in the five volumes of

J. Dorfman, *The Economic Mind in American Civilization*, 5 vols., New York: Viking, 1946–59.

Volumes 3–5 are particularly useful for the material covered here.

The transformation of American economics in the first half of the twentieth century is covered in the many essays in

M. S. Morgan and M. Rutherford (eds.), *From Interwar Pluralism to Postwar Neoclassicism*, Durham, N.C.: Duke University Press, 1998;

M. Rutherford, *The Economic Mind in America: Essays in the History of American Economics*, London: Routledge, 1998.

The period's monetary economics is brilliantly surveyed in

D. Laidler, *The Golden Age of the Quantity Theory*, Deddington: Philip Allan, 1991.

Also useful is

T. M. Humphrey, *Money, Banking and Inflation*, Cheltenham: Edward Elgar, 1993.

Microeconomics and Mathematical Economics in the Twentieth Century

This is a topic on which widely divergent views can be found, ranging from accounts premissed on the assumption that the mathematization of economics has been a great success to ones that regard it as a total failure. From this large literature, a helpful starting point can be found in a symposium in *Daedalus*, 1997, especially in contributions by R. M. Solow and D. Kreps, two eminent economic theorists. Another excellent short account is

M. S. Morgan, 'The formation of "modern" economics: engineering and ideology', in T. H. Porter and D. Ross (eds.), *The Cambridge History of Science*, Vol. 7, *Modern Social and Behavioural Sciences*, Cambridge: Cambridge University Press, forthcoming.

For very critical views of these developments see

M. Blaug, 'The formalist revolution or what happened to orthodox economics after World War II?', in R. E. Backhouse and J. Creedy (eds.), *From Classical Economics to the Theory of the Firm: Essays in Honour of D. P. O'Brien*, Cheltenham: Edward Elgar, 1999;

T. W. Hutchison, *Changing Aims in Economics*, Oxford: Basil Blackwell, 1992.

The history of general-equilibrium theory has been tackled by several people (the following will provide references to other works by the same authors):

B. Ingrao and G. Israel, *The Invisible Hand: Economic Equilibrium in the History of Science*, Cambridge, Mass.: MIT Press, 1990;

M. Mandler, *Dilemmas in Economic Theory: Persisting Foundational Problems of Microeconomics*, Oxford: Oxford University Press, 1999;

P. Mirowski, 'The when, the how and the why of mathematical expression in the history of economic analysis', *Journal of Economic Perspectives* 5, 1991, pp. 145–57;

E. R. Weintraub, *How Economics Became a Mathematical Science*, Durham, N.C.: Duke University Press, forthcoming.

The book by Mandler offers observations on a variety of aspects of microeconomics.

For reprints and translations of some influential works, see

W. J. Baumol and S. M. Goldfield (eds.), *Precursors in Mathematical Economics: An Anthology*. Series of Reprints of Scarce Works on Political Economy, 19, London: London School of Economics, 1968.

On game theory, Leonard's works are crucial:

R. J. Leonard, 'From parlor games to social science: von Neumann, Morgenstern and the creation of game theory, 1928–1944', *Journal of Economic Literature*, 33 (2), 1995, pp. 730–61;

R. J. Leonard, 'Reading Cournot, reading Nash: the creation and stabilisation of the Nash equilibrium', *Economic Journal*, 104, 1994, pp. 492–511.

See also

S. Nasar, *A Beautiful Mind*, London: Faber and Faber, 1999;

E. R. Weintraub (ed.), *Toward a History of Game Theory*, Durham, N.C.: Duke University Press, 1992.

The former is a biography of Nash.

One of the leading players in the rise of mathematical economics has given his own account of the genesis of his work:

P. A. Samuelson, 'How *Foundations* came to be', *Journal of Economic Literature*, 36 (3), 1998, pp. 1375–86.

The conceptions of competition in the socialist-calculation debate are thoroughly discussed in

D. Lavoie, *Rivalry and Central Planning*, Cambridge: Cambridge University Press, 1985.

Several of Hayek's articles and some useful modern commentaries are reprinted in

S. Littlechild (ed.), *Austrian Economics*, Vol. 3, Cheltenham: Edward Elgar, 1990.

The best introduction to theories of imperfect competition and the theory of the firm are

D. P. O'Brien, 'Research programmes in competitive structure', *Journal of Economic Studies*, 10, 1983, pp. 29–51, and 'The evolution of the theory of the firm', in F. H. Stephen (ed.), *Firms, Organization and Labour*, London: Macmillan, 1984. Both are reprinted in *Methodology, Money and the Firm: The Collected Essays of D. P. O'Brien*. 2 vols., Cheltenham: Edward Elgar, 1994;

A. Skinner, 'E. H. Chamberlin: the origins and development of monopolistic competition', *Journal of Economic Studies*, 10, 1983, pp. 52–67.

Quantitative Economics

On the history of US national-income accounting, see

C. Carson, 'The history of the United States national income and product accounts: the development of an analytical tool', *Review of Income and Wealth*, 21, 1975, pp. 153–81;

J. W. Duncan and W. C. Shelton, *Revolution in United States Government Statistics, 1926–1976*, Washington, DC: US Department of Commerce, 1978;

J. W. Kendrick, 'The historical development of national accounts', *History of Political Economy*, 2, 1970, pp. 284–315;

M. Perlman, 'Political purpose and the national accounts', in *The Character of Economic Thought, Economic Characters and Economic Institutions: Selected Essays of Mark Perlman*, Ann Arbor, Mich.: University of Michigan Press, 1996.

Stone's contribution is discussed in

L. Johansen, 'Richard Stone's contributions to economics', *Scandinavian Journal of Economics* 87 (1), 1985, pp. 4–32.

On the development of econometric techniques, see

R. J. Epstein, *A History of Econometrics*, Amsterdam: North Holland, 1987;

M. S. Morgan, *A History of Econometric Ideas*, Cambridge: Cambridge University Press, 1990.

Edited versions of early articles on the subject are reprinted with substantial commentary in

D. F. Hendry and M. S. Morgan (eds.), *The Foundations of Econometric Analysis*, Cambridge: Cambridge University Press, 1995.

There are several pieces on the history of the Cowles Commission, including

C. F. Christ, 'The Cowles Commission's contributions to econometrics at Chicago, 1939–55', *Journal of Economic Literature*, 32 (1), 1994, pp. 30–59;

C. F. Christ, 'History of the Cowles Commission 1932–1952', in Cowles Commission (ed.), *Economic Theory and Measurement*, Chicago: Cowles Commission, 1953.

Macroeconomics in the Twentieth Century

By far the best source on inter-war macroeconomics is

D. Laidler, *Fabricating the Keynesian Revolution: Studies in the Inter-War Literature on Money, the Cycle and Unemployment*, Cambridge: Cambridge University Press, 1999.

The literature on Keynes is vast. A good starting point is recent biographies:

D. Moggridge, *Maynard Keynes: An Economist's Biography*, London: Routledge, 1992;

R. Skidelsky, *John Maynard Keynes: Vol. 1, Hopes Betrayed, 1883–1920*; Vol. 2, *The Economist as Saviour, 1920–1937*; Vol. 3, *Fighting for Britain, 1937–1946*, London: Macmillan, 1983, 1992, 2000.

These authors have both also written much shorter biographies:

D. E. Moggridge, *Keynes*, London: Fontana, 1976;

R. Skidelsky, *Keynes*, Oxford: Oxford University Press, 1996.

A simpler account is offered in:

M. Blaug, *John Maynard Keynes: Life, Ideas, Legacy*, London: Macmillan, 1990.

From the rest of the literature on Keynes, I list just two pieces by one of the leading post-war macroeconomic theorists:

D. Patinkin, *Anticipations of the General Theory?*, Oxford: Basil Blackwell, 1982;

D. Patinkin, 'On different interpretations of the General Theory', *Journal of Monetary Economics*, 26, 1990, pp. 205–43.

Macroeconomics since Keynes has not been comprehensively surveyed. Works that provide detailed coverage of particular themes include

W. Young, *Interpreting Mr Keynes: The IS–LM Enigma*, Cambridge: Polity Press, 1987.

This discusses the way in which the IS–LM model emerged from discussions of the *General Theory*.

P. G. Mehrling, *The Money Interest and the Public Interest: American Monetary Thought, 1920–1970*, Cambridge, Mass., and London: Harvard University Press, 1997.

This explores the role of non-Keynesian monetary thought on post-war macroeconomics.

J. D. Hammond, *Theory and Measurement: Causality Issues in Milton Friedman's Monetary Economics*, Cambridge: Cambridge University Press, 1996;

K. D. Hoover, *The New Classical Macroeconomics*, Oxford: Basil Blackwell, 1988.

The titles of these are self-explanatory.

R. E. Backhouse, *Interpreting Macroeconomics: Explorations in the History of Macroeconomic Thought*, London: Routledge, 1995, Chapters 8–10;

R. E. Backhouse, 'The rhetoric and methodology of modern macroeconomics', in B. Snowdon and H. R. Vane (eds.), *Reflections on the Development of Modern Macroeconomics*, Cheltenham: Edward Elgar, 1997.

These provide brief surveys of post-war macroeconomics from a variety of perspectives.

Finally, a revealing way into modern macroeconomics is to read some of the many interviews that have been conducted with leading economists:

A. Klamer, *The New Classical Macroeconomics: Conversations with New Classical Economists and their Opponents*, Brighton: Wheatsheaf Books, 1987;

B. Snowdon and H. R. Vane (eds.), *Conversations with Leading Economists: Interpreting Modern Macroeconomics*, Cheltenham: Edward Elgar, 1999.

Heterodoxy, Applied Economics and the Broadening of the Economics Discipline

The varieties of American institutionalism – perhaps the most important twentieth-century heterodoxy – are discussed in several of the books cited in the section on early-twentieth-century economics. Useful overviews are

M. Rutherford, 'American institutionalism and the history of economics', *Journal of the History of Economic Thought*, 19, 1997, pp. 178–95;

M. Rutherford, 'Institutionalism as "scientific" economics', in R. E. Backhouse and J. Creedy (eds.), *From Classical Economics to the Theory of the Firm: Essays in Honour of D. P. O'Brien*, Cheltenham: Edward Elgar, 1999;

M. Rutherford, *Institutions in Economics: The Old and the New Institutionalism*, Cambridge: Cambridge University Press, 1994.

The last of these also covers the new institutionalism centred on transaction costs.

The phenomenon of heterodoxy is discussed in a symposium in the *Journal of the History of Economic Thought*, 22 (2), June 2000, and in

M. Desai, 'The underworld of economics: heresy and heterodoxy in the history of economic thought', in G. K. Shaw (ed.), *Economics, Culture and Education: Essays in Honour of Mark Blaug*, Cheltenham: Edward Elgar, 1991.

The origins of modern Austrian economics are chronicled in

K. Vaughn, *Austrian Economics in America: The Migration of a Tradition*, Cambridge: Cambridge University Press, 1994.

Essays on applied economics – interpreted as referring both to applied fields and to the application of techniques – are brought together in

R. E. Backhouse and J. Biddle (eds.), *Toward a History of Applied Economics*, Durham, N.C.: Duke University Press, 2000.

Further such essays can be found in Part 2 of

J. B. Davis (ed.), *New Economics and its History*, Durham, N.C.: Duke University Press, 1988.

For other essays on specific fields see

C. D. Goodwin, *Economics and National Security: A History of their Interaction*, Durham, N.C.: Duke University Press, 1991;

I. McLean, 'Economics and politics', in D. Greenaway, M. Bleaney and I. Stewart (eds.), *Companion to Contemporary Economic Thought*, London: Routledge, 1991;

W. C. Mitchell, 'Political science and public choice: 1950–70', *Public Choice*, 98, 1999, pp. 237–49;

A. Peacock, *Public Choice Analysis in Historical Perspective*, Raffaele Mattioli Lectures, Cambridge: Cambridge University Press, 1992;

W. W. Rostow, *Theorists of Economic Growth from David Hume to the Present: With a Perspective on the Next Century*, New York and Oxford: Oxford University Press, 1990.

During the past two decades there have been many volumes of autobiographical essays published which give a picture of the burgeoning variety of approaches to economics, including

R. E. Backhouse and R. Middleton (eds.), *Exemplary Economists*: Vol. 1, *North America*; Vol. 2, *Europe, Asia and Australasia*, Cheltenham: Edward Elgar, 1999;

G. M. Meier and D. Seers (eds.), *Pioneers in Development*, and G. M. Meier (ed.), *Pioneers in Development*, Second Series, Oxford: Oxford University Press, 1984, 1987.

The former contains references to many more volumes of such essays.

For examples of biographical essays, see

R. Holt and S. Pressman (eds.), *Economics and its Discontents: Twentieth Century Dissenting Economists*, Cheltenham: Edward Elgar, 1998;

W. J. Samuels, *American Economists of the Late Twentieth Century*, Cheltenham: Edward Elgar, 1996.

The international dimension of economic ideas is explored in:

A. W. Coats (ed.), *The Development of Economics in Western Europe since 1945*, London: Routledge, 2000;

A. W. Coats (ed.), *The Post-1945 Internationalization of Economics*, Durham, N.C.: Duke University Press, 1996.

References

Prologue

1. L. C. Robbins, *An Essay on the Nature and Significance of Economic Science* (1932), 2nd edn, London: Macmillan, 1935, p. 16.
2. A. Marshall, *Principles of Economics* (1890), 8th edn, London: Macmillan, 1920, p. 1.

1 The Ancient World

1. Hesiod, *Theogony and Works and Days*, trans. M. L. West, Oxford: Oxford University Press, 1988, p. 39.
2. Ibid., p. 38.
3. B. F. Gordon, *Economic Analysis before Adam Smith: Hesiod to Lessius*, London: Macmillan, 1975, p. 11.
4. W. I. Matson, *A New History of Philosophy*, Vol. 1, London: Harcourt Brace Jovanovich, 1987, p. 67.
5. This term is taken from S. T. Lowry, *The Archaeology of Economic Ideas: The Classical Greek Tradition*, Durham, N.C.: Duke University Press, 1987.
6. Aristotle, *Nichomachean Ethics*, trans. David Ross, Oxford: Oxford University Press, 1980, p. 110.

2 The Middle Ages

1. Genesis 1:28, 2:15.
2. Isaiah 2:6–8.
3. Amos 8:4–6.

344

4. Exodus 22:25–6.

5. Ecclesiastes 11:1–2.

6. J. J. Spengler, 'Economic thought of Islam: Ibn Khaldun', *Comparative Studies in Society and History*, 6, April 1964, p. 290.

7. Quoted in O. Langholm, *Economics in the Medieval Schools*, Leiden: E. J. Brill, 1992, pp. 54–5.

8. *Summa Aurea*, quoted in Langholm, *Economics in the Medieval Schools*, p. 71.

9. Langholm, *Economics in the Medieval Schools*, p. 71.

10. Quoted in Langholm, *Economics in the Medieval Schools*, p. 187.

11. Luke 6:35.

12. Quoted in O. Langholm, *The Legacy of Scholasticism in Economic Thought: Antecedents of Choice and Power*, Cambridge: Cambridge University Press, 1998, p. 59.

13. Quoted in A. E. Monroe, *Early Economic Thought: Selections from Economic Literature Prior to Adam Smith*, Cambridge, Mass.: Harvard University Press, 1965, p. 101.

3 The Emergence of the Modern World View – the Sixteenth Century

1. Quoted in M. Grice Hutchison, *The School of Salamanca: Readings in Spanish Monetary Theory, 1544–1605*, Oxford: Clarendon Press, 1952, p. 94.

2. Ibid., p. 95.

3. It has also been attributed to John Hales (d. 1571), a Member of Parliament. For a detailed discussion see D. Palliser, *The Age of Elizabeth: England under the Later Tudors, 1547–1603*, London: Longman, 1983, Appendix 2.

4. M. Dewar (ed.), *A Discourse of the Common Weal of this Realm of England*, Charlottesville: University Press of Virginia, 1959, p. 59.

5. Ibid., p. 54.

4 Science, Politics and Trade in Seventeenth-Century England

1. W. Petty, *The Economic Writings of Sir William Petty*, Vol. 1, ed. C. H. Hull, Cambridge: Cambridge University Press, 1899, p. 244.

2. Ibid., pp. 244–5.

References

3. Ibid., p. 304.

4. Quoted in A. O. Hirschman, *The Passions and the Interests: Political Arguments for Capitalism before its Triumph*, Princeton: Princeton University Press, 1977, p. 39.

5. Quoted in Hirschman, *The Passions and the Interests*, pp. 25–6.

6. T. Mun, *England's Treasure by Forraign Trade* (1664), quoted in A. E. Monroe, *Early Economic Thought: Selections from Economic Literature Prior to Adam Smith*, Cambridge, Mass.: Harvard University Press, 1965, p. 180.

7. W. Letwin, *The Origins of Scientific Economics: English Economic Thought, 1660–1776*, London: Methuen, 1963, p. 3.

8. J. Child, *Brief Observations Concerning Trade and Interest of Money* (1668), at http://www.ecn.bris.ac.uk/het/child/trade.txt, accessed 24 May 2001.

9. J. Locke, *Locke on Money*, Vol. 1, ed. P. H. Kelly, Oxford: Clarendon Press, 1991, p. 216.

10. Ibid., pp. 235–6.

11. J. R. McCulloch (ed.), *Early English Tracts on Commerce*, London: Political Economy Club, 1856; reprinted Cambridge: The Economic History Society, 1952, p. 510.

12. Ibid., p. 516.

13. Ibid., p. 525.

14. Ibid., pp. 529–30.

15. Ibid., p. 528.

16. Ibid., pp. 513–14.

5 Absolutism and Enlightenment in Eighteenth-Century France

1. Quoted in T. W. Hutchison, *Before Adam Smith: The Emergence of Political Economy, 1662–1776*, Oxford: Basil Blackwell, 1988, p. 111.

2. R. Cantillon, *Essai sur la Nature du Commerce en Générale* (1755), trans. and ed. H. Higgs, London: Macmillan, 1931, p. 3.

3. Ibid., p. 59.

4. Ibid., pp. 61–3.

5. Ibid., p. 65.

6. Ibid., p. 161.

7. Ibid., p. 185.

8. Ibid., p. 189.

9. Quoted in P. D. Groenewegen, *The Economics of A. R. J. Turgot*, The Hague: Martinus Nijhoff, 1977, p. 26.

10. Ibid., p. 29.

11. Ibid., p. 84.

12. Ibid., p. 141.

6 The Scottish Enlightenment of the Eighteenth Century

1. Quoted in A. S. Skinner, *A System of Social Science: Papers Relating to Adam Smith*, Oxford: Clarendon Press, 1979, p. 1.

2. Ibid., p. 5.

3. A. Ferguson, *Principles of Moral and Political Science*, Vol. 1, Edinburgh, 1792, p. 47.

4. D. Hume, *Writings on Economics*, ed. E. Rotwein, Edinburgh: Nelson, 1955, p. 5.

5. Ibid., p. 11.

6. Ibid., pp. 11–12.

7. Ibid., p. 33.

8. Ibid., p. 37.

9. J. Steuart, *An Inquiry into the Principles of Political Economy* (1767), ed. A. S. Skinner, Edinburgh: Oliver & Boyd, 1966, p. 153.

10. Ibid., p. 5.

11. Ibid., p. 12.

12. Ibid., pp. 40, 41.

13. Ibid., p. 195.

14. Ibid., p. 198.

15. Ibid., p. 339.

16. Ibid., p. 345.

17. Ibid., pp. 142–3.

18. A. Smith, *The Theory of Moral Sentiments* (1759–90), ed. D. D. Raphael and A. L. Macfie, Oxford: Oxford University Press, 1976, p. 3.

19. Ibid., p. 86.

20. Ibid.

21. A. Smith, *An Inquiry into the Nature and Causes of the Wealth of Nations* (1776), ed. R. H. Campbell, A. S. Skinner and W. B. Todd, Oxford: Oxford University Press, 1976, p. 25.

22. Ibid., p. 75.

23. Ibid., p. 330.
24. Ibid., p. 337.
25. Ibid., pp. 337–8.
26. Ibid., pp. 163–4.
27. Ibid., p. 456.
28. Ibid., p. 723.

7 Classical Political Economy, 1790–1870

1. T. R. Malthus, *An Essay on the Principle of Population* (1798), ed. A. Flew, Harmondsworth: Penguin Books, 1970, p. 100.
2. D. P. O'Brien, *The Classical Economists*, Oxford: Oxford University Press, 1975, p. 45.
3. S. Bailey, *A Critical Dissertation on the Nature, Measure and Causes of Value* (1825), London: LSE Reprints, 1925, p. 1.
4. J. S. Mill, *Principles of Political Economy with Some of their Applications to Social Philosophy* (1848), London: Longmans, 1873, 'Preliminary remarks', p. 13.
5. Ibid, pp. 13–14.
6. Ibid., Book V, Chapter IX, Section 16, p. 590.
7. K. Marx, *Capital*, Vol. 2 (1885), London: Lawrence & Wishart, 1974, p. 189.
8. Ibid., Vol. 1 (1867), trans. S. Moore and E. Aveling, pp. 714–15.
9. Ibid., p. 715.
10. Ibid.

8 The Split between History and Theory in Europe, 1870–1914

1. W. S. Jevons, *The Theory of Political Economy* (1871), ed. R. D. C. Black, Harmondsworth: Penguin Books, 1970, p. 187.
2. C. Menger, *Principles of Economics* (1871), trans. J. Dingwall and B. F. Hoselitz, Grove City, Pa.: Libertarian Press, 1994, p. 52.
3. Ibid., p. 164.
4. Ibid., p. 217.
5. Ibid., p. 97.
6. A. Marshall, *Principles of Economics* (1890), 8th edn, London: Macmillan, 1920, p. 315.

9 The Rise of American Economics, 1870–1939

1. J. B. Clark, *The Philosophy of Wealth* (1886), 2nd edn, Boston, 1887, pp. 151.
2. J. B. Clark, *The Distribution of Wealth* (1899), 2nd edn, New York, Macmillan, 1902, pp. 401–2.
3. This and the following diagram are taken from I. Fisher, *The Purchasing Power of Money*, New York: Macmillan, 1911.
4. T. B. Veblen, *Theory of Business Enterprise*, New York: Scribners, 1904, p. 67.
5. Ibid., p. 66.
6. T. B. Veblen, *The Engineers and the Price System* (1921), New York: A. M. Kelley, 1965, pp. 81–2.
7. T. B. Veblen, 'The preconceptions of economic science II', *Quarterly Journal of Economics*, 13, 1899, p. 422.
8. W. C. Mitchell, 'Quantitative analysis in economic theory', *American Economic Review*, 15, 1925, p. 5.
9. F. H. Knight, *Risk, Uncertainty and Profit* (1921), London: LSE Reprints, 1933, p. vii.
10. Ibid., pp. 52–3.
11. F. H. Knight, *The Ethics of Competition* (1935), New Brunswick, N.J.: Transaction Publishers, 1997, p. 87.
12. E. H. Chamberlin, *The Theory of Monopolistic Competition*, Cambridge, Mass.: Harvard University Press, 1933, p. 10.

10 Money and the Business Cycle, 1898–1939

1. A. Marshall and M. P. Marshall, *The Economics of Industry* (1879), Bristol: Thoemmes Press, 1994, pp. 154–5.
2. J. M. Keynes, *The Collected Writings of John Maynard Keynes*: Vol. 4, *A Tract on Monetary Reform* (1923), London: Macmillan, 1971, p. 65.
3. Ibid., p. 138.
4. D. Laidler, *Fabricating the Keynesian Revolution: Studies of the Inter-war Literature on Money, the Cycle and Unemployment*, Cambridge: Cambridge University Press, 1999, p. 243.
5. Quoted in Laidler, *Fabricating the Keynesian Revolution*, p. 215.
6. Ibid., p. 241.
7. J. M. Keynes, *The Collected Writings of John Maynard Keynes*: Vol. 7,

The General Theory of Employment, Interest and Money (1936), London: Macmillan, 1971, pp. 149–50.

8. Ibid., p. 152.

9. Ibid., p. 3.

10. This way of putting it is due to Laidler, *Fabricating the Keynesian Revolution*.

11 Econometrics and Mathematical Economics, 1930 to the Present

1. R. Stone, 'The accounts of society', *American Economic Review*, 87 (6), 1997, p. 20.

2. Quoted in R. Frisch, 'Editorial', *Econometrica*, 1, 1933, p. 1.

3. T. Haavelmo, 'The probability approach in econometrics', *Econometrica*, 12 (supplement), 1944, p. iii. (Italics have been removed from the original.)

4. T. Haavelmo, 'The statistical implications of a system of simultaneous equations', *Econometrica*, 11, 1943, p. 1.

5. M. S. Morgan, *A History of Econometric Ideas*, Cambridge: Cambridge University Press, 1990, p. 264.

6. P. A. Samuelson, *Foundations of Economic Analysis*, Cambridge, Mass.: Harvard University Press, 1947, p. 4. ('Hypothesis' has been changed to the plural.)

7. P. A. Samuelson, 'How *Foundations* came to be', *Journal of Economic Literature*, 36 (3), 1998, p. 1382.

8. G. Debreu, *Theory of Value: An Axiomatic Theory of Economic Equilibrium*, New Haven: Yale University Press, 1959, p. x.

9. J. von Neumann and O. Morgenstern, *The Theory of Games and Economic Behavior*, Princeton: Princeton University Press, 1944, p. 38.

12 Welfare Economics and Socialism, 1870 to the Present

1. W. S. Jevons, *The State in Relation to Labour* (1882), 3rd edn, London, 1894, p. 14.

2. H. Sidgwick, *The Principles of Political Economy* (1883), 2nd edn, London: Macmillan, 1887, p. 71.

3. A. Marshall, *Principles of Economics* (1890), 8th edn, London: Macmillan, 1920, p. 108.

4. A. C. Pigou, *The Economics of Welfare*, London: Macmillan, 1920, p. 10.

5. Ibid., p. 11.

6. V. Pareto, *Manual of Political Economy* (1906), trans. A. S. Schwier, New York: A. M. Kelley, 1971, p. 155.

7. Ibid., p. 268.

13 Economists and Policy, 1939 to the Present

1. M. Perlman, *The Character of Economic Thought, Economic Characters and Economic Institutions: Selected Essays of Mark Perlman*, Ann Arbor, Mich.: University of Michigan Press, 1996, p. 217.

14 Expanding the Discipline, 1960 to the Present

1. J. A. Schumpeter, *A History of Economic Analysis*, London: Allen & Unwin, 1954, p. 23.

2. A. Blinder, 'The economics of brushing teeth', *Journal of Political Economy*, 82, 1974, pp. 887–91.

3. A. O. Hirschman, *Essays in Trespassing: Economics to Politics and Beyond*, Cambridge: Cambridge University Press, 1981; *Crossing Boundaries: Selected Writings*, New York: Zone Books, 1998.

4. J. Niehans, 'Transactions costs', in J. Eatwell, M. Milgate and P. Newman (eds.), *The New Palgrave: A Dictionary of Economics*, London: Macmillan, 1987, Vol. 4, p. 676.

5. R. Coase, 'The problem of social cost', *Journal of Law and Economics*, 3, 1960, pp. 1–44.

6. J. A. Schumpeter, *Economic Doctrine and Method* (1912), trans. R. Aris, London: Allen & Unwin, 1954, p. 152.

7. Ibid.

Epilogue: Economists and Their History

1. J. A. Schumpeter, *A History of Economic Analysis*, London: Allen & Unwin, 1954, p. 754.
2. Ibid., p. 827.
3. E. H. Chamberlin, *The Theory of Monopolistic Competition*, Cambridge, Mass.: Harvard University Press, 1933, p. 10.

Index

Index

Index

Index

Index

mainstream, homogeneity of 316

Malthus, Thomas Robert 2, 133–5, 137–8, 140, 149, 166–7, 177

Malynes, Gerard 3, 77, 78, 84

management 313

Mandeville, Bernard 112–13, 130, 132

Mangoldt, Hans von 146, 203

manufacturing, growth of 133, 139

Marcus Aurelius 26

marginal efficiency of investment 230–31

marginal private and social products 273–4

marginal utility 169, 172, 175, 182, 188, 284

marginalism 269–70, 313

market, extent of 124

market structure 206, 265

markets, and coordination 49, 64, 85, 91–2, 103, 113, 284

Marschak, Jacob 250–51, 317

Marshall, Alfred 4, 154, 178–83, 189, 192, 201, 203, 207, 209, 219–20, 222, 254, 258–9, 270, 272–3, 282, 285, 318, 322, 325

Marshall, Mary Paley 219, 220

Martel, Charles 35, 39–40

Marx, Karl 1, 8, 109, 141, 156–65, 183–4, 195, 197–8, 237

Marxism 184, 269, 314–15

Massachusetts Institute of Technology 316

mathematics

twentieth-century developments in 259–61

use of 21–2, 142–3, 167–8, 170, 179, 181, 183, 190–93, 201, 229, 232–5, 237–8, 245, 255–6, 258–9, 263–8, 301, 306–7, 309, 312, 314, 316

maximization 169, 176, 182, 201, 258–9, 270, 320

see also optimization

Meade, James 243–4, 291

measurement 168–9, 252

mechanical laws 53

mechanical reasoning 82

Menger, Carl 174–7, 188, 255, 316, 325

Menger, Karl 255–6, 263, 266

Mercado, Thomas de 62

mercantililsm 57–9, 70, 87, 89, 91, 98, 104, 113, 116, 121, 129, 132, 148

merchant adventurers 66, 77

Mercier de la Rivière, Pierre-Paul 100

metallic fluctuation, principle of 153

Methodenstreit 177

methodological individualism 316

Michelangelo 52

Middle Ages, end of 51

migration

of European economists 207, 210, 266, 307

under Colbert 90

Mill, James 136–7, 142

Mill, John Stuart 236–7, 153–6, 164–5, 168, 172, 179, 198, 203, 219, 270, 272

Minard, Joseph 145

Mirabeau, Marquis de 58, 89, 100–101

Mirrlees, James 305

mirror for princes 36

Mises, Ludwig von 217–18, 224, 276–7, 285–6, 316

Misselden, Edward 78, 87, 129

Index

Index

READ MORE IN PENGUIN

In every corner of the world, on every subject under the sun, Penguin represents quality and variety – the very best in publishing today.

For complete information about books available from Penguin – including Puffins, Penguin Classics and Arkana – and how to order them, write to us at the appropriate address below. Please note that for copyright reasons the selection of books varies from country to country.

In the United Kingdom: Please write to *Dept. EP, Penguin Books Ltd, Bath Road, Harmondsworth, West Drayton, Middlesex UB7 0DA*

In the United States: Please write to *Consumer Services, Penguin Putnam Inc., 405 Murray Hill Parkway, East Rutherford, New Jersey 07073-2136.* VISA and MasterCard holders call 1-800-631-8571 to order Penguin titles

In Canada: Please write to *Penguin Books Canada Ltd, 10 Alcorn Avenue, Suite 300, Toronto, Ontario M4V 3B2*

In Australia: Please write to *Penguin Books Australia Ltd, 487 Maroondah Highway, Ringwood, Victoria 3134*

In New Zealand: Please write to *Penguin Books (NZ) Ltd, Private Bag 102902, North Shore Mail Centre, Auckland 10*

In India: Please write to *Penguin Books India Pvt Ltd, 11 Community Centre, Panchsheel Park, New Delhi 110017*

In the Netherlands: Please write to *Penguin Books Netherlands bv, Postbus 3507, NL-1001 AH Amsterdam*

In Germany: Please write to *Penguin Books Deutschland GmbH, Metzlerstrasse 26, 60594 Frankfurt am Main*

In Spain: Please write to *Penguin Books S. A., Bravo Murillo 19, 1ºB, 28015 Madrid*

In Italy: Please write to *Penguin Italia s.r.l., Via Vittorio Emanuele 45/a, 20094 Corsico, Milano*

In France: Please write to *Penguin France, 12, Rue Prosper Ferradou, 31700 Blagnac*

In Japan: Please write to *Penguin Books Japan Ltd, Iidabashi KM-Bldg, 2-23-9 Koraku, Bunkyo-Ku, Tokyo 112-0004*

In South Africa: Please write to *Penguin Books South Africa (Pty) Ltd, P.O. Box 751093, Gardenview, 2047 Johannesburg*

READ MORE IN PENGUIN

BUSINESS AND ECONOMICS

Webonomics Evan I. Schwartz

In *Webonomics*, Evan I. Schwartz defines nine essential principles for growing your business on the Web. Using case studies of corporations such as IBM and Volvo, as well as smaller companies and web-based start-ups, Schwartz documents both the tremendous failures and the successes on the Web in a multitude of industries.

Inside Organizations Charles B. Handy

Whatever we do, whatever our profession, organizing is a part of our lives. This book brings together twenty-one ideas which show you how to work with and through other people. There are also questions at the end of each chapter to get you thinking on your own and in a group.

Lloyds Bank Small Business Guide Sara Williams

This long-running guide to making a success of your small business deals with real issues in a practical way. 'As comprehensive an introduction to setting up a business as anyone could need' *Daily Telegraph*

Teach Yourself to Think Edward de Bono

Edward de Bono's masterly book offers a structure that broadens our ability to respond to and cope with a vast range of situations. *Teach Yourself to Think* is software for the brain, turning it into a successful thinking mechanism, and, as such, will prove of immense value to us all.

The Road Ahead Bill Gates

Bill Gates – the man who built Microsoft – takes us back to when he dropped out of Harvard to start his own software company and discusses how we stand on the brink of a new technology revolution that will for ever change and enhance the way we buy, work, learn and communicate with each other.